Chamorro Reference Grammar

PALI LANGUAGE TEXTS: MICRONESIA

Social Science Research Institute
University of Hawaii

Donald M. Topping
Editor

Chamorro Reference Grammar

DONALD M. TOPPING

with the assistance of
BERNADITA C. DUNGCA

University of Hawaii Press

HONOLULU

The research reported herein was partially supported by the Government of the Trust Territory of the Pacific. Publication of the finished book was financed by the Trust Territory Government. Mrs. Dungca's assistance was made possible through support received from the Government of Guam and the Culture Learning Institute of the East-West Center at the University of Hawaii.

Contents

Preface

This grammar of the Chamorro language has been in the planning stage for a long time. Parts of the grammar were presented in my doctoral dissertation in 1963. Additional pieces were published in 1968. Many scattered fragments were incorporated in the footnotes of *Spoken Chamorro* (1969). But this is the first attempt on my part to assemble enough pieces of the language in a sufficiently systematic way to deserve to be called a reference grammar.

There are, of course, other grammars of the Chamorro language, some of which are fairly well known. I am indebted to all of them for insights into the language which I was able to get from studying them. I do not wish to claim that the present grammar is any better than the earlier ones, but I would like to justify its compilation (as an addition to the earlier ones) on three counts: (1) it includes some data that the earlier grammars do not; (2) it offers a different interpretation of some of the data based upon more recent concepts in the field of linguistics; (3) it is written primarily to help Chamorro speakers learn something of the complexities of their language. It is hoped that interested non-Chamorro speakers will also be able to learn something about the language through studying this work.

Because language is so complex and constantly changing, a grammar can never be complete. There are usually exceptions to every rule and new rules are constantly being made by the native speakers of the language. This grammar is an attempt to describe the rules of the language, not to prescribe them. All of the rules given in this book are based on actual language used by numerous native speakers of Chamorro throughout the Mariana Islands. In addition to the rules, attempts are sometimes made to "explain" the rules—to give the reason for them. In most cases, however, no explanation is offered simply because there is usually no reason for any rule in any language.

Throughout the text can be found "Notes to Linguists." In these sections I have taken the liberty of using slightly technical terms and concepts for fellow linguists who may be interested in Chamorro grammar from a scientific point of view. In the main body of the text I have tried to avoid technical terminology as much as possible. Where such terms are used they are italicized and are included in the Glossary of Linguistic Terms at the end of the book.

While I cannot single out each individual who assisted me in discovering the grammatical system of the Chamorro language, I would like to give special thanks to Mrs. Bernadita C. Dungca (Guam), Mrs. Lagrimas Untalan (Guam), Mr. Pedro M. Ogo (Rota), Mrs. Rosa Roberto Carter (Guam), and Mr. Jose S. Pangelinan (Saipan) for their invaluable assistance and patience.

1   Introduction

Before jumping into the structure of the language itself, we should take some time to consider the cultural background, past and present, of the Chamorro language and people. There are several books of historical and cultural interest which are listed in the bibliography and should be consulted by everyone interested in Chamorro. I say this because of my belief that a language can never be effectively studied apart from its cultural setting. In addition, the surface changes that have taken place in the Mariana Islands during the past twenty-five years tend to give a distorted view of Chamorro culture to the eye of the unwary beholder. While much of the old Chamorro way of life is apparently disappearing, which is a universal social phenomenon, many distinctly Chamorro cultural patterns still persist, especially on the islands of Rota, Tinian, and Saipan. Even in the face of the rapid changes that are taking place in the Marianas, we can hope that the Chamorro way of life will continue to retain some of its distinctive features.

For works of historical and cultural interest, I would especially recommend the following books:

Paul Carano and Pedro C. Sanchez, *History of Guam;*
Alexander Spoehr, *Marianas Prehistory;*
          Saipan: the Ethnology of a War Devastated Island;
Laura Thompson, *The Native Culture of the Marianas Islands; Guam and Its People.*

THE CHAMORRO PEOPLE: WHERE AND WHEN?

1.1   At the present time there are approximately 40,000 native Chamorro speakers living in Guam and approximately 12,000 living in the other islands of the Marianas, with the following break-down by inhabited islands. Saipan-9,000; Rota-1,500; Tinian-1,000; Pagan-30; Anatahan-25; Alamagan-10. (Note: all of the above figures are approximations.)

The term "Chamorro speaker" is used to refer to the inhabitants of the Marianas who speak Chamorro as their native, or first language. It is somewhat difficult to define a Chamorro "people" or "race" because the present-day Chamorros are a heterogeneous racial group. Perhaps this fact has helped give rise to the use of such terms as Guamanian, Rotanese, and Saipanese for purposes of cultural and social identification.

Nobody knows for sure where the first Chamorros came from. It is safe to assume that the original Chamorros belonged to the large group of Pacific peoples known generally as Malayo-Polynesian, but there is no certain evidence to tell us where the first inhabitants of the Mariana Islands came from. Laura Thompson has suggested that the first inhabitants of the Mariana Islands were the descendants of seafaring folk who migrated westward from Asia to the Philippines to the Western Carolines and, finally, to the Marianas (Thompson 1947). According to Spoehr (1954:38), there is good evidence (from the Chalan Piao site in Saipan) that the first settlers of the Marianas arrived somewhere around 1527 B.C. ± 200 years, or approximately 3,500 years ago! And there they lived in relative isolation until the pale voyagers from the sea landed upon their shores in 1521. Magellan was only the first of hundreds of thousands of subsequent travelers who were to cause great changes in the Chamorro people and culture during the next 450 years.

After the near extermination of the pre-Spanish Chamorros through epidemic diseases and mass murders, outbreeding was most common, especially with Spanish and Filipino groups. These admixtures were then further modified by later contacts with other Europeans, Americans, and Japanese. According to Spoehr, "Many present-day Chamorros are physically indistinguishable from Europeans, while others display general Mongoloid features" (1954:26).

THE CHAMORRO LANGUAGE: ITS ORIGINS, RELATIVES, AND TENACITY

1.2   The origins of the Chamorro language are very nearly as obscure as the origins of the people. Since there are no written records before the work of Father Sanvitores in 1668, we have no way to ascertain what the language was like when the first people came to the Marianas. Even the records left by Father Sanvitores, which constitute one of the earliest grammars of any Pacific language, are too sketchy to give a very clear picture of what the language was like in his day. Hence, we can not be certain as to what the language of the original Chamorro settlers was like. We can only speculate, with perhaps some help from current comparative evidence. At least one scholar of comparative languages in the Pacific area claims that the closest relatives to Chamorro are Maanyan (of Borneo) and West Futuna, in the New Hebrides (Dyen 1962:43). His claims are based upon the relatively high percentage of common vocabulary items that are shared among these languages.

Chamorro belongs to the family of languages known as Austronesian. My own opinion is that Chamorro is a Philippine type language, and its closest linguistic relatives are probably Ilokano and Tagalog. This opinion is based on the many similarities in the grammatical structures of the languages and, in particular, the focus system of the languages. (More will be said about this later in the section on grammar.) It is quite possible that these similarities in the grammatical devices were borrowed from Filipinos with whom the Chamorros traded. However, this is very unlikely. Speakers of one language often borrow words from another language, but very seldom, if ever, do they borrow grammatical features.

We will leave the question of when and how the Chamorro language first became a separate language to those who are more interested in reconstructing history. The important thing for modern students of Chamorro—both native speakers and others—to bear in mind is that Chamorro is *not* a dialect of any other known language. It is a separate and distinct language in itself, just as German, Japanese, and English are separate and distinct languages. There are dialects of Chamorro, namely the dialects of central Guam, southern Guam, Rota, and Saipan. But these dialects simply reflect slightly different ways of speaking the same language —Chamorro. As we will see, Chamorro has all of the regular rules and complexities that are found in all languages of the world. Some of the rules for Chamorro are similar to rules found in related languages. But most of them are distinctly Chamorro.

One very remarkable thing about the history of the Chamorro language is its ability to survive. In spite of the drastic reduction in population during Spanish times to an estimated 3,678 speakers (Thompson 1947:57), the language survived. In spite of intensive efforts by Spanish and American administrative authorities to "stamp out" Chamorro, the language survived. In spite of the current "Americanization" of the Marianas, complete with mass communications and education in English, the language is still surviving. I, for one, hope that it will continue to survive.

There are those who maintain that the Chamorro language is dying out. There are even those who are anxious to hasten its death. If such is indeed the case, let us hope that something can be done to stop this trend. Chamorro is the native language of the Chamorro people. It forms a very critical part of their social and personal vitality. It is the language they use to communicate their most intimate thoughts to their God and their loved ones. It is the language they use for fun by playing with both the sounds and meanings of words. It is the language they use to create dreams and fantasies and for secret thoughts. For the Chamorro people to lose this language would be a great loss indeed, one that could never be replaced.

I am hopeful that the Chamorro language will continue to survive. People without a language are poor people indeed. I hope, too, that this grammar may contribute in some small way to its survival.

EARLIER STUDIES OF CHAMORRO

1.3   In addition to the complete listing of studies of the Chamorro language given in the bibliography, I would like to single out seven of them for special mention. They are listed in chronological order.

Father Sanvitores. The earliest known grammar of Chamorro was written by Father Sanvitores in 1668. This work, of considerable interest to the comparative or historical linguist, doubtless bears the distinction of being the first grammar of any Micronesian language. Written in Latin, it follows the pattern of most other grammars of the seventeenth century. For example, the author takes such a word as *taotao* 'man' and puts it through the nominative, genitive, dative and accusative cases, even though the word remains as *taotao*, with no change, throughout the declension. Father Sanvitores claims to have been divinely inspired to learn Chamorro in an incredibly short period of time.

William Safford. Aside from a Spanish grammar by Mata y Araujo in 1865, William E. Safford's *The Chamorro Language of Guam* (1903–1905) was the next study of the language after an interim of well over a hundred years. (A Spanish grammar of Chamorro by del Carmen is reported to have been published in Manila in 1865, but I have not been able to obtain it.)

Safford was undoubtedly one of the most perceptive Americans ever to visit the Marianas, for after spending only one year (1899–1900) on Guam as an aide to the first American governor, he made significant contributions in several areas, notably botany and language. Considering that he had no previous material to go by, Safford's two separate works on the plants and language of Guam are quite remarkable.

No linguist, Safford reacted to this new language in a predictable manner: in addition to making frequent comparisons with similar words from other Austronesian* languages, he set up a Latin grammar framework and discussed the features of Chamorro grammar that would fit into the framework. He included long lists of "irregular" forms of verbs and nouns, but they were irregular only because Safford did not see the regularity of the patterns since he was looking at them from the point of view of Latin grammar.

Fritz, P. Callistus, and Kats. The grammars by Fritz (1909) and Kats (1917) are basically restatements of Safford in German and Dutch respectively. Neither of them contributes anything new, except for Fritz's accompanying dictionary. Father Callistus, who was a Capuchin missionary, offered only a dictionary with an accompanying "gefasste Grammatik und Sprachübungen," a work doubtless designed for the use of missionaries, and also based upon Latin grammar.

Von Preissig. E.R. von Preissig, a United States Navy Chief Pay Clerk who was stationed on Guam, compiled the first English-Chamorro Dictionary, which was published in 1917. His work also contains a very short and concise "grammar," the basis of which is acknowledged to be that of Safford. Von Preissig's misunderstanding of the complex system of affixation in Chamor-

---

*The term Austronesian is now used by most linguists to refer to the family of languages formerly known as Malayo-Polynesian.

ro grammar led to incorrect arrangement and classification of many words. Yet, it is still a most useful dictionary for English speakers studying Chamorro.

H. Costenoble. H. Costenoble was the last of the German grammarians who worked on Chamorro. Having learned to speak the language as a child on Guam (from 1905 to 1913), he is the first of the grammarians to have a high degree of fluency in the language, at least by his own account. His work, *Die Chamoro Sprache* (1940), the result of over fifteen years' work, is a complete grammar, filling 550 pages and containing a vast amount of illustrative material. Unfortunately, its contents are not accessible to most Chamorros and Americans because they are written in German. Also, many of his examples are rejected by Chamorro speakers because they are ungrammatical.

The Present Study. It is hoped that the present study will include as much information about Chamorro as the preceding ones and will present it in a way that will reveal as clearly as possible its very complex grammatical system. As stated previously, it is hoped that Chamorro people—especially the students—will be able to learn about and have respect for their language through using this book.

FOREIGN INFLUENCES ON CHAMORRO

1.4   Like a canoe blown by many winds, the Chamorro people and language have been subjected to several different foreign influences. All of these have left some mark on the language.

Spanish. The most notable influence on Chamorro language and culture came from the Spanish. In addition to bringing Christianity and its many cultural by-products to the Marianas, they brought a language which left a permanent mark on Chamorro. There was wholesale borrowing of Spanish words and phrases into Chamorro, and there was even some borrowing from the Spanish sound system. But this borrowing was linguistically superficial. The bones of the Chamorro language remained intact; a little Spanish flesh was added through vocabulary borrowing, but Chamorro remained basically Chamorro.

In virtually all cases of borrowing, Spanish words were forced to conform to the Chamorro sound system. For example, from Spanish *verde* 'green' we get Chamorro *betde*, and from Spanish *libro* 'book' we get Chamorro *lepblo*. The substitution of

Chamorro sounds for Spanish sounds is quite consistent, and is discussed under section 2.9 "Chamorrocized Spanish."

For examples of how Spanish words were forced to conform to the rules of Chamorro grammar, note the following:

Spanish:	cuentos 'to talk'
Chamorro:	Kumekuentos hao.
	'You are talking.'

Spanish:	cuenta 'count'
Chamorro:	Hu kuentatayi hao.
	'I am substituting for you.'

Spanish:	espia 'spy'; adelantar 'to advance'
Chamorro:	Ha espipiha mo'na i adelanton i tano'.
	'He is looking for improvement of the land.'

Spanish:	ganar 'to gain'
Chamorro:	Kuarentai tres ha' i tata gi ora ginanna-ña.
	'The father earned only forty-three cents an hour.'

(Notice that in the last Chamorro sentence three additional Spanish words occur—*kuarenta, tres, ora*— in unaltered forms.)

While Spanish may have left a lasting mark on Chamorro vocabulary, as it did on many Philippine and South American languages, it had virtually no effect on Chamorro grammar.

German. The German period of influence in the Marianas was relatively brief (1899–1914) and was confined largely to Saipan. Since the Germans did not set up an elaborate administrative system for their new colony, they exerted much less influence, both cultural and linguistic, than did the Spanish. Very few German vocabulary items found their way into Chamorro, and the German influence on Chamorro grammar was nil.

Japanese. Japanese influence on Chamorro was much greater than that of German, but much less than Spanish. The Japanese influence, like the German, was pretty well confined to the northern Marianas, especially Saipan. Once again, the linguistic influence was restricted exclusively to vocabulary items, many of which refer to manufactured objects such as *denke'* 'flashlight' and *chirigame'* 'toilet paper'. Many Saipanese became fluent and literate in the Japanese language; if the period of Japanese domination of the Marianas had been longer, the linguistic influence would undoubtedly have been much greater.

English. The influence of English on Chamorro has been great, especially in Guam. Since 1898, when Captain Henry Glass sailed

The Charleston into Apra Harbor, English has been used in Guam in an ever-increasing amount. It is the official language of Guam, is used as the medium of instruction in both public and private schools, and is used almost exclusively for newspaper, radio and TV communication. In Guam, most people know some English, and literacy in English is practically universal among the younger generation.

In the northern Marianas, English in not so widely used as it is in Guam. It was not used at all in the northern islands until after World War II, and then only sparingly by the administering authorities and in the schools. It was not until after 1961, when the Trust Territory Headquarters moved to Saipan, that English came to be used widely, both in the schools and the communications media.

The influence of English on the Chamorro language is very much like the influence of Spanish. Many words have been borrowed from English into Chamorro; but Chamorro grammar has not taken on any of the features of English grammar. Most of the borrowed words are names of newly introduced objects, such as "washing machine, Jeep, lighter, pizza" and so on. Occasionally one hears a complete English phrase in the middle of a Chamorro stream of speech. One that I have heard frequently is "I mean . . ." which is used, as in English, when one wishes to try to clarify something he has just said.

English Loanblends. As was the case with Spanish, many English words have been made to conform to Chamorro grammar and pronunciation rules. These are cases of "loanblends." Some examples of these loanblends are *bumóling* (from "bowling"), *lumáns* (from "lunch"), and *mantataip* (from "type"). (For a more complete discussion of these loanblends and how they are made to conform to the Chamorro system, see Topping 1963b.)

Influence of Foreign Languages on Chamorro Spelling. Of the various foreign language influences on the spelling of Chamorro, that of Spanish has been the greatest. Since the Spanish priests were the first to spell the Chamorro language, it is not surprising that they used their own alphabet. Considering the vast differences in the two languages, the Spanish alphabet served surprisingly well and is still used today by many people who write Chamorro.

German appears to have had some influence on the spelling

of Chamorro. This can be seen in some writings where the letter *k* is used in place of Spanish *c* or *qu, gw* for *gu, h* for *j,* and *j* for *y,* as pronounced in the English word "yes."

Since Japanese does not use the Roman alphabet for writing, it had no influence on the Chamorro writing system.

The influence of English on everyday written Chamorro has not been very great. This is probably due to the fact that most people who can write English seldom have the need to write anything in Chamorro. The influence of English writing did play some part in the official Chamorro Orthography which was adopted in Saipan in January, 1971. This is discussed in Section 2.8.1 below.

DIALECTS OF CHAMORRO

1.5   As stated in 1.2 above, there are differences in the *dialects of Chamorro* that are spoken in different areas. The dialect of the southern villages of Guam—Inarajan, Merizo, Umatac—differs from the dialect spoken in Yoña, Agaña, or Yigo. The dialect of Rota differs from the dialect of Saipan or Guam. Although these dialect differences have never been formally described, a native speaker of Chamorro has no difficulty in detecting a dialect that is different from his own. And in most cases he can identify the dialect being spoken.

The dialect differences are not great enough to cause any difficulty in communication.

The major dialect differences are between Rota and all the other islands. The Saipan dialect and the dialect of central and northern Guam are very similar, while the dialects of southern Guam and Rota have certain common features. The major difference between the dialects of Saipan and Guam are found in vocabulary; Saipanese tend to use more loanwords from Japanese while Guamanians use more loanwords from English.

If a native speaker is asked to describe the distinctive features of the Rota dialect, he usually says that the people from Rota speak in a "sing-song" manner. This description is a fairly accurate one. In linguistic terms we might say that the Rota dialect is characterized by more frequent non-terminal junctures which cause more frequent rising and falling of pitch levels. These junctures make the Rota dialect sound more "rhythmical" or "sing-song."

In addition to the characteristic intonation of the Rota dialect, there are certain other general features that can be described. They are as follows:

    a. Absence of geminate consonants. (Cf. 2.4.3.)

    b. Absence of syllable-final *h*. (Cf. 2.4.3.)

    c. Insertion of *h* in Spanish loan words, especially preceding glides.

Some examples which will illustrate these differences between the Rota dialect and the Guam/Saipan dialect are given here:

Guam/Saipan		*Rota*
a.	tommo 'knee'	tomo
	meggai 'many'	megai
b.	mamahlao 'bashful'	mamalao
	tohge 'stand up'	toge
c.	espia 'look for'	espiha
	tieras 'scissors'	tiheras

In the words of the a. group, both consonants (mm, gg) are pronounced clearly in the Guam/Saipan dialect, while only a single consonant is pronounced in the Rota dialect. In the words of the b. group, the h is clearly pronounced in the Guam/Saipan dialect, but is omitted in the Rota dialect.

There are other formal differences in the different dialects of Chamorro, but these have not been sufficiently investigated to attempt to describe them here.

2 The Sound System of Chamorro

INTRODUCTION

Most of the older grammar books for the European languages did not have very much information on the sound systems of those languages. It was just assumed that the spelling system was adequate to represent the actual sounds of the language. Perhaps the reason for this is that most of the older grammar books of European languages that we may have studied were written before grammarians clearly understood the importance of differentiating between the spelling system of a language and the actual sounds that occur in the language. As we will see, the spelling system and the sound system of a language are two different things.

If we are to understand the entire system of the Chamorro language, it is important to have a clear understanding of the sound system, which involves the separate sounds that occur in the language and the changes that they undergo when they occur in different environments. This is the reason why the first section of this grammar—and it is a fairly long section—concentrates exclusively on the sound system of Chamorro.

We are taking the approach here that Chamorro speech can be broken up into separate sounds, or *segments,* This concept of breaking a "word" or a "stream of speech" into separate segments of sound is not a new one. When the Greeks devised an alphabetic writing system some 3,000 years ago, they were devising a method to represent individual segments of sound. The writing systems for the languages of the world that use alphabets (as opposed to the Chinese writing system, for example) are based on this concept. All alphabetic writing systems are an attempt to represent separate segments of sound by separate written symbols.

The question has been raised more than once as to whether it is possible to break up a stream of speech into separate, discrete sounds, or *segments*. (The term segment is used here to refer to a single sound unit.) For example, in a simple word such as the English word "yes," how many separate segments of sound are found? Most people would probably answer "three." They are *y*, *e*, and *s*. But, one might ask the question, "Where does the *y*-sound stop and the *e*-sound begin? Or where does the *e*-sound stop and the *s*-sound begin?" The question is not an easy one to answer.

The situation is probably further complicated by our preconceptions about sounds and spelling. We tend to think that the letters of the alphabet represent the sounds of the language. We do not have to look very far to find evidence that this assumption is not correct. For example, the English word "checks" has six letters. How many separate sounds—or segments of sound—does the word have? Most linguists would agree that the word "checks" has four separate sounds. The first segment of sound is represented by the letters *ch*. The second segment is represented by the letter *e*, the third by *ck*, and the fourth by s. Thus, we have a word that contains four separate segments of sound that are represented by six letters.

A different, but related, situation is found in a word like "box." It has three letters. How many segments of sound does the word have? Most linguists would agree that it has four separate sounds. One sound is represented by *b*. The second sound is represented by *o*. However, the last two segments of sound (which might be spelled phonetically as *ks*) are represented by the single letter x.

These examples from English are used to illustrate that there can be a significant difference between the spelling system adopted for a language and the sound system. In the pages to follow we will concentrate on the sound system of Chamorro. The spelling system will be discussed later in section 2.8.

In order to discuss the segments of the sound system of Chamorro, it will be necessary to use a few technical terms and symbols. These technical terms will be used as sparingly as possible.

In learning to use an English dictionary, most people learn something about phonetic spelling. For example, in the Webster's *Seventh New Collegiate Dictionary,* the word "cancel" is followed immediately by the phonetic respelling ['kan (t)-sel]; the word "write" is respelled as ['rit]. These phonetic respellings are an attempt to show by using the written symbols of the International

Phonetic Alphabet how a word is pronounced by native speakers of the language. In phonetics, we try to show how each segment of the word is actually pronounced. (Generally speaking, linguists do not use the symbols of the International Phonetic Alphabet (IPA) because the symbols available in the IPA are often not adequate to represent the sounds of some of the more "exotic" languages of the world. The few phonetic symbols used in the discussion of Chamorro will be explained as they are introduced.)

Linguists—and especially phoneticians—usually go a little further with phonetics than dictionary makers do. Linguists sometimes wish to show all of the fine distinctions of the sounds of a language. They do this by using various systems of phonetic spelling and by describing how sounds are made by referring to the parts of the body that are used in making the sounds. In order to make our discussion easier and perhaps more meaningful, a drawing is given here. Various parts of this drawing are labeled. The names of these parts will be used from time to time in the discussion of the sounds of Chamorro.

THE ORGANS OF SPEECH

To illustrate how linguists would treat the fine phonetic distinctions of sounds, we will examine the pronunciation of the sound represented by the letter k̲ in the following three Chamorro words:

kilili*   'carry along'
katta   'letter'
falak   'go to'

(The words spelled here with k̲ may be spelled differently by some people who write Chamorro. The word *kilili* might be spelled *quilili*, the word *katta* is often spelled *catta*: and *falak* is usually spelled *falag*. The spellings given here using k̲ represent the spelling system that will be used throughout this book. The entire spelling system of Chamorro will be discussed in section 2.8 below.)

Most native speakers of Chamorro would probably feel that the k̲ sound in the three words listed above is the same. (Some might feel that the k̲ in falak is really a g̲.) For all practical purposes of communication they are the same. However, linguists—and particularly those who specialize in phonetics— would take note that the three k̲ sounds are phonetically different. In other words, there are differences in the three k̲ sounds that a phonetician can detect, but the differences would not be noticed by the average native speaker of Chamorro.

What are the differences in the pronunciation of the three *k*'s? We will describe the differences and then suggest a way for Chamorro speakers to discover the differences for themselves.

The k̲ of *kilili* could be described as "fronted k." It is called "fronted" because in producing it the back part of the "blade" of the tongue (see chart) presses against the roof of the mouth in order to stop the flow of air. Try pronouncing just the first syllable of *kilili* to feel which part of the tongue is touching the roof of the mouth. Then pronounce only the k̲ of *kilili* and pretend that you are going to pronounce the first syllable (k̲i). Do this several times.

The k̲ of *katta* could be described as a "backed k." It is called "backed" because in producing it the dorsum (the very back part of the tongue) presses against the back part of the roof of the mouth in order to stop the flow of air. Try pronouncing just the

*The stress, or accent mark is used only where it is not predictable. See section 2.6.1.

first syllable of *katta* and the first syllable of *kilili* and you should feel a difference in where the tongue is placed for the k̲ in each word. Now try pronouncing just the first sound of *katta* and *kilili* and you should have no difficulty feeling the difference between a fronted k̲ and a backed k̲.

The k̲ sound of *falak* is different from the other two because when the word *falak* is said by itself, the final k̲ may be "unreleased." That means that the speaker tends to hold the tongue against the back part of the roof of the mouth for a fraction of a second, or possibly longer. Because the sound is unreleased, it is phonetically different from the k̲ of *kilili* or *katta*; the k̲ in both of those words is released.

In phonetic writing we could write the k of *kilili* as [k̲]. The k of *katta* could be written as [k]. And the k̲ of *falak* could be written as [k̓].

NOTE: *Whenever phonetic spelling is used, it will be enclosed in square brackets* [ ].

As stated earlier, these differences in the pronunciation of k̲ are not really noticeable to the native speaker of Chamorro. Since the differences are not noticeable, the Chamorro speaker is generally not aware that they even exist. There are many sounds in Chamorro that are phonetically different, but which sound the same to the Chamorro speaker. These differences are of interest to the linguist and are important in describing the complete sound system of the language. We will make no attempt to describe all of the phonetic differences of the sounds of Chamorro, but it will be necessary to examine some of them as we continue.

When the differences in the sound of a particular language are not generally significant, the linguist calls these "phonetic differences." However, when the differences in the sounds are significant, then the linguist calls these "phonemic differences." To illustrate two sounds that are "phonemically" different in Chamorro, let us consider the first consonant of the two words *lata* 'can' and *rata* 'surface'. In these two words l̲ and r̲ are *contrastive sounds*. When the two sounds contrast with each other, i.e., when the substitution of one sound for the other causes a difference in meaning, the linguist would call them different *phonemes*.

Since the differences in the three k̲'s discussed above are not contrastive, the linguist says that these are *phonetic differences*. He can further say that the "fronted k," the "backed k," and the "unreleased k" all belong to the same *phoneme* /k/. Another way of describing the three k̲'s is to say that they are "non-phonemic." On the other hand, the difference between 1̲ and r̲ is phonemic because 1̲ and r̲ contrast. That is to say, if we substitute 1̲ for r̲, or vice-versa, the meaning of the word will change.

NOTE: *Whenever phonemic spelling is used it will be enclosed in slant lines / /.*

When two or more phonetically different sounds belong to the same phoneme, they are called *allophones.* In Chamorro, [k̲], [k], and [k̆] are allophones of the phoneme /k/.

All languages have phonemes and allophones. No two languages of the world have exactly the same sets of phonemes and allophones. The phonemes (contrastive sounds) and allophones (non-contrastive sounds) of Chamorro will be discussed below.

CHAMORRO VOWELS

2.1   There are six vowel phonemes in Chamorro. These can be distinguished very easily when they occur in the loudest syllable in the word and when they are not followed by a consonant in the same syllable. These six vowels are illustrated in the following six Chamorro words. (Traditional spelling is followed and the vowel being illustrated is underlined.)

híta	'we'	úchan	'rain'
epanglao	'hunt for crabs'	oppe	'respond'
baba	'open'	baba	'bad'

A phonemic chart of the above vowels and phonemic respelling of the words would look like this:

Phonemic Vowel Chart

	Front		Back	
High	i	/hita/	u	/uchan/
Mid	e	/épanglao/	o	/oppe/
Low	æ	/bæba/	a	/baba/

(Note to non-Chamorro speakers: The six vowel phonemes in Chamorro have *approximate* equivalents in English. They are not the same in both languages. The approximate English equivalents of the six Chamorro vowels can be seen in the following examples:

Chamorro Vowel	Word Showing Approximate English Equivalent
/i/	beet
/e/	bait
/æ/	bat
/u/	boot
/o/	boat
/a/	father

Remember that the Chamorro vowels are not the same as the English vowels. In general, the English vowels are longer in duration and they tend to have an accompanying glide, while the Chamorro vowels do not.)

There are three things that should be noticed about the phonemic chart and respelling. One is the particular arrangement of the vowels. (It does not follow the alphabetic sequence a, e, i, o, u.) Another is the labels given on the chart (Front, Back, etc.). The third is the use of a new symbol /æ/ in place of a regular letter of the alphabet. There are reasons, which are given below, for these three differences.

Arrangement of the Vowels and Labels. The Chamorro vowels are arranged in two columns labeled "front" and "back." This is to help illustrate the fact that the vowels /i, e, æ/ are pronounced with the *front* part of the tongue, including the tip and the blade, serving as the primary articulator. When the vowel /i/ as in *hita* is pronounced, the front part of the tongue is very high in the mouth. When the vowel /æ/ as in *baba* 'open' is pronounced, the front part of the tongue is very low. Compare the different positions of the front part of the tongue when you pronounce the two words *hita* and *baba*. Check the height of the tongue by looking in a mirror.

Another method to help detect the different levels of vowel height is place your hand on your chin and then say the sound of the first vowel in *hita* (/i/). While still holding your chin, say the first vowel sound of *baba* (/æ/). Then try saying the two vowels /i/ and /æ/ rapidly a number of times in succession. You will notice your chin moving up and down in order to permit raising and lowering of the tongue for high and low vowels respectively.

When the vowel /e/ as in *épanglao* 'hunt for crabs' is pronounced, the front part of the tongue is neither high nor low, but is somewhere in between, or in the middle of the two extremes. This is why the term "mid" is used for this sort of vowel.

The vowels listed under the "back" column—/u, o, a/—are produced by using the back part of the tongue as the primary articulator. When the high vowel /u/ is pronounced, as in *uchan* 'rain', the back part of the tongue is relatively high in the mouth. When the low vowel /a/ is pronounced, as in *baba* 'bad', the back part of the tongue is relatively low in the mouth. And when /o/ is pronounced, as in *oppe* 'answer', the back part of the tongue is somewhere in between high and low. Hence, we can call it "mid."

When the three back vowels of Chamorro are pronounced, the lips are automatically rounded; that is to say, the lips form a kind of circular shape as though one is getting ready to whistle. The u and o are more rounded than the a. All three of the back vowels contrast in terms of lip rounding with the three front vowels. This phenomenon is clearly visible when looking in a mirror.

It will be noticed that there are six contrastive vowels in Chamorro. In the Roman alphabet there are only five vowel letters. In order to show the six contrastive vowels in Chamorro we have had to use one additional phonetic vowel symbol /æ/ for the low front vowel. This symbol is usually called "digraph." Special symbols will be used only when necessary in this discussion.

Phonemic Status of Chamorro Vowels

2.1.1   We can offer evidence in Chamorro that each of the six vowels is significant in the language, that each one is *phonemic*. We can show this by finding pairs of words in the language that have different meanings. The difference in meaning between the pairs of words rests on the difference in a single vowel. Everything else in the pair of words remains the same. We call a pair of words in which there is only one difference in the sound structure a *minimal pair*. Note the following minimal pairs in Chamorro which contrast vowels that are fairly close to each other in sound. The words are written in phonemic transcription.

Vowels Contrasted	Chamorro Words and Meanings			
/i/—/e/	/in/	'we (exclusive)'	/en/	'you (plural)'
/e/—/æ/	/edda'/	'soil'	/ædda'/	'mimic'
/u/—/o/	/bula/	'full'	/bola/	'ball'
/o/—/a/	/bola/	ball'	/bala/	'bullet'

/æ/—/a/   /bæba/ 'open'   /baba/ 'bad'

Vowel Allophones

2.1.2   In all languages of the world, the phonemes—the significant sounds—of a language have one or more *allophones*—different pronunciations of the same phoneme. These allophones sound very different to the trained linguist, but to the native speaker of a language these differences usually need to be pointed out. In order to have a clear understanding of the vowel system of Chamorro, we need to examine the allophones of the six vowel phonemes.

The allophones (phonetic variants) of a single phoneme are usually caused by the immediate environment in which the particular sound occurs. For example, the different types of Chamorro /k/ that were discussed earlier are different because of the immediate environment in which each occurs. The k of *kilili* is fronted because it immediately precedes a "front" vowel. The k of *katta* is backed because it immediately precedes a "back" vowel. The k of *falak* is unreleased because it occurs at the end of a word.

The six vowel phonemes of Chamorro also have allophones. And these allophones are conditioned by their immediate environment. The pattern of variation among the vowels is very regular, and each allophone is always predictable.

Allophones of /i/ and /u/. The two high vowels /i/ and /u/ both have slightly lower allophones in certain environments. By lower allophones we mean that the tongue is slightly lower in the mouth when they are produced. These two lower allophones will be represented by the symbols [ɪ] and [ʊ]. The allophone [ɪ] is slightly lower than [i] and the allophone [ʊ] is slightly lower than [u]. Thus, each of the two high vowels of Chamorro have allophones as follows:

Phoneme	Allophones	Chamorro	Illustrative Words	English*
/i/	[i]	[hita]	'we'	beat
	[ɪ]	[hɪt]	'us'	bit
/u/	[u]	[uchan]	'rain'	boot
	[ʊ]	[utʊt]	'cut'	could

*Remember that the vowels of the English words are only approximate equivalents of the Chamorro vowel sounds.

The rules for the distribution of these allophones are as follows:

> Vowel Rule 1: If the vowel is *stressed*—that is, if it sounds louder than the other vowels in the word—and if it is not followed by a consonant in the same syllable, then the higher allophones [i] and [u] will occur.
>
> Vowel Rule 2: If the vowel is *unstressed*—if it sounds less loud than the other vowels in the word—or if it is followed by a consonant in the same syllable, then the lower allophones [ɪ] and [ʊ] will occur.

Here are some additional examples of Chamorro words with the higher vowel allophones. Notice that the immediate environment corresponds with Rule #1. The period following the vowel marks syllable division. The accent mark (') over the vowel indicates stress or loudness.

Front Vowel /i/		*Back Vowel /u/*	
[hí.hʊt]	'near'	[pú.gas]	'rice'
[ní.gap]	'yesterday'	[mú.mʊ]	'fight'
[a.lí.gao]	'look for'	[a.gú.pa']	'tomorrow'

Following are some additional examples of Chamorro words with the lower vowel allophones. Note that the environment for these allophones corresponds with Rule #2. The lower allophones are underlined.

Front Vowel /i/		*Back Vowel /u/*	
[lá.hɪ]	'male'	[hí.hʊt]	'near'
[mə.ga.hɪt]	'truly'	[mú.mʊ]	'fight'
[ɪt.más]	'most'	[bʊn.mʊ.cha.chʊ]	'industrious'

Allophones of /e/ and /o/. In all probability the phonemes /e/ and /o/ became significantly different sounds (phonemic sounds) in Chamorro after Spanish loan words began to be used frequently. For a brief explanation of this, see the "Notes to Linguists" section following this discussion of the vowels.

The phonemes /e/ and /o/ are somewhat different from the vowels /i/ and /u/. Both /e/ and /o/ have three allophones each. It may be somewhat confusing because one of the allophones of /e/ (namely [ɪ]) is similar to one of the allophones of /i/, and one of the allophones of /o/ (namely [ʊ]) is similar to one of the allophones of /u/. The patterns for the allophones of /e/ and /o/ are somewhat different from each other; hence they will be treated separately.

Phoneme /e/ has higher and lower allophones. They can be represented as follows:

Phoneme	Allophone	Illustrative Words	
		Chamorro	English
	[ɪ]	[óp.pɪ]	'respond'	bit
/e/	[e]	[pe.ga]	'attach'	bait
	[ɛ]	[mɛ́g.gai]	'many'	bet

Vowel Rule 3: If the vowel is stressed (loud), and if it is not followed by a consonant in the same syllable, the allophone [e] will occur ([pe.ga]). If the vowel is stressed or unstressed and followed by a consonant in the same syllable, the lower allophone [ɛ] will occur (mɛ́g.gai], [lɛk.tú.ra]). If the vowel is unstressed (not loud) and is not followed by a consonant in the same syllable, the higher allophone [ɪ] will occur ([óp.pɪ]).

Phoneme /o/ also has three allophones. One of the allophones is the same as one of the allophones of /u/, namely [ʊ]. The allophones of /o/ can be represented as follows:

Phoneme	Allophones	Illustrative Words	
		Chamorro	English
	[ʊ]	[máp.pʊt]	'difficult'	put
/o/	[o]	[óp.pɪ]	'respond'	boat
	[ɔ]	[tɔ́k.tʊk]	'hug'	log

Vowel Rule 4: If the vowel is stressed, and if it is not followed by the consonants *k* or *ng* in the same syllable, the allophone [o] will occur ([ó.chū] 'eight', [óp.pɪ]). If the vowel is unstressed— whether it is followed by a consonant or not—the higher allophone [ʊ] will occur ([ó.chʊ], [máp.pʊt]). If the vowel is stressed and is followed by the consonants *k* or *ng* in the same syllable, the lower allophone [ɔ] will occur ([tɔ́k.tʊk], [trɔ́ng.kɪn] 'tree').

Following are some additional examples of Chamorro words with the different vowel allophones of /e/ and /o/. Note that the environment for these allophones corresponds with Rules 3 and 4.

Front Vowel /e/		Back Vowel /o/	
[hót.nɪ]	'thread needle'	[hót.nɪ]	'thread needle'
[sé.bʊ]	'grease'	[hú.yʊng]	'out'
[sɛ́s.sʊ]	'often'	[hɔ́k.sɪ]	'hold down'

Allophones of /æ/ and /a/. The vowels /æ/ and /a/ do not have as many allophones (or variant pronunciations) as the other vowels.

When the vowel is stressed, it is easy to determine whether the vowel is the front vowel /æ/ or the back vowel /a/. Note the following pairs of words:

Front Vowel		Back Vowel	
[bǽ.bə]	'open'	[bá.bə]	'bad'
[fǽ.tə]	'boast'	[fát.tə]	'absent'

However, when the vowel is unstressed—as in the final syllable of all four of the above words—we get a different phonetic vowel [ə]. (Linguists call this vowel "schwa" and it is described as a mid-central vowel.) There is actually no sure way to determine whether [ə] is an allophone of /æ/ or /a/. We might say, then, that both low vowels have allophone [ə], as stated in the following rule:

Vowel Rule 5: If either /æ/ or /a/ is unstressed, the allophone [ə] will occur.

Following are some additional Chamorro words showing this allophone of /æ/ and /a/:

[há.fə]	'what'
[sí.hə]	'they'
[hí.tə]	'we'
[kə.tót.sɪ]	'fourteen'

Chamorro speakers are well aware of the fact that /a/ in many words becomes /æ/ when preceded by words containing /i/. For example, [má. tə] becomes [i mæ.te]. This type of change will be discussed later in section 2.7, Morphophonemics.

Summary of Chamorro Vowels

2.1.3   We have seen that Chamorro has six phonemic vowels. They are called phonemic because the substitution of one of these vowels for another in a pair of words that are identical except for one vowel—a minimal pair—will cause a change in meaning. Note the following minimal pairs:

/bula/	'full'	/bola/	'ball'
/bæba/	'open'	/baba/	'bad'
/in/	'we (exclusive)'	/en/	'you (plural)'

The six phonemic vowels of Chamorro can be charted so as to show their relationship to each other in terms of highness versus lowness and frontness versus backness. All of the back vowels are produced with the lips rounded; the front vowels are produced with the lips unrounded. (cf. Phonemic Vowel Chart, section 2.1)

There are at least eleven vowel allophones of the six phonemic vowels in Chamorro. They can be charted as follows so as to show relative highness-lowness and frontness-backness:

Phonetic Vowel Chart

	Front	Central	Back
High	i		u
Lower High	ɪ		ʊ
Mid	e	ə	o
Lower Mid	ɛ		ɔ
Low	æ		a

Notice that the vowels on the phonetic chart are not arranged vertically. This is done purposely in order to show that the vowel [ɪ] is a little bit less fronted than [i], that [e] is less fronted than [ɪ], and so on. Likewise, for the back vowels, [ʊ] is a little bit less back than [u], [o] a little less back than [ʊ], and so on.

A good phonetician could undoubtedly find more phonetic variation among the vowels than is shown here. Also, the amount of variation may well vary from one speaker to another. The above phonetic chart can be regarded as a general approximation of the phonetic variations of the six vowel phonemes in Chamorro.

Notes to Linguists: Chamorro Vowels. Before Spanish contact, Chamorro probably had a four-vowel system: /i u æ a/. The mid vowels [e o] were allophones of /i/ and /u/ in closed syllables and following medial consonant clusters. Through the introduction of high vowels in closed syllables and mid vowels in open syllables in Spanish loan words, the phonemic inventory of Chamorro was expanded to include the mid vowels.

The low front vowel seems anomalous. It is usually found in words in which the /a/ has been fronted by vowel harmony rules. But, there are still pairs of words such as /bǽba/ 'open' and /bába/ 'bad', /fǽta/ 'boast' and /fátta/ 'absent', which suggest that the two low vowels did not result from Spanish influence.

The apparent overlapping of allophones [ɪ] and [ʊ] described above is a very real problem. Stem-final unstressed /i/ and /e/ both occur as [ɪ]. Likewise, stem-final unstressed /u/ and /o/ both occur as [ʊ]. Bi-uniqueness can be achieved by considering the preceding stressed vowel of the stem and/or whether there is a medial consonant cluster in the stem. If the preceding stressed vowel of the stem is mid, the final unstressed vowel is also mid. If the preceding stressed vowel of the stem is high, the final unstressed vowel is high. If there is a medial consonant cluster, the final unstressed vowel is mid, and in native Chamorro words the stressed vowel is also mid. The only stressed high vowels preceding a consonant cluster are found in Spanish loan words. For a complete discussion of the rules governing the vowels in Chamorro, see Topping 1968.

Diphthongs

2.1.4   When two or more vowels come together within a single syllable, they form a *diphthong* (pronounced [dɪpθɔng] or [dɪfθɔng]). Diphthongs are also referred to as *glides* because the articulator—primarily the tongue—glides from one position to another to cause a change in the sound. The most common diphthongs in Chamorro are as follows:

Diphthong	*Example*	*Words*
ai	/taitai/	'to read'
	/matai/	'to die'
ao	/taotao/	'person'
	/lao/	'but'

Some additional diphthongs are found in loan words which have been borrowed from Spanish, English, and possibly other languages. Some examples are given below:

Diphthong	*Chamorro Word*
/oi/	boi (from English 'boy')
/ia/	espia (from Spanish 'espia')
/ea/	manea (also maneha, from Sp. 'manejar')
/oe/	hagoe (source unknown)
/iu/	tiu (from Spanish 'tio')

It is possible to have almost any combination of vowels forming diphthongs in Chamorro when loanwords are included. The only diphthongs typically found in native Chamorro words are /ao/ and /ai/.

The sequences of vowels found in words like *Guam, guihi,*

buente, and *dueño* are not diphthongs, even though it appears that two vowels occur in the same syllable. The above words spelled phonemically would look like this: /gwam/, /gwihi/, /bwente/, /dweño/. Since the phoneme /w/ replaces the letter *u,* we don't really have two vowels in the same syllable after all.

Notes to Linguists: Diphthongs. I prefer to analyze the diphthongs in Chamorro as a sequence of vowel and semivowel, i.e., /ay/ and /aw/. This interpretation precludes any occurrences of /VV/ in the language, thus simplifying the description.

The cluster represented as /gw/ in my phonemic analysis (Cf. Topping 1969a) could well be considered a single labio-velar phoneme, although I have not suggested this as a solution.

Interestingly, the two Chamorro diphthongs /aw/ and /ay/ are in complementary distribution with /gw/ and /z/ (voiced alveo-palatal affricate) respectively. It is arguable that these pairs should be listed as allophones, e.g., /gw/ has allophones [gʷ] and [aw]; /z/ has allophones [z] and [ay].

This interpretation of diphthongs as vowel plus semi-vowel is confirmed by evidence from the process of reduplication. The rule in Chamorro for reduplication is to repeat the (C)V́ of the stem. Notice the following stems containing diphthongs and their respective reduplicated forms. (Conventional spelling is used here.)

Stem		*Reduplicated Form*	
taitai	'to read'	tátaitai	'reading'
taotao	'people'	tátaotao	'body'
saosao	'wipe'	sásaosao	'wiping'

CHAMORRO CONSONANTS

2.2   It is not unusual for a language to have more than one phonemic analysis and interpretation. Two different linguists might work with the same informant and come up with different analyses of the same data. A phonemic analysis can be considered an "interpretation" of the phonetic data. The phonemic analysis of Chamorro consonants presented here is the one that corresponds most closely with the writing system. (For different interpretations of Chamorro phonology see Mathiot 1955; Seiden 1960; Topping 1963, 1969a.)

There are eighteen consonants in Chamorro and one semi-consonant /w/ (also known as semivowel). (For a discussion of the semiconsonant see 2.3.1 below.) The semiconsonant is not used in the writing system but is included here as part of the discussion of how the consonant system of Chamorro works. Remember that we are still talking in terms of the *phonemic* system of Chamorro, not the writing system.

In this discussion of the Chamorro consonant phonemes, we shall adhere to the writing system as much as possible. It is very important to bear in mind the following points:

> a. The consonant represented by *ch* is a single consonant, not a sequence of two consonants. In the articles on Chamorro phonology listed above, it is represented by the symbol /c/.
> b. The consonant represented by *y* is a voiced, alveolar affricate. In the articles on Chamorro phonology listed above, it is represented by /z/ and /ʒ/.
> c. The consonant represented by ng is a single consonant, not a sequence of two consonants. In the articles on Chamorro phonology listed above, it is represented by the symbol /ŋ/.
> d. The semiconsonant /w/ is spelled with *u* in the standard spelling system when it follows a consonant. In diphthongs the semiconsonant /w/ is spelled with an *o*, as in the word *taotao* 'people'. In this section on phonology, the /w/ spelling will be used.

The consonants are illustrated in the following Chamorro words. The approximate English equivalents of the Chamorro consonants in English are also included.

Chamorro Consonant	Chamorro Phonemic	Word Spelling	Chamorro Word New Spelling	Approximate English Equivalent
/p/	/paharu/	'bird'	páharu	pat
/t/	/tata/	'father'	tata	tap
/k/	/kada/	'each'	kada	king
/'/	/haga'/	'blood'	haga'	No English Equiv.
/b/	/baba/	'bad'	baba	bat
/d/	/dagu/	'yam'	dagu	dock
/g/	/gaige/	'here'	gaige	get
/ch/	/chægi/	'try'	chagi	tsar
/y/	/yema/	'egg yolk'	yema	floods
/f/	/foggon/	'stove'	foggon	fast
/s/	/saga/	'stay'	saga	say
/h/	/hatsa/	'lift'	hatsa	hot
/m/	/mata/	'face'	mata	mama

/n/	/napu/	'wave'	napu	<u>n</u>ot
/ñ/	/ñamu/	'mosquito'	ñamu	ca<u>ny</u>on
/ng/	/ngayu/	'collect firewood'	ngayu	si<u>ng</u>ing
/l/	/lahi/	'male'	lahi	<u>l</u>ong
/r/	/ratu/	'little while'	ratu	<u>r</u>at
/w/	/gwihi/	'there'	guihi	<u>Gw</u>endolyn

Consonant Chart

2.2.1   The consonants of Chamorro can be charted in the following manner:

Phonemic Consonant Chart

	Bilabial	Labio-dental	Alveolar	Palatal	Velar	Glottal
Stops						
Voiceless	p		t		k	'
Voiced	b		d		g	
Affricates						
Voiceless			ch			
Voiced			y			
Fricatives		f	s			h
Nasals	m		n	ñ	ng	
Liquids			l,r			
Semi-Consonant	w					

There are several linguistic terms used on the consonant chart. They are helpful in describing the manner in which each sound is made. The labels across the top of the chart describe the *point of articulation* in producing the particular sound. The labels along the left-hand column describe the *manner* in which the sounds are articulated. These terms will be defined in connection with the particular consonants they are associated with. It will be helpful to refer to the following diagram which shows the various points of articulation.

Stops

2.2.2   There are seven consonants in Chamorro that are called *stops*. (The terms *obstruent* and *plosive* are also used by many linguists to describe this type of sound.) The term *stop* is used to suggest

POINTS OF ARTICULATION

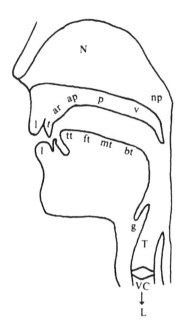

N = nasal cavity
T = throat
L = to the lungs
VC = vocal cords
l = lip (upper and lower)
t = teeth
ap = alveo-palatal
p = hard palate
v = velum
g = glottis
tt = tip of tongue
ft = front of tongue
mt = middle of tongue
bt = back of tongue
np = nasal passage
ar = alveolar ridge

that the flow of air from the lungs is momentarily stopped (or checked) in the production of the sound. The air flow may be stopped by closing the two lips, by placing the tip of the tongue a-gainst the teeth, or by bringing together any of the several points of articulation to form a closure, and consequent stoppage of air.

Bilabial Stops

2.2.3   The *bilabial stops* /p/ and /b/ are described thus because the two lips are brought completely together in order to stop the flow of air momentarily before releasing it. They are made at the same *point of articulation*. There are several differences between /p/ and /b/. The most significant difference is that /p/ is *voiceless* and /b/ is *voiced*.

Voiceless and voiced consonants are found in most languages of the world. The articulatory organs used to control voicing are the *vocal cords*. The vocal cords are twin membranes in the throat. (See diagram showing Points of Articulation.) These vocal cords behave somewhat like strings on a guitar. They can be made to vibrate, thus producing noise, or voicing; or they can be allowed to relax loosely in the throat, in which case there is no noise, or voicing. Control of these membranes is completely automatic in human speech, so that people don't have to stop and think about whether they should stretch the vocal cords or let them relax. When a voiceless sound (such as /p/) is pronounced, the membranes are opened and relaxed, allowing the air to come through them unimpeded. When a voiced sound (such as /b/) is pronounced, the membranes are drawn taut and are made to vibrate by the air passing through them. This, then, is the major difference between voiceless and voiced consonants.

In Chamorro there are pairs of voiceless versus voiced stops and affricates (see 2.2.7). All of the fricatives (see 2.2.8) are voiceless, and all of the remaining consonants are voiced. It is important to understand this distinction between voiceless and voiced consonants.

The other very noticeable differences between /p/ and /b/ are that /p/ is accompanied by a slight puff of air while /b/ is not, and that the muscles of the face—particularly those around the lips—are more *tense* when pronouncing /p/ than when pronouncing /b/. /p/ is often described as a *tense* (or fortis) consonant, while /b/ is described as a *lax* (or lenis) consonant. All voiceless stops in Chamorro are tense; all voiced stops in Chamorro are lax.

Alveolar Stops

2.2.4   The stops /t/ and /d/ are also made at the same point of articulation by placing the tip of the tongue against the *alveolar ridge* and stopping the flow of air. The *alveolar ridge* (see chart) is the very front part of the roof of the mouth just behind the point where the upper teeth go into the upper gums. Some speakers of Chamorro may actually place their tongue tip against the back of the upper teeth in order to form the closure. /t/ is voiceless and tense; /d/ is voiced and lax.

Velar Stops

2.2.5   /k/ and /g/—the *velar* stops—follow the pattern of voiceless-voiced that we have seen in /p-b/ and /t-d/. /k/ is voiceless and tense; /g/ is voiced and lax. They are both made at the same point of articulation by placing the back of the tongue against the velum to form closure to stop the flow of air. This is why they are called "velar stops."

Glottal Stop

2.2.6   This is a very important consonant in Chamorro and in many other languages of the world. Unfortunately, the earlier grammars and dictionaries of Chamorro have, for the most part, ignored it because it is not a phonemic consonant in European languages. This consonant is symbolized in different ways in different languages of the Pacific. In Cebuano, for example, it is often represented by *q*; in Palauan it is represented by *ch*; and in Hawaiian it is represented by ' (apostrophe mark). Since the apostrophe is found on all standard typewriters and is widely used in other Pacific languages, it has been adopted for Chamorro.

The important thing to remember is that the glottal stop is a genuine consonant, just as *p*, *t*, and *k* are genuine consonants. The presence or absence of the glottal stop can determine the difference in meanings of words. Note the following pairs of words:

haga	'daughter'	haga'	'blood'
baba	'bad'	ba'ba'	'spank'

In producing the glottal stop the vocal cords are briefly closed completely by muscular tension, and air pressure from the lungs builds up behind them. Then the vocal cords are opened quickly and the air is released. The glottal stop in Chamorro usually occurs at the end of a word (as in *haga'*) or between two vowels (as in *li'e'* 'to see'), but it also occurs between a vowel and a following consonant (as in *ba'ba'*). The glottal stop is always voiceless.

Affricates

2.2.7   The two *affricates* in Chamorro /ch/ and /y/ are sometimes classified as stops. Technically, they should be placed in a different class of consonants from the stops. In the production of stops the air flow is stopped completely and then cleanly released. In the production of affricates, the air flow is stopped completely by the articulators, then released with an audible hissing or buzzing noise through a partial opening.

In producing /ch/ and /y/ the tip of the tongue is placed against the alveolar ridge in order to stop the air flow. The front part of the tongue comes very close to the alveo-palatal area. (See chart of Points of Articulation.) During release the air is allowed to escape through a partial opening.

The voiceless-voiced distinction applies to the affricates in the same way that it is observed among the stops. When /ch/ is produced, the vocal cords are at rest; when /y/ is produced, the vocal cords are vibrating.

Some examples of Chamorro words containing the affricates are:

/chægi/	'to try'	/yæyæs/	'tired'
/cho' cho'/	'work'	/yema/	'egg yolk'
/chomma'/	'forbid'	/yommok/	'fat'

For practice in hearing the difference between voiceless and voiced affricates try pronouncing only the first consonant of the words *chomma'* and *yommok* while holding your hands over your ears or on your throat. When the voiced affricate is pronounced, you can hear the "buzzing" sound. When the voiceless affricate is pronounced, you should hear nothing except the hissing sound of air escaping between the tongue and the alveolar ridge. Notice that these sounds cannot be sustained like the nasal or fricative sounds.

Fricatives

2.2.8   There are three consonants in Chamorro that belong to the class of sounds known as *fricatives* (or *spirants*). All three of them are voiceless. The term fricative is used to describe the hissing sound—friction—when these consonants are produced. In producing a fricative, the articulators form only partial closure, and the air is forced through the opening thus creating the hissing sound. (Remember that in producing stops and affricates, the air flow is blocked completely; in producing fricatives, it is only partially blocked.) The space between the articulator and the point of articulation is so narrow that the air being forced through it is impeded. This impedence causes a turbulence that makes the hissing sound.

The fricatives (as well as the nasals and liquids) are also classed as *continuants,* as opposed to stops, because the sound can be sustained for as long as the flow of air can be maintained.

The consonant /f/ is described as a *labio-dental fricative* because the articulator used in producing it is the lower lip against the upper teeth. It is easily identifiable in such words as /fatto/ 'come' and /taftaf/ 'early'.

The consonant /s/ is described as an *alveolar fricative.*

In making this sound, the tip of the tongue touches against the front part of the roof of the mouth just behind the front upper teeth and the air is forced through the narrow opening causing the hissing noise. The front part of the tongue comes very close to the alveo-palatal area. This consonant is found in such words as /saga/ 'to stay' and /gasgas/ 'clean'.

The phoneme /s/ has one allophone which should be mentioned here. When /s/ occurs immediately preceding the high front vowel /i/, it frequently sounds like the "sh" sound in English (as in "she"). The phonetic symbol for this allophone is [š], and it is often heard in words such as [šiʊk] 'stab' and [šia] 'they' when the words are spoken in rapid speech. (In slow speech the above words would be pronounced [sihʊk] and [sihə].)

The consonant /h/ is described on the consonant chart as a glottal fricative. This description is actually misleading because the point of articulation for /h/ varys widely depending on the immediate environment. The constriction (or partial closure) for /h/ is in the throat; the vocal cords are not vibrated, so, like /p t k s f/ there is no voicing. The point at which the constriction is formed is more forward when /h/ precedes a front vowel (as in /hita/) than it is when /h/ precedes a back vowel (as in /hatsa/). Try pronouncing just the /h/ of /hita/ and /hatsa/ and you will be able to detect a difference in quality.

Nasals

2.2.9   There are four *nasal* consonants in Chamorro. They are called nasal because in producing them the velum is lowered and the air flow is directed through the nose. This lowering and raising of the velum is done automatically during the flow of speech. It is, in fact, one of the earliest articulatory movements that an infant learns to control.

The consonant /m/ is described as a *bilabial nasal* because the two lips are completely closed when making this sound. Even though the air is coming out through the nose, the closure of the lips affects the quality of the sound. This consonant is found in such words as /mata/ 'face' and /hanom/ 'water'.

The consonant /n/ is described as an alveolar nasal. This sound is made by placing the tongue in the same position against the alveolar ridge as it is for the consonants /t/ and /d/. This consonant is found in such words as /napu/ 'wave' and /nifen/ 'tooth'.

The consonant /ñ/ is described as a *palatal nasal*. When making this sound, the tip of the tongue is usually placed down behind the lower teeth, and the middle part of the tongue is pressed against the palate well behind the alveolar ridge. When this consonant is released, there is usually a "y" like sound associated with it, as in the English word "canyon." This consonant is found in such words as /ñamu/ 'mosquito' and /taña'/ 'try'.

The consonant /ng/ is described as a *velar nasal*. When making this sound, the back part of the tongue is pressed against the velum as it is for the consonants /k/ and /g/. This consonant is found in such words as /ngai'an/ 'when' and /poddong/ 'fall down'.

Liquids

2.3.0   The consonants /l/ and /r/ are quite distinct from each other in modern Chamorro, but in pre-Spanish Chamorro they were both probably variants of the same sound. In modern Chamorro we can find minimal pairs of words such as /lata/ 'can' and /rata/ 'low pitch' in which /l/ and /r/ contrast. It will be noticed, however, that one of the words is a Spanish loanword (lata). Further evidence that /l/ and /r/ were allophones in pre-Spanish Chamorro is the way in which /l/ replaced /r/ in some Spanish loanwords but not in others. See the following examples:

Spanish		*Chamorro*	*Sound Change*
frito	'fry'	aflitu	r became l
franela	'flannel'	franela	r remained r
		—flanela	r became l
lata	'can'	lata	l remained l

(Final l in Spanish words became t in Chamorro; this is discussed in section 2.4 on Distribution of the Consonants.)

To pronounce the Chamorro /l/, the tip of the tongue is placed against the alveolar ridge, as it is when pronouncing /t d n/. The sides of the tongue are then lowered so that the air passes over the sides of the tongue rather than over the center of the tongue. Since the air is released laterally, the consonant /l/ is usually called a *lateral*. Sample words in which this consonant is found are /lamlam/ 'shiny' and /chalan/ 'road'.

The other liquid consonant /r/ has two allophones in Chamorro. When it occurs at the beginning of a word, it is pronounced by curling the tip of the tongue back towards the palate, but without touching the roof of the mouth. The tongue is then in a *retroflex* position; this type of /r/ is a retroflex r. It is found in words such as /ratu/ 'little while' and /risaki/ 'receding wave'.

The other allophone of /r/ is called a *flapped r*; it is usually symbolized in phonetic writing as [ř]. When the flapped r is pronounced, the tip of the tongue quickly touches the front part of the palate behind the alveolar ridge. This allophone occurs in the middle of words between two vowels. The following words contain the flapped r:

[pařa] 'towards'
[ořa] 'hour'

The "flap" is more noticeable in rapid speech than in slow speech.

Semiconsonant

2.3.1 The semiconsonant /w/ is a linguistic invention for Chamorro. It could be eliminated from the phonemic inventory. We could consider the initial sound of the word *Guam* a single consonant and transcribe it phonemically as /g^w/; or, we could consider it a consonant plus vowel /gu/ as is suggested by the writing system. For the present, let us consider the semiconsonant /w/ one of the Chamorro consonant phonemes.

There is no single point of articulation for /w/, even though it is described as bilabial. It is placed at this point of articulation because the two lips are rounded and are brought almost together in making this sound. The semiconsonant /w/ never occurs by itself as a consonant, but always with another consonant, as in the following examples:

/gwiya/	'him'	/kumwentos/	'talk'
/kwentos/	'talk'	/dweño/	'owner'
/pwenge/	'night'	/rweda/	'wheel'
/bwente/	'maybe'	/swetdo/	'wage'

It will be noticed that most of the above words are Spanish in origin. Pre-Spanish Chamorro undoubtedly had /gw/ and /pw/ as in /gwiya/ and /pwenge/, but the other combinations of consonant plus /w/ were introduced through Spanish loan words.

Summary of Chamorro Consonant Phonemes

2.3.2 To facilitate the learning of the sound system of Chamorro and the articulatory description of the consonants, the following list is given. The articulatory terms are conventional descriptions of the consonants.

/p/	voiceless bilabial stop
/t/	voiceless alveolar stop
/k/	voiceless velar stop
/'/	glottal stop
/b/	voiced bilabial stop
/d/	voiced alveolar stop
/g/	voiced velar stop
/ch/	voiceless alveolar affricate
/y/	voiced alveolar affricate
/f/	voiceless labio-dental fricative
/s/	voiceless alveolar fricative
/h/	voiceless glottal fricative
/m/	bilabial nasal
/n/	alveolar nasal
/ñ/	palatal nasal
/ng/	velar nasal
/l/	lateral
/r/	retroflex
/w/	bilabial semiconsonant

DISTRIBUTION OF THE VOWELS AND CONSONANTS

2.4   In order to have a good understanding of the sound system of a language, it is necessary to know the *distribution* of the sounds. In considering the distribution of the sounds we must consider whether there are *distributional limitations* on where each of the sounds may occur. There are always such limitations in every language, and these limitations are not the same for any two languages.

Distributional Limitations of Vowels

2.4.1   The Vowels in Chamorro have almost complete freedom of occurrence: that is, all of the six vowels may occur at the beginning middle, or end of a word.

Distributional Limitations of Consonants

2.4.2   There are several distributional limitations on the consonants of Chamorro that should be noted. The following consonants never occur at the end of a word: /b d g ch y h ñ l r/. In the traditional writing systems of Chamorro, many words were spelled with final *g* (for example, *niyog* 'coconut'), but the actual final consonant that occurs in that word is a voiceless /k/. We could summarize this rule of the language as follows: voiced stops, affricates, liquids, /ñ/, and /h/ never occur at the end of a word in Chamorro.

Another distributional limitation of the consonants is that the two sounds /'/ and /w/ never occur at the beginning of a word in Chamorro. (Phonetically there is a glottal stop preceding every word-initial vowel, but this is not phonemic. For example, the phonemic representation of /alu/ 'baracuda' and the phonetic representation of the same word ['alu] are different.)

All of the other consonants in Chamorro may occur at the beginning, middle, or end of a word.

It might be pointed out that, since voiced stops do not occur at the end of a word in Chamorro, this often causes difficulties for Chamorro speakers learning English. In English, final voiced and voiceless stops occur in minimal contrast. For example, see the following pairs of English words: rip-rib; bet-bed; duck-dug. The Chamorro speaker who is just beginning to learn English is very likely to confuse the sets of words listed above because of the rule in Chamorro that voiced stops do not occur in word-final position.

Consonant Clusters

2.4.3   A *consonant cluster* consists of two or more consonants together in the same syllable without any intervening vowels. In Chamorro, as in all other languages, there are limitations on the number and types of consonants that can form clusters.

In modern Chamorro the permissible consonant clusters are as follows: (The semiconsonant /w/ is considered a consonant for purposes of this aspect of the language.)

pl-	/planu/	'plan'
kl-	/klasi/	'class'
bl-	/blusa/	'blouse'
gl-	/gloria/	'glory'
fl-	/flores/	'flowers'
pr-	/primu/	'cousin'

tr-	/trabiha/	'still'
kr-	/kristo/	'Christ'
br-	/brasu/	'arm'
gr-	/grifu/	'faucet'
fr-	/franela/	'T-shirt'
pw-	/pwenge/	'night'
kw-	/kwentos/	'talk'
bw-	/bwente/	'maybe'
gw-	/gwihæn/	'fish'
mw-	/kumwentos/	'talk'
ngw-	/fangwentos/	'talk'

It should be pointed out that all of the words listed above containing consonant clusters except for /pwenge/ and /gwihæn/ are loanwords from Spanish. If we interpreted the /pw/ and /gw/ as single consonants instead of consonant clusters, we could then conclude that the only consonant clusters found in Chamorro are in Spanish loanwords.

It is fairly safe to conclude that in pre-Spanish Chamorro there were no consonant clusters, unless we wish to interpret /pw/ and /gw/ as clusters instead of independent consonants. Even in modern Chamorro, including the Spanish loanwords, the consonant clusters are limited to sequences of two consonants only. (English has consonant clusters of three or more.) The second consonant in each Chamorro consonant cluster must be either a liquid /l r/ or the semiconsonant /w/.

Chamorro does not permit any consonant clusters at the end of a word.

Geminate Consonants. When two identical consonants come together across a syllable boundary, they are described as *geminate consonants.* (The term "syllable boundary" is used to describe the point where one syllable stops and the following syllable begins. The syllable boundary in a word like *baba* is clearly after the first a. The syllable boundary in the word *tommo* is somewhere between the two m's.) More than half of the consonants in Chamorro occur as geminate consonants, which form a type of consonant cluster. The geminate consonants with example words are as follows:

pp	/goppe/	'jump over'
tt	/fatto/	'come'
kk	/akka'/	'bite'

bb	/yabbao/	'reap'
dd	/ædda'/	'imitate'
gg	/meggai/	'many'
ss	/sesso/	'often'
mm	/tommo/	'knee'
nn	/konne'/	'catch'
ll	/halla/	'pull'

There may be examples of other geminate consonants in Chamorro, but they have not turned up in the data on which this grammar is based.

The consonants that do not geminate are: /'ch y h ñ ng r/.

These geminate consonants are very important in determining the spelling rules for Chamorro. They are sometimes difficult to identify, especially for the non-Chamorro speaker, for three reasons: 1) Geminate consonants do not occur in modern English and are consequently difficult for the English speaker to hear; 2) The speakers of the dialect of Chamorro spoken on Rota do not pronounce geminate consonants; 3) Many younger speakers of Chamorro do not pronounce the geminate consonants, especially in rapid speech. Hence the word /tommo/, spoken by a young Guamanian or Rotanese, would probably sound like [tómʊ] instead of [tómmʊ].

It might also be pointed out here that the same speakers who do not pronounce geminate consonants usually do not pronounce syllable-final /h/. Hence, the word /sahyan/ 'set the table' would be pronounced with the /h/ at the end of the first syllable by most Saipanese and Guamanians, but it would be pronounced as /sayan/ by most Rotanese and younger Guamanians. The occurrence of the syllable-final /h/ is also important for the spelling rules, as we shall see later on.

These differences in pronunciation of the geminate consonants and the syllable-final /h/ help account for the so-called Rota dialect.

Although we have said that the consonant c̲h̲ does not geminate, there appears to be partial gemination. For instance, the word /acho'/ 'stone' might be spelled phonetically as [atchʊ'], with the t̲ representing partial gemination of the consonant c̲h̲.

THE SYLLABLE

2.5   Although the terms *syllable* and *syllable boundary* have already been used in the preceding discussion of the sound system, no attempt has been made to define what constitutes a syllable in Chamorro. Rules for syllable division are not always easy to discover and they vary from language to language.

Each syllable in Chamorro contains a vowel. The vowel forms the peak of the syllable. All Chamorro vowels are syllabic. Chamorro has a range of syllabic patterns as follows:

(Syllable division is marked by .)
(V = Vowel C = Consonant)

Syllable Structure	Sample Word	English Gloss
V	/a.lu/	'barracuda'
CV	/a.gu.pa'/	'tomorrow'
CVC	/ses.so/	'often'
VC	/æd.da/	'imitate'
CCV	/pla.nu/	'plan'
CCVC	/blang.ko/	'throw'
C + diphthong	/tai.tai/	'read'
	/tao.tao/	'person'
diphthong	/ao.to.ri.dát/	'authority'
C + /w/ + V	/hwe.gu/	'game'
C + /w/ + VC	/swet.to/	'free'

The syllables of Chamorro are isolated by the following principles. Syllable division occurs—

a. after vowels when they are followed by a single consonant except the glottal stop /'/;

/a.lu/	'barracuda'
/i.pe'/	'to cut'
/u.chan/	'rain'
/na.pu/	'wave'

These constitute *open syllables*; that is, when the syllable ends with a vowel. Syllables that end with consonants are *closed syllables*.

b. after /'/;

/na'.i/	'to give'
/gwi'.eng/	'nose'
/i'.e'/	'baby skipjack'

c. after the first consonant of a medial consonant cluster (in the middle of the word) except when the second consonant is /r l/ or /w/;

/it.mas/	'superlative'
/blang.ko/	'throw'
/gwet.gwe.ru/	'throat'
/dop.bla/	'bend'
/hom.lo'/	'heal'

but note:

/a.brít/	'April'
/a.fli.tu/	'fry'
/pu.gwa'/	'betel nut'
/ma.blang.ko/	'be thrown'
/a.rek.glao/	'ready'

d. between geminate consonants.

/hal.la/	'pull'
/gop.pe/	'step over'
/god.de/	'tie'

The transition between syllables in which geminate consonants are involved is not as clear as that between other syllables. This is sometimes referred to as *muddy transition*.

STRESS AND INTONATION

2.6   The linguistic term *stress* was used earlier in the discussion of the vowels in Section 2.1. It was there stated that a stressed vowel sounds louder than the other vowels in the word. The term *stress* refers to the *degree of loudness* of a syllable (which always contains a vowel as its peak) in the speech of an individual. The fact that one individual may habitually speak in a louder voice than someone else has nothing to do with stress as used in linguistic descriptions. Stress refers to the relative degrees of loudness in the speech of a single person. The term *accent* is used by some people to refer to stress, or loudness. Unfortunately, the term accent is also confusing because of its common usage when referring to a "foreign accent."

The *intonation* of a language refers to the characteristic patterns of rising and falling of the pitch levels of the voice and the types of juncture (pauses) that are significant in the language.

Each language has its own distinct patterns of stress and intonation, and it is very important to consider these patterns as part of the overall sound system of a language. A child learns the intonational system of his native language long before he learns to control the consonants and vowels. Also, the intonational system of a language is probably the most difficult thing for an adult learner of a foreign language to master.

And, even more important from a linguistic point of view, stress and intonation are (1) inseparable and (2) phonemic.

Stress Pattern of Chamorro.

2.6.1 Although not everything is known about the stress pattern of Chamorro, we do know that *stress is phonemic*. There are minimal pairs of utterances where the difference in meaning is determined by a difference in stress. Note the following pairs of words: (Primary stress is indicated by ′.)

| /móhon/ | 'want, desire' | /mohón/ | 'boundary' |
| /aságwa/ | 'spouse' | /ásagwa/ | 'get married' |

In the two examples above we can see that, by placing the primary stress on a different syllable of a word, we get a different meaning.

In Chamorro there are at least three noticeable degrees of stress. There is *primary stress,* which is the loudest. There is also *weak stress,* which is considerably less loud than primary stress. Then, in between primary stress and weak stress there is *secondary stress,* which will be indicated by ∧. Any word of more than two syllables will probably have all three levels of stress present.

For example, in the word /aságwa/ 'spouse', the second syllable is clearly the loudest of the three. But what about the other two syllables? Do they share the same degree of loudness? Careful listening will show that the last syllable is not quite as loud as the first syllable, and the the first syllable is not quite as loud as the second. These differences can be shown in the phonetic transcription as follows: [âságwə] 'spouse'

Although Chamorro has three measurable degrees of stress, these differences are not phonemic. For example, it would not make any difference in meaning if we put secondary stress on the last syllable of /asagwa/ instead of weak stress. Since primary stress is phonemic, we can now group secondary stress and weak stress into one category, namely weak stress. This will stand in opposition. to primary stress, and in the phonemic transcription system it will be left unmarked.

Since primary stress is phonemic, it cannot always be predicted. However, certain significant generalizations can be made about its occurrence.

Word Stress. Most native Chamorro words of two syllables or more carry primary stress on the next to the last syllable. This is known as *penultimate stress*. In words of only two syllables, the primary stress, since it is penultimate, would also be on the first syllable of the word. In order to make more generalized statements about the rules of stress in Chamorro, it will be better to continue to describe this as penultimate stress even though the primary stress is on the first syllable. Note the following examples of primary stress in multi-syllabic (more than one syllable) Chamorro words:

/ápu/	'ash'
/sága/	'stay'
/atúhong/	'large parrot fish'
/tuláika/	'exchange'
/halomtáno'/	'forest'

The last item in the list (/halomtáno'/) is a compound word consisting of /hálom/ and /táno'/. Notice that when the two words are combined, only one of the primary stresses occurs on the penultimate syllable.

There are a number of exceptions to the "penultimate rule." Many words from Spanish retain their original primary stress pattern. Notice the following Spanish loan words:

/asút/	'blue'
/estómagu/	'stomach'
/bapót/	'steam'

Also, some non-Spanish (presumably Chamorro) words violate the general rule. Examples are the words /la'ún/ 'sea urchin' and /dángkolo/ 'big'. Such exceptions, however, are rare.

The penultimate stress rule is so strong in Chamorro that the primary stress shifts from one syllable to another when suffixes are added, so that the penultimate syllable is always the loudest one. Notice how the primary stress keeps moving to the right in the following examples:

/hásso/	'think'
/hinásso/	'thought'
/hinassómu/	'your thought'
/hinassonmámi/	'our thought'

When certain suffixes are added, even the primary stress of Spanish words gets moved to the penultimate syllable:

/estómagu/   'stomach'
/estomagúña/   'his stomach'

When other types of grammatical affixes are attached to words, the penultimate rule does not apply. These affixes always take primary stress. They will be discussed in detail in the section on affixation. Some examples are:

/pácha/   'touch'
/umápacha/   'touch each other'
/tága'/   'chop'
/tátaga'/   'chopper' (also name of surgeon fish)
/salápe'/   'money'
/mísalape'/   'lots of money'

Phrase Stress

2.6.2   The penultimate rule discussed above also applies generally to Chamorro phrases. For example, the two words /háfa/ 'what' and /maléego'/ 'want' both have penultimate primary stress. Notice where the primary stress occurs when the words are strung together in a phrase:

/hafa malægó'mu/   'What do you want?'

In general, all Chamorro phrases and sentences follow the penultimate rule; that is, the next to last syllable will carry a primary stress. Of course, if the phrase or sentence is long, there may be other primary stresses as well. Regardless of whether the utterance is long or short, the penultimate syllable will usually carry a primary stress. Note the following individual words and phrase:

/pára/   'towards'
/ténda/   'store'
/filipínu/   'Filipino'
/para i tendan filipínu/   'toward the Filipino store'

The primary stress of the individual words is reduced to secondary stress (or perhaps even weaker) when the words come together to form a phrase.

Intonation Pattern of Chamorro

2.6.3   In the discussion of Chamorro intonation our primary concern will be the significant features of *pitch* and *juncture* and their relationship to the stress pattern discussed above. (For a very detailed discussion of Chamorro intonation see Mathiot 1955.)

Pitch. The term *pitch* is used in linguistics to refer to the relative highness and lowness of a person's voice while he is speaking. Of course, certain people have a very high pitched voice while others have a low pitched, bass voice. We are not concerned with the differences in pitch that are found in different peoples' voices. We are concerned only with the *relative highness and lowness in an individual's speech.* And, we must be careful not to confuse pitch with stress (or loudness). Since the pitch patterns of one native speaker of a language are characteristic of the speech of all the native speakers of that language, we can make certain valid generalizations.

If we were to measure all of the pitch levels in a person's speech with electronic devices, we would probably find dozens, or perhaps hundreds, of different pitch levels occurring. However, not all of these different levels would be linguistically significant and therefore might be considered allophonic. The number of pitch levels in Chamorro that are linguistically significant is probably three. Other linguists have suggested that there are more than three (cf. Mathiot 1955); but, for our purposes, three different levels of pitch will suffice. These will be called *low, high,* and *extra high.* For purposes of transcription low pitch will be marked with a superscript[1], high with superscript[2], and extra high with superscript[3].

The phonemic status of pitch in Chamorro can perhaps be shown by contrasting two different ways of saying the same word with a resultant difference in meaning—in other words, a minimal pair. Note the following examples. The pitch levels are marked by superscript numbers and by lines which show the relative levels of pitch as well as the "slide" from one pitch level to another.

/[1]bas[2]ta/   (bas/ta)   'Enough!'   (Statement)
/[1]bas[3]ta/   (bas/ta)   'Enough?'   (Question)

Also note the following exchange which was recorded in Yoña, Guam, after a fishing expedition. A statement was made by one of the fisherman that he had speared many fish, but none over three pounds. The other fisherman then queried.

Question: /[1]sák[3]sak/   (sák/sak)   'Saksak? (a type of fish)'
Answer: /[1]sák[2]sak/   (sák/sak)   'Saksak.'

Question: /¹kinenné'³mu/   (kinnené'/mu) 'Your catch?'
Answer: /¹kinenné'²hu/   (kinnené'/hu) 'My catch.'

These examples indicate that pitch is used as a phonemic device in Chamorro in the same way that it is used in English. One can change a statement into a question by changing the pitch pattern of the utterance. For the sake of comparison, see the following examples from English with the pitch patterns shown by lines:

He went ⌐ home.   (Statement)
He went ⌐ home?   (Question)

Even though pitch is used as a phonemic device in Chamorro in the same way that it is used in English, the similarity between the two languages stops there. In fact, the pitch patterns of the two languages are quite different from each other.

Stress-Pitch Relationship. There is a very close relationship between stress and pitch in all languages. But this relationship is not always the same. Chamorro appears to be very different in this respect.

In European languages and in many other languages of the world, a syllable that carries a heavy (or loud) stress is accompanied by a higher pitch level. Note the following examples from English:

télephone
appliance
óperator
operátion

In Chamorro, we find just the opposite relationship between stress and pitch in native Chamorro words and phrases. Primary (or loud) stress is accompanied by a lower pitch level. Note the following examples:

/falágu/   'to run'
/halom táno'/   'forest'
/háfa ïlékmu/   'What did you say?'

The relationship between pitch and streess in Chamorro is unique as far as this writer knows. There may be other languages in which loud stress is accompanied by low pitch as it is in Chamorro, but if there are, I have not heard of them. It is this relationship between pitch and stress in Chamorro that gives the language its own unique "accent."

Pitch Patterns in Phrases. Since the pitch patterns in Chamorro are largely determined by the occurrences of primary stress, the pitch patterns found in phrases are for the most part predictable. In isolated words primary stress is accompanied by low pitch level (level 1). Secondary and weak stress carry the higher pitch level (level 2). Special emphasis and questions can be produced by using the extra high pitch (level 3). In continuous speech— phrases and longer sequences—primary stress is accompanied by pitch level 1. The pitch level rises to 2 or 3 in the syllables following stress and remains there until the next juncture or the next primary stress. Some examples follow:

/¹és²te   es¹tór²ian   un ¹táo²tao/
  this is the story of a man

/²kume¹kwén²tos i   ¹pa²le′ ha fa¹fái²sen i   ¹táo²tao/
  talked   the   priest asking   the   man

/²hu   ¹tú²ngo′   ¹á²yu na   ¹pát²gon/
  I   knew   that   child

/¹gwá²ha nai gwaha   chi¹pá²ña/
  sometimes he has   cigarettes

In the last example, one could also put primary stress on the second occurrence of /gwáha/, in which case there would be an additional fall and rise in pitch caused by the additional primary stress in the phrase.

    This suggests that the rule governing the relationship between primary stress and low pitch is a highly regular rule. However, in continuous rapid speech a speaker may choose not to give primary stress to every syllable where it might be possible.

    The usual stress-pitch relationship found in Chamorro is distorted by loan words from Spanish and English. For example, such words as /asút/ 'blue', /okasión/ 'occasion', and /idát/ 'age' carry primary stress *and* high pitch on the final syllable. The above words would be transcribed as follows when we include the pitch levels:

/¹a²sút/,   /¹okasi²ón/,   /¹i²dát/.

As can be seen, these words go against the regular rules for Chamorro stress and pitch.

    Since stress is usually penultimate in Chamorro and since it is usually accompanied by a low pitch level, we can predict that most Chamorro utterances will end with a rising intonation. This rising intonation at the end of utterances is another of the distinguishing features of Chamorro.

Juncture

2.6.4 *Juncture* was defined earlier as "pause." Actually there is more involved than just the period of pause or silence. The accompanying pitch level is also a feature of the juncture that should be taken into account as part of the intonation pattern of the language.

There are three measurable types of juncture in Chamorro which are discussed briefly here.

Internal Open Juncture. Internal Open juncture (symbolized by /+/) is marked by a slight pause with no accompanying rise in pitch and is ordinarily used to set off word boundaries. This may be described as a "sharper" transition than that found between syllables of a word. Contrasting examples for /+/ are:

/humánao/	'to go'	/hu + manman/	'I wonder'
/i + nána/	'the mother'	/in + atan/	'we look at'
/i + na'na'lo/		/in + na'na'lo/	'we returned'
'the restitution'			
/pwes + sumásaga + si + nanáhu/			
'then my mother was staying'			
/pwes + umásagwa + si + nanáhu/			
'then my mother married'			

The pitch level is not related to /+/, but is governed by the stress pattern of the utterance.

Phrase Final Juncture. Phrase final juncture is characterized by a pause accompanied by a rising pitch level. It is found at the end of phrases and most sentences where discourse is to be continued, and it is the most frequently used juncture in Chamorro. It will be marked by / ↑ /. It is the form of juncture that always occurs at the end of a question. It does not convey the tone of finality that is found in paragraph final juncture discussed below (and marked by /#/). The following paragraph shows some occurrences of phrase final juncture with accompanying changes in pitch levels:

/éste gwíya un estó²ria ↑ estórian dos kumon¹pái²re ↑
 This   is a story   a story of two (father and godfather)

éste i umá'adibi i ²dós ↑
  crediting one another.

| hágas | na | tiémpo | este | i | un táotao i kumon¹pái²re ↑ |
| A long | time | ago | this | one man (father or godfather) |

| ha dídibi este i | un | ¹tao²tao¹ # |
| owed | this | other | man. |

Paragraph Final Juncture. Paragraph final juncture is characterized by a long pause and a falling pitch level. It denotes the end of a paragraph or the completion of discourse, except when a question occurs as the final sentence. If a question occurs at the end of discourse, the final pitch level will be rising instead of falling.

In addition to the three types of juncture discussed above, there is another type which might be described as "hesitation juncture." This type of pause is accompanied by sustained pitch— neither rising nor falling—and it usually occurs after particles such as /nu na gi i/. It is used to break up long utterances and as a "think" break. This type of juncture is completely unpredictable, will vary from speaker to speaker, and depends to a large extent on the speaking situation. The more strained the situation, the more frequent the pauses. Very often the particle itself will be sustained (nuuuu) while the speaker is reconstructing his thoughts or planning how the rest of his sentence is going to come out.

MORPHOPHONEMICS

2.7   *Morphophonemics* is a term used to refer to the changes in the phonemes—or sounds—of a language when two or more words or word-like items are brought together. For example, in Chamorro the first sound of the word *saga* changes when the prefix *man-* is added. The resulting word is *mañaga*. What happened to the s of *saga*? This is one example of a morphophonemic change in Chamorro.

There are quite a few morphophonemic changes that occur among the consonants and vowels in Chamorro. The most common ones will be discussed here under this general heading. Additional examples of morphophonemic changes will be given later in the grammar.

Consonant Assimilation

2.7.1   The term *assimilation* is used in linguistics to describe a phonetic process in which two sounds which are adjacent or very near to each other acquire certain phonetic characteristics of each other. At times they become identical to each other.

Consonant assimilation is the term used to describe what happens when one consonant assimilates or takes on some of the features of another consonant. A consonant may assimilate the point of articulation of another consonant or it may assimilate the manner of articulation. (Cf. 2.2.1.)

The most common type of consonant assimilation occurs when the prefix *man-* (or *fan-*) is attached to a word that begins with a consonant. When this prefix is added, one or two things happen, depending on whether the first consonant of the stem— the word to which the prefix is added—is voiceless or voiced. (Cf. 2.2.1.)

The first thing that happens is that the n of *man-* (or *fan-*) assimilates to the point of articulation of the first consonant of the stem. Thus, if the first consonant of the stem is a labial consonant (such as b), then *man-* changes to *mam-*. {man + bende→ /mambende/ 'to sell'.} Similarly, if the first consonant of the stem is a velar consonant (such as g), *man-* changes to *mang-*. {man + godde → /manggodde/ 'to tie'}

If the first consonant of the stem is voiceless, an additional change takes place: the first consonant of the stem is deleted, or disappears. Note the following examples:

man + po'lo	/mamo'lo/	'to put'
man + taña'	/manaña'/	'to taste'
man + kati	/mangati/	'to cry out'

Notice that the p of *po'lo*, the t of *taña'*, and the k of *kati* all disappear (become deleted) when the prefix *man-* is added. This is also part of the morphophonemic change.

The entire set of changes that occur when *man-* is attached to a stem can be phrased in two simple rules. (For these rules, the consonants /ch y s/ must be considered palatal.)

> Consonant Rule 1: (Assimilation) The /n/ of prefix *man-* assimilates to the point of articulation of the first consonant of the stem, except when the first consonant is *m*.
> Consonant Rule 2: (Consonant Loss) The initial voiceless consonant of the stem is deleted. (This rule applies *only* if the initial consonant of the stem is voiceless.)

Examples for these rules follow. The intermediate stage which requires the application of rule 2 is marked by*.

Stem		Cons. Rule 1	Cons. Rule 2
/po'lo	'put'	*mampo'lo	mamo'lo
bende	'sell'	mambende	
taña'	'taste'	*mantaña'	manaña'
daggao	'throw'	mandaggao	
kati	'cry out'	*mangkati	mangati
godde	'tie'	manggodde	
fa'om	'clobber'	*mamfa'om	mama'om
hanao	'go'	*manhanao	mananao
na'i	'give'	manna'i	
ngangas	'chew'	mangngangas	
yute'	'throw'	manyute'	
saga	'stay'	*mañsaga	mañaga
chægi	'try'	*mañchægi	mañægi/

NOTE: It may be argued by some that the h̲ of *hanao* is not lost when *man-* is added. I have found that some speakers say /manhanao/ when they speak slowly, but will omit the /h/ in rapid speech.

Excrescent Consonants

2.7.2   In some places in Chamorro it is necessary to add a consonant in order to make the words "sound right." These are called *excrescent consonants* because they have no other function than to make the words sound good to the native speaker's ear.

The most common of these excrescent consonants is n̲. It is found, for example, at the end of a stem which ends in a vowel before the plural possessive pronouns for first person exclusive, second person and third person. For example, the word /lepblo/ 'book' is pronounced /lepblon/ when the above pronouns are added:

/lepblon-mami/	'our book'
/lepblon-miyu/	'your book'
/lepblon-ñiha/	'their book'

An excrescent n̲ is also added in certain modification constructions when the modifier follows the *headword*. (The term *headword* is used here to mean the word that is modified.) For example, the word /tenda/ 'store' becomes /tendan/ in the construction /tendan filipinu/ 'Filipino store.' Another example of this excrescent n̲ is found in the name of the old Chamorro bull cart where the word /kareta/ 'car' becomes /karetan gwaka/.

Another example of an excrescent consonant is the addition of the glottal stop when two vowels are brought together as the result of some grammatical process. The word /ædda'/ 'mimic' can take the affix /æ/ to become /æ'ædda'/ 'mimicker'. The glottal stop that comes between the two vowels is excrescent. Furthermore, we can always predict that when two vowels are brought together in Chamorro, they will be separated by an excrescent glottal stop.

Still a third example of an excrescent consonant is the addition of /gw/ following the diphthong /ao/ and preceding the suffix -i. Thus, from /hanao/ 'to go' we get /hanagwi/ 'to go for someone.' (Note that the final portion of the diphthong is also dropped before adding /gw/.)

We may encounter additional types of excrescent consonants in our discussion of Chamorro grammar, but the above are by far the most common types.

Vowel Harmony

2.7.3   Vowel harmony in Chamorro is one of the most interesting phonological features of the language. To my knowledge, Chamorro is the only language of Micronesia or the Philippines that has this feature.

The term *vowel harmony* means that vowels in many words may change according to their immediate environment. Another way to view it is that the vowels in Chamorro must, under certain conditions, agree with each other in terms of whether they are front or back vowels, and whether they are high, mid or low. (See section 2.1.)

There are two types of vowel changes that occur in Chamorro. Both of these are considered to be types of vowel harmony. They are subcategorized as vowel fronting and vowel raising and are discussed separately below. The vowel chart is given again here for quick and easy reference.

Phonemic Vowel Chart

	Front	Back
High	i	u
Mid	e	o
Low	æ	a

Vowel Fronting. The most common type of vowel harmony in Chamorro is *vowel fronting.* This is the term used to describe the change that occurs when a back vowel is drawn forward in the mouth to become a front vowel of the same height. Specifically, a high back vowel /u/ is changed to a high front vowel /i/, a mid back vowel /o/ becomes a mid front vowel /e/, and a low back vowel /a/ becomes a low front vowel /æ/. When the back vowels are fronted, they always remain at the same height.

The condition for vowel fronting is as follows: when a word which has a stressed back vowel is preceded by one of several particles that has a front vowel, then the back vowel of the stem is drawn forward, or fronted. Some of the particles that cause vowel fronting are listed here. (Do not worry about some of the definitions of the particles given here. They will be explained in the section on grammar.)

i	definite, common article
ni	non-focus marking common article
gi	'to, at'
in	'we (exclusive)'
en	'you (plural)'
-in-	goal focus infix
sæn-	directional prefix
mi-	'lots of'

Following are some examples which illustrate vowel fronting when the above particles occur with words. (Affixes are set off by hyphens).

Free Words (Stressed Back Vowels)		Particle and Word (Fronted Vowels)	
guma'	'house'	i gima'	'the house'
foggon	'stove'	ni feggon	'the stove'
okso'	'hill'	gi ekso'	'at the hill'
tungo'	'to know'	in tingo'	'we know'
tungo'	'to know'	en tingo'	'you (pl.) know'
godde	'to tie'	g-in-edde	'thing tied'
lagu	'north'	sæn-lægu	'towards north'
otdot	'ant'	mi-etdot	'lots of ants'

It may also be noticed that back vowels of stems are fronted when the possessive pronouns are attached. For example, from /guma'/ 'house' we find /gima'-mu/ 'your house', and from

/tokcha'/ 'spear' we find /tekcha'-mu/ 'your spear'. It is not the addition of these suffixes that causes the vowel to be fronted. Rather, the fronting of the vowel is caused by one of the particles i, ni, or gi which must precede a possessed noun. What we really have then are phrases consisting of the particle i, ni, or gi plus the possessed noun, as in the following examples:

| /i gima'-mu/ | 'your house' |
| /ni tekcha'-mu/ | 'your spear' |

Vowel Raising. When certain suffixes are attached to Chamorro words *vowel raising* may take place. This means that one of the two mid vowels—either /e/ or /o/—will be raised to its corresponding high vowel—either /i/ or /u/.

The suffixes that cause vowel raising with an example for each of them are as follows. The stem word is given first, followed by the suffixed form.

(1) Abilitative Suffix -on
/tago'/ 'to command'   /tagu'on/ 'able to command'

(2) fan . . . an 'place of'
/maigo'/ 'sleep'   /fanmaigu'an/ 'sleeping place'

(3) Referential Focus Suffix -i
/tuge'/ 'to write'   /tugi'i/ 'write to someone'

(4) Benefactive Suffix -iyi
/kwentos/ 'to talk'   /kwentusiyi/ 'talk for someone'

The vowel raising that is observed in these examples is not due to the quality of the vowels in the suffixes. Rather, it is due to the fact that when any one of these suffixes is added in the above examples, it has the effect of converting a *closed syllable* to an *open syllable*. (Cf. 2.7.4.) Let us look at the same examples where syllable division is marked by a period.

/ta.go'/	/ta.gu.'on/
/mai.go'/	/fan.mai.gu.'an/
/tu.ge'/	/tu.gi.'i/
/kwen.tos/	/kwen.tu.si.yi/

This phenomenon of vowel raising is closely tied to a general rule about vowels in open and closed syllables which is discussed in the following section.

Before going on to that discussion, it should be pointed out that the first three of the suffixes listed above have alternate forms beginning with /y/ when they are attached to a stem that ends with a vowel. Vowel raising still occurs, as the following examples show:

/bende/	'sell'	/bendiyon/	'salable'
/chocho/	'eat'	/fañochuyan/	'eating place'
/godde/	'tie'	/goddiyi/	'tie for someone'

In the above examples, the /y/ is an *excrescent consonant* which has the same function as those described in section 2.7.2. above.

Chamorro Vowels and Syllable Structure

2.7.4   A general rule that operates throughout the Chamorro language and applies to native Chamorro words is this: high and low vowels occur in open syllables, while mid and low vowels occur in closed syllables. Also, if a word of two syllables has a mid vowel in the first syllable which is followed by two or more consonants, then the vowel of the second syllable will usually be mid.

The rule stated above may sound complicated, but it is actually quite simple, as will be demonstrated below. One word of caution should be added. This rule, like most other rules about language, has certain exceptions, and it applies specifically to native Chamorro words. It is an important rule for a thorough understanding of the new spelling system for Chamorro, as discussed in 2.8.1. below.

Stated again—hopefully in clearer terms—the rule goes like this. In native Chamorro words, open syllables which carry primary stress must contain either high or low vowels /i u æ a/, but never the mid vowels /e o/. Thus we find such words as the following:

/nífen/	'teeth'	/húyong/	'outside'
/bǽba/	'open'	/bába/	'bad'

On the other hand, in native Chamorro words which have closed stressed syllables, we find only the mid vowels /e/ and /o/ or the low vowels /æ/ and /a/. But we never find the high vowels /i/ and /u/ in these closed syllables. Note the following examples:

/lémmai/	'breadfruit'	/tómmo/	'knee'
/dé'on/	'pinch'	/lókka'/	'tall'

There is good evidence in support of this rule in Chamorro. In modern Chamorro we sometimes find two seemingly different but closely related words which mean virtually the same thing. It is fairly obvious that these pairs of words came from the same source. By tracing their development we can see that the above rules concerning Chamorro vowels and syllable structure are valid ones.

If we take a stem such as /hutu/ 'louse', we can derive two forms meaning 'lousy' or 'full of lice'. The word used in formal speech is derived by simply adding the prefix *mi-* to the stem. This prefix now carries the primary stress, and so the resultant form is /míhitu/ meaning 'lots of lice'. (The first u̱ of /hutu/ changes to i̱ due to the first rule of vowel harmony.)

An alternate form of the word meaning 'lousy'—the form which is most often heard in fast speech—is /méhto/. It is obvious that both /míhitu/ and /méhto/ come from the same source. The word /méhto/ is derived from /míhitu/ in the following manner.

The first step in the derivational process is that the second vowel from /míhitu/ is dropped, thus giving /mihtu/. We now have a high vowel in a closed syllable, which Chamorro does not permit. The next step, then, is to lower the first vowel because it is in a closed syllable, thus giving /méhtu/. Now the rule of vowel harmony steps in. This rule says that if we have a stressed mid vowel in the first syllable, then the unstressed vowel in the second syllable must also be mid. The application of this rule then gives us /méhto/.

Another set of words that will serve to illustrate this pattern is the following pair both of which mean 'killer':

    /pípino'/   /pékno'/

Both of the above words come from the root word /puno'/ 'to kill'.

The first word is formed by the process of reduplicating the stressed syllable. Thus, from /púno'/ we get /púpuno'/. Due to vowel harmony rules we then get /pípino'/.

The second word /pékno'/ is derived from /pípino'/ in almost the same way that /mehto/ was derived from /míhitu/. The second vowel of /pípino'/ is lost, thus producing /pípno'/. Since the stressed syllable is now closed, the high vowel /i/ is lowered to /e/. In this particular word, the /p/ changes to /k/ to give us finally /pékno'/. (Actually the sounds /p/ and /k/ share certain acoustic features, but we will not go into those at this time.)

Some additional examples that will help illustrate what happens when a vowel is lost in Chamorro are given here:

mi + chugo' →míchigo' 'juicy'
Unstressed vowel is lost: *michgo'
Since <u>ch</u> does not occur in syllable final position,
it becomes s: *misgo'
The high vowel becomes lowered in a closed
syllable: mesgo' 'juicy'
kanno' 'to eat' → kákanno' 'eater'
Unstressed vowel is lost: *kaknno'
Geminate consonant is reduced to single C:kakno' 'eater'

In some cases the consonants are also affected. For example,

man + tufok → manufok 'to weave'
Vowel loss: *manfok
Consonant assimilation: mamfok 'to weave'
man + tuge' → manuge' 'to write'
Vowel loss: *mange'
Consonant assimilation: mangge' 'to write'

In extreme cases entire words are lost, as in the following example:

manu nai gaige → mangge 'where is'

Some additional examples that will illustrate what happens when vowels are lost follow:

ma + funot	→	mafnot	'tight'
mi + haga'	→	mehga'	'bloody'
mi + fino'	→	mefno'	'lots of talk'
mi + sungon	→	mesngon	'lots of patience'
mi + pilu	→	mepplo	'hairy'

It is probable that many Chamorro words that have a mid vowel in the first syllable that is followed by two consonants that are not the same have developed from this process. The original words from which they came often cannot be reconstructed.

One final example showing vowel loss can be seen in the expression *afan* which is often used when addressing a group of people.

Formal Speech	Rapid Speech
Hafa mañe'lo(s). 'Greetings brothers and sisters.'	Afañe'lo(s).
Hafa mangga'chong. 'Greetings, friends.'	Affangga'chong.
Hafa manátungo'. 'Greetings, friends.'	Afanátungo'.

Final Vowels Following Closed Syllables. We have seen that in native Chamorro words mid vowels occur in stressed closed syllables while high vowels occur in stressed open syllables. Low vowels may occur in either kind of syllable.

Another aspect of the vowel harmony system which should be pointed out is that mid vowels must occur in final unstressed open syllables which follow closed syllables. Another way of stating this is to say that words of two syllables that have medial consonant clusters will not contain high vowels. (This rule applies to native Chamorro words only.) Notice the final vowels in the following examples:

/momye/	'scold'
/sahnge/	'strange'
/totche/	'dunk'
/mepplo/	'hairy'

Chamorro Vowels in Spanish Loanwords

2.7.5 None of the rules given above applies consistently to Spanish loanwords. For example, we find high vowels in closed syllables:

/lísto/	'quick'
/asút/	'blue'
/hatdín/	'garden'

And we find mid vowels in stressed open syllables:

/sébu/	'grease'
/bóta/	'vote'

However, there are some very obvious instances where the rules governing Chamorro vowels have found their way into Spanish loan words. For example, from Spanish *paloma* 'dove' we get Chamorro /palúma/, where the open syllable requires the high vowel /u/ in place of the Spanish mid vowel /o/.

CHAMORRO SPELLING: BACKGROUND

2.8 The history of Chamorro spelling is one of change and inconsistency. There is no evidence to indicate that there was any attempt to write the language before the Spanish colonization in 1668. Presumably Father Sanvitores, who wrote his Chamorro grammar in that same year, was the first person to write the language. Since that time a considerable amount of literature has been written in the language, a good bit of it by Spanish priests. It is not surprising, therefore, that the writing system shows striking influences of the Spanish system of spelling.

In the northern Marianas one can also detect traces of the German spelling system in some of the Chamorro writings that were produced there between 1899 and 1914. But the German influence was very slight when compared with that of the Spanish.

Unfortunately, the Spanish writers did not detect all of the significant sounds of the language; and hence they did not write them. The glottal stop, for example, is not represented at all in any of the early writings. Geminate consonants and syllable-final h̲ were seldom written. There was also considerable variation in the writing of unstressed vowels. The result was a rather inaccurate, underspecified writing system inherited from the Spanish.

Prior to World War II, reading and writing in Chamorro were taught in most of the schools in the Mariana Islands. The system that was taught was basically that used by Father Aniceto Ibañez del Carmen in his Spanish-Chamorro Dictionary published in 1865. Even though there were differences in the way people spelled different words, there was sufficient agreement to permit people to understand one another's writing.

After World War II the teaching of Chamorro in school was completely abandoned in Guam. In the northern Marianas Chamorro was used as the language of instruction in the elementary schools until the 1960's when English became the official language for instructional purposes.

Since very few people of the post-war generation learned to read or write Chamorro in any systematic way, there existed a need to reexamine the situation and, if feasible, to attempt to establish a systematic orthography for the language. Such an orthography was recommended and was presented for formal adoption by the Marianas Orthography Committee in January, 1971. This committee, which included members from Guam, Rota, and Saipan, formally adopted the spelling system presented below. This is also the spelling system that will be used in the remainder of this book and in the companion Chamorro-English Dictionary.

Chamorro Spelling: The New System

2.8.1   Only time will tell whether the spelling system adopted by the

Marianas Orthography Committee will be widely used. If it is used in bilingual education programs in the schools, then its chances for survival are pretty good. On the other hand, Chamorro speakers may prefer to follow their own individual ways of spelling the language.

The rules for the new spelling system as adopted by the Committee in January, 1971 are presented here. The Committee included the following officially designated members: Judge Ignacio V. Benavente (Saipan), Mr. Jose S. Pangelinan (Saipan), Dr. Manuel M. Aldan (Saipan), Mr. Vicente N. Santos (Saipan), Mr. Luis A. Benavente (Saipan), Mr. Justin S. Manglona (Rota), Mrs. Lagrimas L. G. Untalan (Guam), and Mrs. Bernadita C. Dungca (Guam).

The rules for Chamorro orthography as adopted by the Committee are as follows:

1. Proper Names.
All proper names in Chamorro (family and place) will retain their traditional spellings as they appear on maps, property deeds, and in other records.

2. Capitalization.
The standard practices of English and Spanish capitalization will continue to be followed.

3. Choice of Alphabetic Symbols.
The following consonant and vowel symbols will be used in Chamorro spelling. They are given here in alphabetic order: a, b, ch, d, e, f, g, h, i, ', k, l, m, n, ñ, ng, o, p, r, s, t, u, y.

(The letters c, j, q, v, w, z will be used in the spelling of proper names only.)

Example words are given to illustrate the phonetic value of each of the spelling symbols.

Symbol	Example Word	English Meaning
a	baba	bad
a	baba	open (Note: the same symbol *a* is used to represent two sounds.)
b	baba	bad
ch	chalan	road
d	dagao	throw
e	ekungok	listen

f	fugo'	squeeze
g	ga'chong	friend
h	hatsa	lift
i	hita	we (inclusive)
'	haga'	blood
k	kada	each
l	litratu	picture
m	malago'	want
n	nana	mother
ñ	ñamu	mosquito
ng	nginge'	sniff
o	oppe	answer
p	pachot	mouth
r	ramas	branch
s	saddok	river
t	taya'	nothing
u	uchan	rain
y	yan	and

For the purpose of alphabetizing words, the glottal stop will be ignored. For example, note the following words listed in alphabetical order:

na'ayao	lend
nabaha	pocketknife
na'balanse	cause to balance
nabegadot	navigator

4. Diphthongs.
The diphthongs in the writing system will be treated as sequences of vowels. The most common diphthongs are as follows:

ao	taotao	person
ai	taitai	read
oi	tatfoi	so much
ea	manea	manage
ia	dia	day

5. Consonant Symbols in Final Position.
The following consonants will not appear at the end of a word: b, d, g, ch, y, ñ, l, r. The consonants b, d, g, l may appear at the end of a syllable only when the consonant is geminate, i.e., when the following syllable of the same word begins with the same consonant. Examples are:

yabbao	slash
godde	to tie
meggai	many
halla	pull

Words that have traditionally been written with final g, such as *maoleg,* will now be written with final k, for example *maolek.*

6. Unstressed Vowels in Open Syllables.

The letters a, i, u will be used to represent unstressed vowels in open syllables (syllables which end in a vowel) when the shape of the word is CV́CV (where C = consonant, V = vowel). Examples are:

lahi	man
hagu	you
na'i	give to
lagu	north, east
mata	eye, face

The same rule applies to unstressed vowels in open syllables of polysyllabic words except when the preceding vowel is o or e. For example:

	sangani	tell to
	dalalaki	follow
but		
	dankolo	big

In the case of *dankolo,* the first o results from the preceding consonant cluster nk (cf. rule No. 7); the final o results from the preceding o.

7. Unstressed Vowels in Open Syllables Following Consonant Cluster.

The unstressed vowels in open syllables following a sequence of consonants will be represented by e, o, and a. Examples are:

tatte	follow
ho'ye	accept, grant
hamyo	you all
listo	ready
halla	pull

8. Unstressed Vowels in Closed Syllables.

The vowels e, o, and a will be used to represent the unstressed vowels in closed syllables, i.e., syllables which end with a consonant. Examples are:

huyong	out
halom	in
lapes	pencil
li'e'	see
hakmang	eel

The letters i and u will be used to represent stressed vowels in closed syllables when the quality of the sound in the word is clearly that which is associated with the symbols i and u. Examples are:

| asút | blue |
| hatdin | garden |

9. Unstressed Vowels in Spanish Loanwords.

For words borrowed from Spanish in which the pronunciation of unstressed vowels is not clear, rules 6, 7, and 8 above will apply. Examples are:

bunita	pretty
asta ki	until
empidi	prohibit
desbela	stay awake
risibi	receipt
difensót	defender

The same rules apply to words borrowed from Japanese where the pronunciation of the unstressed vowel is not perfectly clear.

10. Spelling of Borrowed Words.

Spanish and Japanese words which have been assimilated into Chamorro will be spelled according to the general rules for Chamorro spelling. The spellings will reflect the changes in pronunciation that the words have undergone. Examples are:

Spanish	*Chamorro*	*English Gloss*
verde	betde	green
la mesa	lamasa	table
paloma	paluma	dove
caballo	kabayu	horse

Recently borrowed English words will retain their English spelling and will be underlined or italicized in print. When the English word contains Chamorro affixes, then it will be spelled according to the general rules for Chamorro spelling. Examples of this latter type are:

> pumipiknik   to go on picnic
> bumabasketbal   to play basketball
> manespleplehen   explaining

11. Consonant Alternation.

When the pronunciation of consonants changes due to affixation, the spelling will be changed accordingly to represent the change in pronunciation. Most of the changes in consonants are caused by the affixation of the prefix *man-*, as in the following examples:

> man + po'lo   → mamo'lo   to put
> man + taña'   → manaña'   to taste
> man + kati   → mangati   to cry
> man + saga   → mañaga   to stay
> man + gupu   → manggupu   to fly

The pronunciation of the first person singular possessive pronoun *hu* is determined by the stem to which it is attached. For example, it is pronounced *tu* when it follows a stem ending with t, as in [pachot-tu], 'my mouth.' It is pronounced *su* when it follows a stem ending with s, as in [lassas-su] 'my skin'. And it is pronounced *ku* when it follows a stem that ends with a vowel preceded by two consonants, as in [lepblo-ku] 'my book'. For purposes of spelling, *hu* and *ku* only will be used. *ku* will be used for spelling when that pronunciation is normal; *hu* will be used elsewhere.

12. Excrescent Consonants.

When additional consonants are added through affixation, they will be represented in the spelling system. The following are examples of excrescent consonants:

> lepblo + mami   →   lepblon-mami   our book
> saga   + ñaihon →   sagannaihon   stay for a while
> hanao + iyi   →   hanaguiyi   go for someone

13. Superfluous Consonants.

When the pronunciation of the consonant ng is predictable (i.e., before k), it will not be written. Instead, only n will be written, as in the following examples:

> dankolo   big
> enkatgao   caretaker
> denkot   peck at

14. Geminate Consonants and Syllable-final h.

Although the pronunciation of geminate consonants and syllable-

final h̲ varies among different speakers of Chamorro (younger
Guamanians and people from Rota tend to omit them), they will
be included in the spelling. The authoratative spelling of such
words will be based on the standard pronunciation of mature
speakers from Guam and Saipan. Some example words are:

tommo	knee
laggua	parrot fish
fatto	come
halla	pull
meggai	many
mohmo	chew for
sahnge	strange
mamahlao	be bashful

15. Fronting of Vowels.

When the pronunciation of a vowel is changed due to vowel
fronting, this change will be reflected in the spelling, as in the
following examples:

foggon	i feggon	the stove
guma'	i gima'	the house

16. Raising of Vowels.

When the pronunciation of a vowel is changed due to vowel
raising, the change in pronunciation will be reflected in the
spelling, as in the following examples:

fugo'	fugu'i	squeeze for
kuentos	kuentusi	speak to
maolek	maoliki	do good for
tatte	tattiyi	return for

17. Free Words.

All *content words* ("adjectives, verbs, nouns") will be written as
separate words in Chamorro. Some examples of content words
are:

kareta	car
dankolo	big
fugo'	squeeze
fata'chong	sit down

The following *function words* (articles, affixes, etc.) will be written
as separate words in Chamorro:

Function Word	Example Phrase	English Meaning
i	i palao'an	the woman
ni	ni palao'an	the woman
si	si Juan	John
as	as Juan	John
nu	nu guahu	me
na	dankolo na taotao	big man
ha'	Hu tungo' ha'.	I really know.
fan	Nangga fan un ratu.	Wait a minute please.
ni	ni hayiyi	no one
sen	sen magof	very happy
gof	gof magof	very happy
sin	sin salape'	without money
tai	tai salape'	without money
gai	gai salape'	have money
u	Para u hanao.	He will go.
bai	Para bai hu hanao.	I will go.

Yo'-type pronouns   yo', hao, gue', hit, ham, hamyo, siha
Hu-type pronouns   hu, un, ha, ta, in, en, ma
Emphatic pronouns   guahu, hagu, guiya, hita, hami, hamyo, siha

gi	gi lancho	at the ranch
iya	iya Guam	Guam
giya	giya Guam	at Guam

18. Prefixes.

The following list contains the prefixes of Chamorro which will be written as part of the word to which they are attached:

a-	umapacha	touch each other
acha-	achalokka'	same height
an-	ansopbla	leftover
chat-	chatbunita	slightly pretty
e-	epanglao	hunt for crabs
ge'-	ge'papa'	further down
gi-	Gilita	person from Rota
hat-	hattalom	further in
ke-	kehatsa	about to lift
la-	lage'hilo'	a little higher up

ma-	maguaiya	be liked (passive)
man-	manmanhasso	thoughts
mi-	misalape'	lots of money
mina'-	mina'tres	third
na'-	na'maolek	make good
san-	sanlagu	towards north/east
tai-	taiguenao	like that
tak-	takkilo'	way up high
ya-	yaguatutu	furthest away

19. Suffixes.

The following list contains the suffixes of Chamorro which will be written as part of the word to which they are attached. (The first item of the list is a *discontinuous affix* which may be considered part prefix and part suffix. It is called "discontinuous" because the stem comes in between the two parts of the affix.)

fan...an(yan)	fanbinaduyan	place of deer
-on	guasa'on	sharpener
-i/-iyi	sangani/sanganiyi	tell to/for
-ñaihon	sagannaihon	stay for a while
-guan	pinalakse'guan	slip of the tongue
-ña	bunitaña	prettier

20. Clitics.

Because of the special relationship that the possessive pronouns have with the stems to which they are related, they will be attached by hyphens, as in the following examples. They are called "clitics" rather than suffixes in order to show this close relationship.

relos-hu	my watch
relos-mu	your (sg.) watch
relos-ña	his/her watch
relos-ta	our (incl.) watch
relos-mami	our (excl.) watch
relos-miyu	your (pl.) watch
relos-ñiha	their watch

21. Reduplication and Infixes.

Reduplicated syllables and infixes will be written as part of the word even though the resulting words may contain an unusually large number of letters. Words will be divided on the basis of the rules presented in this paper, not on the basis of length. Some examples of long words resulting from multiple affixation and reduplication are given here:

manachachama'a'ñao
na'lage'hilu'i
manmangguaguaiya

This concludes the general spelling rules for the Chamorro language as adopted by the Marianas Orthography Committee in Saipan, M.I., January 21, 1971.

CHAMORROCIZED SPANISH

2.9   Perhaps it should be mentioned again that Chamorro is not a dialect of Spanish. Nor is it a creolized version of Spanish. Like several of the languages of the Philippines and South America, Chamorro contains many words of Spanish origin which were borrowed over a period of more than 250 years.

When these Spanish words were borrowed, the pronunciation of them was usually changed to conform to the sound system of Chamorro. The most important of these sound changes are given here.

The following examples illustrate sound changes that were very regular as words were borrowed from Spanish into Chamorro:

Spanish Sound	Chamorro Sound	Example Words	
		Spanish	Chamorro
v (in all positions)	b	viva	biba
		verde	betde
z (in all positions)	s	zapato	sapatos
		destrozar	destrosa
-d (final position)	-t*	ciudad	siudat
		felicidad	felisidat
-1 (final position)	-t	asul	asut
		animal	animat
-r (final position)	-t	lugar	lugat
		hablador	abladot
-11- (medial position)	-y-	caballo	kabayu
		llave	yabi
-rr- (medial position)	-r-	arreglar	arekla
		barrena	barena

*Sometimes the final-*d* in Spanish words was simply not pronounced when used by Chamorro speakers, e.g., *Siuda*.

The sound changes listed above show the result of what happens when a word is borrowed from one language into another and when the sound systems of the two languages are different from each other. In the examples listed above, Chamorro made the Spanish words conform to the Chamorro sound system. In some cases, Chamorro simply did not have the sound (i.e., v, -ll-, -rr-); in other cases, Chamorro had the sound, but the distributional limitations were different (i.e. final -l, -r and -d).

The sound changes listed above were highly regular. In addition to those, there were some irregular sound changes. They are called irregular because the sound change has proved to be inconsistent, and therefore unpredictable. They involve the sounds l, r, and h.

In some instances, Spanish r became Chamorro r or was omitted entirely. For example:

Spanish	Chamorro
franela	franela—flanela

In other instances, Spanish r became Chamorro l:

frito	aflitu

And, in a few instances, Chamorro added h where there was none in Spanish:

espia	espiha

For the most part, the sound changes that occurred when Spanish words were borrowed into Chamorro were very regular. Hence, when we hear a Chamorro word that is Spanish in origin, we can usually reconstruct the original Spanish word accurately simply by following the rules of sound changes listed above.

Following are some Chamorrocized Spanish words with the original Spanish words from which they came. See if you can describe the sound changes that took place in each word.

Chamorro	Spanish	English Gloss
destiniyadot	destornillador	screwdriver
satmon	salmon	salmon
bende	vender	sell
yetba	hierba	grass
bos	voz	voice

Of course, there are always cases of sound change that don't appear to follow the regular rules. Such examples are often found in words that occur very often. This high frequency of occurrence may cause the sounds in the word to undergo further change. An example of such a word in Chamorro is *Yu'us* from Spanish *Dios* meaning 'God'.

3   Morphology:
Words and Their Structure

In this section we will give close attention to the *morphology* of Chamorro—the stock of *morphemes* and the way words (sometimes phrases) are built out of them. Before proceding any further it will first be necessary to define and illustrate some of the new terms that will be used frequently throughout this section. Traditional grammatical terminology will be used where appropriate. But since Chamorro is such a different language from those of western Europe where the "traditional" terms were coined, it will be necessary from time to time to use new terms that are more appropriate for Chamorro.

It should be pointed out that it is not always possible to draw a clear line marking the boundary of words and syntax, or grammar. This is especially true of Chamorro where a large portion of the syntax is found in the formation of words. Every effort will be made to keep the discussion of syntax to a minimum in this section of the book. The reader should not be surprised, however, to find some overlapping between this section and the following one on syntax.

MORPHEME

3.1   The *morpheme* is a very important concept in linguistic analysis. Although it is not a difficult concept, it is sometimes confused with the word or syllable. Sometimes a morpheme is equivalent to a word, but at other times it isn't. Also, a morpheme is sometimes a single syllable; but at other times a morpheme may be polysyllabic—it may have several syllables.

A morpheme is defined by C. F. Hockett as "the smallest individually meaningful element in the utterances of a language." (Hockett 1958: 123) Unlike the phoneme, a morpheme conveys meaning, and it cannot be analyzed into any smaller unit that also has meaning.

The following illustrations from English may help clarify this concept. Consider the following pair:

daughter
hotter

We will assume that both of these items are words because they are both usually written as separate words. (No attempt will be made to give a more formal definition of the word at this point.) Notice that both of these words contain two syllables. The second syllable of each word sounds the same. But the question is does the *-er* of *daughter* mean the same as the *-er* of *hotter*? The answer, of course, is "no."

Another question to ask is whether the *-er* of either word has any meaning by itself and if it recurs with other words with the same meaning? Another way of phrasing the question is this: can the *-er* of either word be detached from the word and re-attached to another word to give it some additional meaning? And, if we remove the *-er* from the word, is the remaining portion a meaningful segment? Let's apply these tests to the two words in question.

First, remove the *-er* from both words:

daught   (er)
hot   (er)

We recognize that *hot* is a word that can stand by itself with the same meaning or can enter into combinations with other words, as in "hot water," "hot days," and "very hot." On the other hand, **daught* cannot stand by itself with the meaning "female offspring."

At the same time, the *-er* of *hotter* can be attached to other words and carry the same meaning that it does in the word *hotter*. For example, we have such words as *younger* meaning "more young," *bigger* meaning "more big," and so on. The *-er* of *hotter* can be readily identified as a segment of the English language that carries meaning. The *-er* of *daughter* is obviously a very different segment for two reasons: (1) If we detach it from the word we are left with the meaningless segment **daught*; (2) We cannot attach it to other words for the purpose of giving them a similar meaning.

(It might be argued that the *-er* of *daughter* is also found on the words *sister, mother, brother,* and *father,* and that its function is to identify membership in the immediate family. However, since its use is not productive for forming new words, it will be considered as an inseparable part of each of the above words.)

What can now be said about the two words *hotter* and *daughter?* In the first place, they are both words. Secondly, they both have two syllables. But there the similarity stops. The word *hotter* can be divided into two morphemes, *hot* and *-er.* The word *daughter* cannot be further analyzed into smaller components; hence, the word *daughter* is a single morpheme.

Some further examples of English words that contain two morphemes are *truly* (*true* and *-ly*), *likeness* (*like* and *-ness*), *electricity* (*electric* and *-ity*), and *boys* (*boy* and *-s*).

Some further examples of words of more than one syllable but which are single morphemes are *expect, cadaver, language,* and *communicate.* These words cannot be broken down into smaller meaningful units. They are minimum semantic units and are therefore morphemes. Again, one could say that we can detach the *ex-* from *expect* and use it with words like *excel.* But, it is doubtful that the *ex-* of *expect* and *excel* have any common meaning. And it is certain that **pect* and **cel* don't mean anything by themselves. Hence, the words *expect* and *excel* cannot be reduced any further.

There are parallel examples in Chamorro which will help to establish the concept of the morpheme. The following pair of words will serve to illustrate:

binaya'	'filled, satiated'
binenu	'poison'

The first word *binaya'* contains two morphemes. One of these is *baya'* meaning 'satiate' or 'fill'; the other is the morpheme *-in-.* We know that *-in-* is a morpheme because it changes the meaning of the word *baya'* in practically the same way that it changes the meaning in other pairs of words, such as *maolek-minaolek, baba-binaba,* and *tanom-tinanom.*

On the other hand, we cannot break down the second word *binenu* 'poison' into two morphemes to get **benu* plus *-in-.* There is no Chamorro word **benu.* Hence, *binenu* is a single word and a single morpheme that cannot be broken down into smaller meaningful units.

Another example from Chamorro can be found in the pair of expressions *yamu* 'you like' and *ñamu* 'mosquito'. In the first expression we know that we have two morphemes. The morpheme

-mu can recur in combination with other morphemes with the same meaning, e.g., *ilekmu* 'you said', *malago'mu* 'you want'. Also, the morpheme *ya-* can recur with other morphemes with the same meaning, e.g., *yahu* 'I like', *yaña* 'he likes'.

The *-mu* of *ñamu* cannot be separated. If we did try to break the word *ñamu* into two morphemes, then we would have a meaningless **ña-* and a meaningless **-mu*, because the *-mu* of *ñamu* has no relationship in meaning to the *-mu* of *yamu*.

(Remember that the *-mu* of *ya-mu* and *ilek-mu* is set off by a hyphen in the writing system.)

The conclusion then is that *yamu* consists of two morphemes —*ya-* and *-mu*—while *ñamu* is a single morpheme.

Some additional Chamorro words that are polysyllabic but consist of a single morpheme are *dánkolo* 'big', *díkike'* 'small', and *lamasa* 'table'. (Note that *lamasa* was originally two morphemes in Spanish—*la mesa*—but in Chamorro usage it is a single morpheme.)

Some Chamorro words that consist of two or more morphemes are *gumupu* 'fly' (from *gupu* plus *-um-*), *guma'yu'os* 'church' (from *guma'* and *yu'os*), and *fina'denne'* 'hot sauce' (from *donne'*, *fa'-*, and *-in-*).

TYPES OF MORPHEMES AND WORDS

3.2   Under the general heading of morpheme come several types. Since it will be necessary to make frequent references to them during the discussion of the grammar, the various types of morphemes found in Chamorro will be presented here.

Free morphemes are morphemes which can stand alone without any other morphemes attached to them. They are always words, and they cannot be reduced to any smaller forms. Some examples of free morphemes are *i* 'the', *dánkolo* 'big', *hatsa* 'to lift', *li'e'* 'to see', and *pachot* 'mouth'.

Bound morphemes can never stand alone, but must always be attached to another morpheme to form a word. Some examples of bound morphemes are *é-* as in *épanglao* 'look for crabs', *-um-* as in *sumasaga* 'be staying', and *-ñaihon* as in *sagañaihon* 'stay for a while'. Bound morphemes cannot be considered as words, but they serve to form *complex words*. (See below for discussion of complex words.)

With these two categories of morphemes we can form three different types of words. The first type of word will be called *simple words.* They are equal to the free morphemes described above. They may also be considered *roots* or *root words.*

The second type of word will be called *compound words* which are composed of two (possibly more) free morphemes. Some examples of compound words are *halomtano'* 'forest', *guma'yu'os* 'church', and *tronkonhayu* 'tree'. It is often difficult to determine whether the Chamorro compound words should be treated as single words or as phrases consisting of two words. (This is often a problem in English as well.) For example, are terms such as *batkon aire* 'airplane' a compound word or a noun phrase? Or what about *botsan alunan* 'pillow case'? Is *halomtano'* a compound word or a series of two words? The question can best be resolved by the intuitive feelings of the native speaker.

The third type of word is the *complex word,* and except for simple words, it is probably the most common type of word found in Chamorro. The complex word consists of either a free morpheme plus one or more bound morphemes, or, on rare occasions, two bound morphemes. Some examples of complex words consisting of free and bound morphemes are *apasi* 'to pay' (from *apas* plus *-i*), *fa'maolek* 'fix' (from *fa'-* plus *maolek*), and *hinasso* 'thought' (from *hasso* plus *-in-*). An example of a complex word consisting of two bound morphemes is *na'i* 'to give' (from *na'-* plus *-i*).

In many cases the bound morpheme of complex words has become "fossilized" so that native speakers tend to think of the word as an indivisible unit. A word such as *ékungok* 'to listen' probably comes from the bound morpheme *e*-plus *hungok* 'to hear'; the word *tattiyi* 'follow' probably comes from the free morpheme *tatte* 'follow' plus the bound morpheme *-yi.*

Allomorphs

3.2.1   In Section 2.1.2, which forms part of the discussion of the sound system of Chamorro, the term *allophone* was explained as "phonetic variants" of a single phoneme. In a manner quite parallel to the phoneme-allophone relationship, we also find a morpheme-allomorph relationship. An *allomorph* is a variant of a morpheme occurring in a specific environment. In other words, the same morpheme may be pronounced differently depending on the immediate environment.

It is important not to confuse allomorphs with the different pronunciations that result from rapid speech or from contractions. In English, for example, *didn't* is a contracted form of *did not*, but it is not an allomorph. In Chamorro, *pon* is frequently used as a contracted form of *para un* (as in *Para un cho'gue*), but it is not an allomorph.

Allomorphs are different forms of a single morpheme and the differences in form are determined by their immediate environment. Some examples from English and Chamorro will help to illustrate this concept.

In English, the morpheme that signifies past tense is written *-ed*. The pronunciation of this morpheme will vary, depending on the pronunciation of the word to which it is attached. The past tense of the verb *walk* is *walked,* pronounced /wɔkt/. The final *-ed* in this case is pronounced /t/. The past tense of the verb *move* is *moved,* pronounced /muvd/. The final *-ed* in this case is pronounced /d/. And the past tense of the verb *treat* is *treated,* pronounced /tritəd/. The final *-ed* in this case is pronounced /əd/.

The above examples illustrate that there are at least three allomorphs of the past tense verb ending in English. (There are actually more, but these are the most common ones.) They are /t/, /d/, and /əd/. The environments for these three allomorphs can be easily stated:

1. If the stem ends with /t/ or /d/, the allomorph /əd/ will occur.
2. If the stem ends with any voiceless consonant except /t/, the allomorph /t/ will occur.
3. The allomorph /d/ occurs elsewhere.

In Chamorro there is a morpheme *-i* that can be attached to many words, and it usually means 'to someone' or 'for someone'. It is found, for example, in the word *sangani* 'tell to', which comes from *sangan* plus *-i*. This morpheme also has three allomorphs— *-i, -yi,* and *-gui*—which are determined by the immediate environment.

In addition to words like *sangani*, which contains the morphemes *sangan* plus *-i*, there are the following: *hatsayi* 'lift for', which comes from *hatsa* plus *-yi*, and *hanagui* 'go for', which comes from *hanao* plus *-gui*. Obviously, the morphemes *-i, -yi,* and *-gui* have the same meaning (or very nearly the same). We can say that they are different forms of the same morpheme; or, to put it in linguistic terms, they are *allomorphs* of a single morpheme. The differences in pronunciation are determined by the immediate environment. The environments for these three allomorphs can be easily stated:

1. If the stem ends with a consonant, the allomorph -*i* will occur.
2. If the stem ends with the diphthong -*ao*, the allomorph -*gui* will occur.
3. The allomorph -yi occurs elsewhere.

NOTE: The morpheme *hanao* also has two allomorphs, as can be seen in the above example. When the morpheme -*gui* is added, then the allomorph *hana* occurs instead of *hanao*. Otherwise we would get **hanaogui* which is not an acceptable form. There are different possible linguistic interpretations of the changes that occur when we go from *hanao* to *hanagui*. The interpretation given here is the simplest one and will suffice to explain the data.

<u>Notes to Linguists: Diphthongs</u>. The allomorphic alternation observed here in *hanao-hanagui* lends further evidence for considering /aw/ and /gw/ as allophones. Also, there is parallel alternation between /ay/ and /z/, as can be seen in the following examples:

     taitai /táytay/ 'read'   /taytázi/ 'read for'

If we posit that [gw] and [z] are in complementary distribution with [aw] and [ay] respectively, then this would simplify the rules for the alternation of the allomorphs -*i*, -*yi*, and -*gui*. It would also allow for a more economical statement of the phonemic inventory.

WORD CLASSES IN CHAMORRO: PARTS OF SPEECH

3.3   In addition to the types of morpheme classification presented in the preceding section, it will be helpful to examine the word classes—parts of speech—in Chamorro. We will begin at the most general level of classification of words and work down to the more specific classes and types of words.

In classifying parts of speech in Chamorro it is tempting to follow the traditional lines of nouns, verbs, adjectives, adverbs, and so forth. Indeed, at some points in the grammar we will do so. It seems reasonable to consider words like *lahi* 'man', *langet* 'sky', and *guma'* 'house' as nouns. Words like *dánkolo* 'big', *dikike'* 'small', and *mannge'* 'delicious' certainly appear to be adjectives. And one could not argue that words like *malagu* 'run', *hatsa* 'lift', and *chumocho* 'eat' are anything but verbs.

This system of classification is based largely on traditional methods for classifying parts of speech in English. Furthermore, the system is based on the meaning of the words. For our present purposes, this system of classification of words does not work very well.

The classification of words in Chamorro requires that we use a system that is suitable for Chamorro. In the Chamorro language we often find the same word functioning as a noun, a verb, and an adjective according to the traditional definitions of those grammatical terms. Consider, for example, the word *dánkolo* 'big' in the following sentences:

> Dánkolo si Juan.
> 'Juan is big.'
>
> Hu li'e' i dánkolo.
> 'I saw the big one.'
>
> Hu li'e' i dánkolo na taotao.
> 'I saw the big person.'

In the first sentence, *dánkolo* functions as the predicate of the sentence where we would normally expect to find a verb. In the second sentence, *dánkolo* appears to be a direct object, where we would normally expect to find a noun. In the third sentence, *dánkolo* is clearly a modifier of the word *taotao*. We would ordinarily call any word that functions in this manner an adjective.

One can see from the above examples that it could be very confusing to try to classify Chamorro parts of speech on the basis of meaning or function alone. It will be necessary, then, to use different methods for classifying words in Chamorro.

Word classification in Chamorro can best be determined on the basis of the grammatical properties of the word, not on the basis of its meaning or its function as a subject, predicate, modifier or whatever. That is to say, words are said to belong to the same class if they can substitute for each other in a grammatical frame, or if they "behave" in the same way. One might also say that words belong to the same class if they can take the same kind of affixation.

Words in Chamorro can be divided into two basic classes, the Major Word Class and the Minor Word Class, each of which has several subclasses.

Major Word Class

3.3.1   The class of words in Chamorro labeled *major word class* consists of words that are traditionally designated by such terms as noun, verb, adjective, and adverb. Since these terms are not entirely appropriate for classifying Chamorro words, we will use the terms "Class I," "Class II," and "Class III" for purposes of basic classification. (This system is also used in the Chamorro-English Dictionary for purposes of classification.)

The major word class consists of *open sets* of words. That is to say, new words are constantly being added to and lost from the class of major words. (The minor word class consists of *closed sets:* words are seldom added to or lost from this class.) One might say that the major class of words forms the more fluid part of the vocabulary of any language. When we invent new words, they are nearly always members of the major class.

Class I Words. Words in Chamorro are said to belong to Class I provided the following two conditions can be met: (1) They must be able to take the passive voice prefix *ma-*; (2) They must be able to form the predicate of a goal focus construction. (More will be said about passive voice and goal focus later.)

Examples of these two constructions follow. The words *hatsa* 'to lift' and *li'e'* 'to see' will be used.

Passive Voice:	Mahatsa i lamasa.
	'The table was lifted.'
	Mali'e' i palao'an.
	'The woman was seen.'
Goal Focus:	Hinatsa i lamasa ni lahi.
	'The man lifted the table.'
	Lini'e' i palao'an ni lahi.
	'The man saw the woman.'

Other words belonging to this class are *pacha* 'to touch', *agang* 'call', *gimen* 'drink', *kanno'* 'eat', and *ha'me* 'singe'. There are, of course, hundreds of other Chamorro words that belong to this class. All of them have all of the features of transitive verbs, as the term is used in traditional grammars. The main reason for not calling them verbs is that many words in Class II also have features of traditional verbs but do not follow the same grammatical rules that the Class I words do.

Class II Words. Words in Chamorro are said to belong to Class II provided they can form the predicate of a sentence with the pronoun *yo'* as the subject pronoun. Some Class II words may require the insertion of the infix *-um-* or the prefix *ma-* before they can form the predicate. Some examples are given here:

Root Word		*Sentence*	*Gloss*
malago'	'want'	Malago' yo'.	'I want.'
malagu	'run'	Malagu yo'.	'I ran.'
taotao	'person'	Taotao yo'.	'I am a person.'
díkike'	'small'	Díkike' yo'.	'I am small.'
dagua	'sunburn'	Dagua yo'.	'I am sun-burned.'
malate'	'intelligent'	Malate' yo'.	'I am intelligent.'

Root Word *Requiring -um-*		*Sentence*	*Gloss*
chocho	'eat'	Chumocho yo'.	'I ate.'
gupu	'fly'	Gumupu yo'.	'I flew.'
saga	'stay'	Sumaga yo'.	'I stayed.'
tohge	'stand up'	Tumohge yo'.	'I stood up.'

Requiring ma-		*Sentence*	*Gloss*
cho'cho'	'work'	Macho'cho' yo'.	'I worked.'
ta'chong	'seat'	Mata'chong yo'.	'I sat down.'
fondo	'bottom'	Mafondo yo'.	'I sank.'
pokkat	'walk'	Mamokkat yo'.	'I walked.'

Special Problem of ma-. According to the present analysis of Chamorro, there are three morphemes that are spelled *ma*. One is the third person plural subject pronoun *ma* meaning 'they'. Another is the passive prefix *ma-* mentioned above in the definition of Class I words. The third is the *verbalizer ma-* seen in the words listed above (*macho'cho'*, *mata'chong*, etc.) See section 3.5.3 for a discussion of *verbalizer*.

It is possible that all three forms of *ma* come from the same historical root. But in the analysis of modern Chamorro, it seems better to treat them as separate morphemes.

For the non-native Chamorro speaker (and for the linguist) it would be very helpful if we could find rules to predict which roots take the infix *-um-* and which roots take the prefix *ma-*. Why, for example, should *chocho* 'eat' take *-um-* to become *chumocho* while *cho'cho'* 'work' becomes *macho'cho'*? Or, why should *tohge* 'stand up' become *tumohge* while *ta'chong* 'seat' becomes *mata'chong* 'sit down'? Unfortunately, we must conclude that the use of *-um-* or *ma-* is unpredictable, but that the majority of the Class II words take *-um-*. *Ma-* as a verbalizer can be considered irregular. It is also possible, and perhaps preferable, to consider the *ma-* as part of the root.

Another peculiar aspect of *ma-* is that it appears to have become fossilized in a fairly large number of words in Chamorro. That is to say it has become an inseparable part of the word. There are quite a few words of three syllables, the first of which is *ma-*. It is tempting to try to separate *ma-* from the rest of the word, the result of which would be a root word of two syllables (e.g., *ta'chong* from *mata'chong*). In the majority of cases, if we remove *ma-*, the remaining two syllables have no meaning. Some words of this type are:

malagu	'run'	malate'	'intelligent'
malago'	'want'	ma'udai	'ride'
maleffa	'forget'	magahet	'truly'

In the above words no further morphemic analysis can be made. We can only suspect that the initial syllable of these words was a prefix that became fossilized and is now inseparable from the original root. The above words now stand as roots.

Class III Words. There is a small group of words that we will arbitrarily put into Class III. It is reasonable to argue that these Class III words are really minor words because they form a closed set. They are included here among the major class only because they all have the characteristics of verbs except that they do not take the full set of verb affixation. They are also different from other verbs in that some of them must occur with a particular type of subject pronoun.

These Class III words can be subclassed into categories a, b, c, etc. They are listed below with examples.

Class IIIa words, with rough translations and examples, are:

gaige	Gaige yo' gi eskuela.
'to be present'	'I am at school.'
taya'	Taya' salape'-hu.
'none'	'I have no money.'
guaha	Guaha salape'-hu.
'exist, have'	'I have money.'
tai	Tai salape' yo'.
'none'	'I have no money.'
gai	Gai salape' yo'.
'exist, have.'	'I have money.'

Class IIIb:

munga	Munga humanao.
'don't, no'	'Don't go.'

siña	Siña yo' humanao.
'be able'	'I can go.'

Class IIIc words are:

cha'-	Cha'-mu humahanao.
'don't'	'Don't go.'

ilek-	Hafa ilek-mu?
'say'	'What did you say?'

ga'o-, ga'ña-	'prefer' (two alternate forms)
Hafa ga'o-mu?	'What do you prefer?'
Hafa ga'ña-mu?	'What do you prefer?'

ya-	Ya-hu humanao.
'like, want'	'I want to go.'

(Words of Class IIIc must take the possessive pronouns as subject pronouns.)

Class IIId words are:

malak	Malak Honolulu yo'.
'go'	'I went to Honolulu.'

mohon	Sumaga yo' mohon giya Honolulu.
'desire'	'I hope I can stay in Honolulu.'

In general, the words we have placed in Class III don't conform to the usual rules of the other words in the major class. It is difficult to make general rules about Class III words; some of them take some affixes, but they do not take the full range of affixes that the words of Class I and Class II can take.

Class III words are considered more like major words because they all seem to act like verbs. This is why they will be taken up again later under the section labeled Irregular Verbs. Class III words are subclassed into a, b, c, and d because they require different grammatical structures when they form part of a sentence. Major Word Class in Chamorro is summarized with the following diagram and brief explanation:

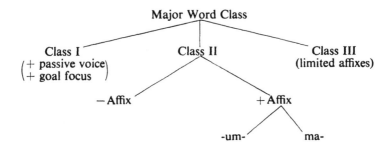

Class I words must be able to take the passive voice prefix and form the predicate of a goal focus construction.

Class II words can form the predicate of statements with *yo'* (or a pronoun of the same class) as a subject. Some Class II words require no affix; others require either the infix *-um-* or the prefix *ma-*. Words of Class I and Class II can take many more affixes, which will be discussed later.

Now that the basic classification of the words of the major word class has been made according to the arbitrary names of Class I, II, and III, we can proceed to consider some of the subclasses of words. In doing this we will use the traditional names such as verb, noun, and modifier. It must be remembered, however, that with few exceptions *any major word in Chamorro can function as a verb, noun, or modifier.*

The problem of verbs in Chamorro will be taken up in the next section.

Verbs

3.3.2   It was suggested above that the traditional method of classifying the parts of speech (verb, noun, adjective, etc.) does not fit the Chamorro language. However, the traditional terms can be used where their use will serve to make the discussion of the grammar more understandable. In our discussion, since we will be referring to the *verb,* which lies at the very heart of Chamorro grammar, it will be necessary to explain some of the features of the Chamorro verb.

It must be remembered that the class of words that we are now calling "verbs" includes words from all three of the classes of major words described above. The different classifications serve different purposes, and they are both equally valid. It is hoped that this dual system of classification will not cause confusion.

Chamorro verbs can be subclassified into three major categories: intransitive verbs, transitive verbs, and irregular verbs. These will be discussed separately below.

Intransitive Verbs. According to traditional definitions, an *intransitive verb* is one that does not require, and often cannot take, a direct object. In addition to this definition, we can make some further specifications for Chamorro intransitive verbs.

When they form the predicate of a non-future statement,

intransitive verbs usually take either the infix -*um*- or the prefix *ma*-, and they are followed by the subject noun or pronoun. If the subject is a pronoun, then it must be of the *yo'*-type. (Cf. section 3.4.1 on pronouns.) Some examples of intransitive verbs with noun and pronoun subjects are given here.

Intransitive Verb Root	Intransitive Sentence (Singular Subject)	Gloss
gupu	Gumupu yo'.	'I flew.'
	Gumupu i paluma.	'The bird flew.'
saga	Sumaga yo'.	'I stayed.'
	Sumaga i palao'an.	'The woman stayed.'
tohge	Tumohge yo'.	'I stood up.'
	Tumohge i lahi.	'The man stood up.'
kuentos	Kumuentos yo'.	'I talked.'
	Kumuentos i lahi.	'The man talked.'
cho'cho'	Macho'cho' yo'.	'I worked.'
	Macho'cho' i lahi.	'The man worked.'
(ma) ta'chong	Mata'chong yo'.	'I sat down.'
	Mata'chong i palao'an.	'The woman sat down.'

There is a group of intransitive verbs in Chamorro that do not require the infix -*um*- or the prefix *ma*- when they form predicates. Several of these verbs appear to contain a fossilized form of *ma*- (cf. section 3.5.3 Additional Problems of *ma*-), but others do not. By "fossilized" we mean that the *ma*- has become an inseparable part of the word. These verbs are considered intransitive verbs because they can be substituted for all of the other intransitive verbs that do take -*um*- or *ma*-. Some of these intransitive verbs that do not require either the infix or the prefix are given here in sentences:

Intransitive Verb Root	Intransitive Sentence (Singular Subject)	Gloss
matai	Matai i lahi.	'The man died.'
magap	Magap yo'.	'I yawned.'
	Magap i lahi.	'The man yawned.'
ma'udai	Ma'udai i lahi.	'The man rode.'
makmata	Makmata yo'.	'I woke up.'
	Makmata i lahi.	'The man woke up.'
ma'ngak	Ma'ngak i patgon.	'The child tottered.'

If the subject of the intransitive sentence is plural, then the prefix *man-* replaces the infix *-um-*. Constrast the following sentences which have plural subjects with the sentences above which have singular subjects: (Note the morphophonemic changes as discussed in section 2.7.)

Intransitive Verb Root	Intransitive Sentence (Plural Subject)	Gloss
gupu	Manggupu siha.	'They flew.'
saga	Mañaga siha.	'They stayed.'
tohge	Manohge siha.	'They stood up.'
kuentos	Manguentos siha.	'They talked.'

If the root word takes the prefix *ma-* or no affix at all, then the prefix *man-* is simply added to the root, as in the following examples:

Intransitive Verb Root	Intransitive Sentence (Plural Subject)	Gloss
(ma) cho′cho′	Manmacho′cho′ siha.	'They worked.'
(ma) ta′chong	Manmata′chong siha.	'They sat down.'
matai	Manmatai siha.	'They died.'
ma′udai	Manma′udai siha.	'They rode.'
makmata	Manmakmata siha.	'They woke up.'

Transitive Verbs. Transitive verbs in traditional terms are verbs that take a direct object. This claim can also be made for transitive verbs in Chamorro. Also, we need to make some further specifications about Chamorro transitive verbs.

In a simple, non-focused sentence, when the direct object is definite then the *hu*-type subject pronouns must precede the verb (cf. 3.4.1 on Pronouns) and the verb stem does not require any affix. Looked at in another way, a regular transitive verb will substitute for the verb *li′e′* in the following sentence:

> Hu li′e′ i lepblo.
> 'I saw the book.'

Some examples of verbs that could substitute for *li′e′* are as follows:

Hu li′e′ i lepblo.	'I saw the book.'
pacha	touched
yute′	threw away

taitai	read
tuge'	wrote
espia	looked for
hatsa	lifted
sodda'	found

Of course, transitive sentences may also take noun subjects, in which case the subject pronoun *ha* must be used with singular subjects and the pronoun *ma* is used with plural subjects, as in the following examples:

I lahi ha li'e' i palao'an.	'The man saw the woman.'
I lalahi ma li'e' i palao'an.	'The men saw the woman.'

When the direct object of a transitive verb is indefinite, then the prefix *man-* is required and the *yo'-type* pronouns are used. These changes in the forms of the verb and pronoun are very confusing to the non-Chamorro speaker because they make the transitive verb constructions resemble intransitive verb constructions. Note the following contrastive examples:

Transitive Sentence with Definite Object	*Transitive Sentence with Indefinite Object*
Hu li'e' i lepblo.	Manli'e' yo' lepblo.
'I saw the book.'	'I saw a book.'
Hu taitai i lepblo.	Manaitai yo' lepblo.
'I read the book.'	'I read a book.'
Hu hatsa i lamasa.	Manhatsa yo' lamasa.
'I lifted the table.'	'I lifted a table.'

(A more detailed discussion of definite and indefinite object constructions will be given later in the section on syntax.)

Special Transitive Verbs. There are three types of *special transitive verbs* in Chamorro. They might be categorized as follows:

1. The form used with the indefinite object is different from the form used with the definite object, but one form is obviously derived from the other.
2. The form used with the indefinite object is different from the form used with the definite object and is not derivable from the same root.
3. There exists a single form only for indefinite objects.

These three types of special transitive verbs will now be illustrated.

Type 1 can be illustrated by the following pairs of words:

With Definite Object	*With Indefinite Object*
tuge'— Hu tuge' i katta.	mangge' —Mangge' yo' katta.
'I wrote the letter.'	'I wrote a letter.'
tufok— Hu tufok i kannastra.	mamfok— Mamfok yo' kannastra.
'I wove the basket.'	'I wove a basket.'

In both of the above examples the verb used with the indefinite object is obviously derived from the verb used with the definite object by the following process:

Root: tuge'—tufok

Object Prefix man-: man + tuge' →manuge'

man + tufok → manufok

Loss of initial
consonant and
vowel of root: manuge' → mange'

manufok → manfok

Assimilation of *n*
of prefix to
following
consonant: mange' → mangge'

manfok → mamfok

There are numerous other Chamorro verbs which have similarly related definite and indefinite object verb forms.

Type 2 can be illustrated by the following pair of words:

With Definite Object	*With Indefinite Object*
kanno'— Hu kanno' i mansana.	chocho— Chumocho yo' mansana.
'to eat' 'I ate the apple.'	'I ate an apple.'

It will be noticed that there is no apparent relationship between these two words meaning 'eat'. Neither form can be derived from the other. Each of these words has become "specialized" in that *kanno'* can only be used with definite objects while *chocho* can only be used with indefinite objects. It will be further noted that *chocho* requires the infix *-um-* that we have observed earlier in the intransitive verbs.

Type 3 probably includes only four verbs which are:

With Indefinite Objects Only

malago'	Malago' yo' mansana.
'to want'	'I want an apple.'
maleffa	Maleffa yo' ni lepblo.
'to forget'	'I forgot the book..'
mañotsot	Mañotsot yo' ni isao.
'to repent'	'I repent the sin.'
munhayan	Munhayan yo' ni lepblo.
'to finish'	'I finished the book.'

In the case of transitive verbs of Type 3, the forms given above are the only existing forms and they are therefore used even when the object appears to be definite, e.g.,

Malago' yo' ayu na lepblo.
'I want that book.'

Mañotsot yo' ni bida-hu.
'I repent what I did.'

Irregular Verbs. The *irregular verbs* of Chamorro were introduced in the discussion of Class III words above. All of the irregular verbs belong to Class III. They are called irregular verbs because they do not conform to the patterns of affixation that the other verbs follow. Safford (1909:97 ff.) lists most of them as "defective verbs." In fact, even within Class III we find several different types of verbs when classified in terms of their grammatical features.

The verbs that fall in this class of irregular verbs are listed here:

gaige	'be, exist'
guaha	'have, exist'
taigue	'not present, absent'
mangge	'where'
taya'	'none'
estaba	'used to be'
gai	'have'
tai	'none'
munga	'don't, no'
cha'—	'don't'
siña	'can'
alok	'say'
ga'o	'prefer'
ya—	'like, prefer'
malak	'go to'

mohon   'desire'
hekkua'   'I don't know'
iyo   'belong to'

The translations given in each case are close approximations. These verbs will now be discussed separately.

Gaige is probably the most common of the irregular verbs in Chamorro. It is usually translated as 'there is' or 'there exists' when the subject is specific:

Gaige yo' gi eskuela.   'I am at school.'
Gaige si Paul gi lancho.   'Paul is at the ranch.'

The verb can take the pluralizing prefix *man-*:

Manggaige siha gi eskuela.   'They are at the school.'

It can also take reduplication:

Gagaige si Paul gi eskuela.   'Paul is being at the school.'

The verb *gaige* cannot take any of the other verbal affixes. Note that it is always followed immediately by the subject noun or pronoun.

Guaha is another very common word in Chamorro. It is usually translated as 'have' or 'exist'. It differs from *gaige* in that it does not take the standard verbal affixes, the sentence structure that *guaha* requires is different, and the subject is relatively non-specific. Note the following examples:

Guaha salape'-hu.   'I have money.'
   exists money-my

Guaha familia-ku.   'I have a family.'
   exists family-my

The two sentences following will illustrate the difference in use between *gaige* and *guaha:*

Gaige i patgon giya Guam.
The child is at Guam.'

Guaha un patgon giya Guam.
'There is a child at Guam.'

Taigue might be considered the negative counterpart of *gaige.* (Note also the positive-negative relationship between *gai* and *tai* discussed below.) It is usually translated as 'it isn't there' or 'it is absent':

Taigue si Paul.
'Paul isn't here (or there).'

Taigue i estudiante.
'The student is absent.'

Like *gaige*, this verb can take the pluralizing prefix *man-* and can be reduplicated:

Manaigue i manestudiante.
'The students are absent.'

Tataigue si Paul.
'Paul is not being here.'

Taigue does not take any of the other verbal affixes.

Mangge is actually a contraction consisting of the question word *manu* 'where', the linking particle *nai*, and the irregular verb *gaige*. Thus, from the formal expression *manu nai gaige* we derive the informal contraction *mangge* 'where is'. Since the contracted form patterns itself very much like *gaige* and *taigue*, it is included here among the irregular verbs.

Mangge si Paul?
'Where is Paul?'

Mangge hao?
'Where are you?'

Manmangge i famagu'on?
Where are the children?'

Taya' is the opposite (or negative) of *guaha*. It is usually translated as 'do not have' or 'does not exist', and it takes the same sentence structure as *guaha*. Examples are:

Taya' salape'-hu.   'I don't have any money.'
 not exist money-my

Taya' familia-ku.   'I don't have any family.'
 not exist family-my

Estaba is a Spanish loan word from the verb *estar*. Since Chamorro does not have a formally marked past tense form for *gaige*, the Spanish loan word *estaba* is used in the sense of 'used to be' or 'was':

Estaba yo' gi gualo' anai matto hao.
'I was at the farm when you came.'

Estaba bula kareta gi pantalán.
'There used to be many cars at the pier.'

Gai and *tai* are probably related to *guaha* and *taya'* respectively. *Gai* has the same meaning as *guaha*, and *tai* means the same as *taya'*. The difference is that *gai* and *tai* require different sentence structures. Compare the following sentences with the ones above:

<u>Gai</u> salape' yo'.   'I have money.'
exists money me

<u>Tai</u> salape' yo'.   'I don't have any money.'
not exist money me

A further difference is that *gai* and *tai* both take the plural marking prefix *man-*, while *guaha* and *taya'* do not. Thus, the following sentences are possible:

<u>Manggai</u> salape' siha. 'They have money.'
exists money they

<u>Mantai</u> salape' siha. 'They don't have any money.'
not exist money they

NOTE: Some speakers might use the plural marking prefix *man-* with *guaha* and *taya'* to form *mangguaha* and *mantaya'*. These "pluralized" forms are not very common. Some speakers would not use them at all, but simply use the following forms:

<u>Guaha</u> salape'-ñiha. 'They have money.'
exists money-their

<u>Taya'</u> salape'-ñiha. 'They don't have any money.'
not exist money-their

Munga is a negative word that behaves more like a verb than like anything else. That is why it is listed as one of the irregular verbs. *Munga* is used most frequently in two somewhat different ways. It is commonly used to decline something that is offered, such as food or drink. A negative response to the question *Kao malago' hao chumocho?* (Would you like to eat?) would be *Munga yo'*.

Munga is also used in the sense of "Don't do" something:

<u>Munga</u> gof atrasao. 'Don't be too late.'
don't very late
<u>Munga</u> manangga yo'. 'Don't wait for me.'
don't wait for me

The irregular verb *munga* does not take any affixes.

Cha'- is similar in meaning to *munga*, but it is quite a different sort of word. When used with the second person pronoun, it carries the meaning 'don't':

Cha'-mu nánangga.
Don't wait.'

When used with other pronouns, it carries a somewhat different negative meaning, such as 'won't' or 'had better not':

Cha'-hu nánangga.
'I won't wait.'

Cha'-ña nánangga.
'She had better not wait.'

It will also be noted that the "main verb" which occurs with *cha'-* is always in the reduplicated form.

NOTE: The reduplicated form of *nangga* has been converted to a noun-like word, so that the sentence *Cha'-mu nánangga* might be translated as 'Don't be a waiter.' More will be said about this type of reduplication later.

Siña 'can, may' is another of the irregular verbs that does not take affixation like the regular verbs. *Siña* might be thought of as an auxiliary verb which functions very much like its English counterpart 'can.' It should be noticed that the subject pronoun patterns with *siña* rather than with the main verb. That is, if the "main verb" takes a specific object, then a *hu*-type pronoun precedes the verb. If the main verb is intransitive, or takes a non-specific object, a *yo'*-type pronoun usually follows *siña*, but may also follow the main verb. See the following examples:

Siña yo' manli'e' palao'an?
'I can see a woman.'

Siña hu li'e' i palao'an?
'I can see the woman.'

Siña yo' gumupu.
'I can fly.'

Siña gumupu yo'.
'I can fly.'

The next three irregular verbs—*alok*, *ga'o-* and *ya*—all have at least one thing in common: they must take possessive subject pronouns in non-future constructions. The examples cited below are given with the first person singular subject pronoun:

Ilek-hu "no".
'I said "no".'

Ga'o-ku guihan.
'I prefer fish.'

Ya-hu guihan.
'I like fish.'

There are further peculiarities of two of these irregular verbs that should be mentioned at this time.

The verb *alok* has the alternate form *ilek* when it occurs in the non-future tense. The form *alok* occurs in future tense (*Para bai hu alok "no"*. 'I will say "no".') *Alok* is the only one of these three verbs that can occur in the future tense. Note that when *alok* occurs, a different type of subject pronoun must be used.

The verb *ga'o* 'prefer' has an alternate form *ga'ña*. Both are used freely with precisely the same meaning:

> Ga'o-ku guihan.
> 'I prefer fish.'
>
> Ga'ña-ku guihan.
> 'I prefer fish.'

The irregular verb *malak* 'go to' stands alone in terms of the syntactic patterns that it requires. Unlike all of the other verbs, regular and irregular, it cannot take a subject pronoun immediately before or after. It appears to have a kind of "built in" preposition, and the subject pronoun must follow the location, as in the following examples:

> Malak Honolulu yo'.
> 'I went to Honolulu.'
>
> Malak i tenda yo'.
> 'I went to the store.'

The initial m̲ of *malak* changes to f̲ in future and imperative statements.

> Para bai hu f̲alak i tenda.
> 'I will go to the store.'
>
> F̲alak i tenda.
> 'Go to the store.'

Malak is also used to form sentences with certain location words, as in the following examples:

> Malak papa' yo'.
> 'I went down.'
>
> Malak tatte yo'.
> 'I went behind.'
>
> F̲alak i me'nan i palao'an.
> 'Go in front of the woman.'

(For further discussion of the *location words* see 3.4.4. below.)

Mohon 'feel sincerely' is classed among the irregular verbs even though it does not conform to the usual rules for verbs or nouns, or anything else. Its meaning is also somewhat difficult to translate. The following examples will illustrate how it can be used:

Sumaga yo' mohon giya Agaña.
'I hope I can stay in Agaña.' or 'I'm looking forward to the chance to stay in Agaña.'

Sumaga mohon gi gima' si Frank.
'I wish Frank would stay at home.'

Hekkua' might be considered a fixed idiomatic expression rather than an irregular verb. Its usage is limited to the single situation when the speaker wishes to express his uncertainty. It is the equivalent of the English expression 'I don't know' given in answer to a question, and it is used only for the first person singular.

Mangge si Jose?
'Where is Jose?'

Hekkua'.
'I don't know.'

Iyo is also listed among the classifiers of Chamorro (see 3.5). It is listed here among the irregular verbs because it also has characteristics of a verb. See the example below:

Iyo-ku i kareta.
'The car belongs to me.'

Auxiliary Verbs. There appear to be a small number of words in Chamorro that may be considered *auxiliary verbs*. For Chamorro, we will define an auxiliary verb as a verblike word that usually occurs with a second verb which carries the primary meaning. The auxiliary verb tends to modify the meaning of the main verb.

Auxiliary verbs can sometimes occur without a main verb, or with the main verb "understood." But, they usually require a second verb to complete the predicate.

These auxiliary verbs may be considered *modal* because they add something to the mood of the utterance.

Some examples of the auxiliary verbs are given below:

Siña	'can'
Siña yo' manli'e' palao'an.	'I can see a woman.'
Siña yo' gumupu.	'I can fly.'

Notice that *siña* does occur without another verb when responding to questions or when the other verb is understood:

Kao siña yo' gumupu?	'Can I fly?'
Ahe', ti siña.	'No, cannot.'
Hunggan, siña yo'.	'Yes, I can.'
tanga	'wish, desire'
Hu tanga lumi'e' Hawaii.	'I desire to see Hawaii.'
atotga	'risk, dare'
Hu atotga humanao para i tasi	'I dared to go to the sea.'
hasngon	'deliberately'
Hu hasngon gumacha' adeng-mu.	'I deliberately stepped on your foot.'
mohon	'wishful feeling'
Sumaga yo' mohon giya Agaña.	'I hope I can stay in Agaña.'

Of course, there are other verbs in Chamorro that often require a second verb in the sentence in order to make it complete. For example, the verbs *malago'*, *ya-*, and *maleffa* may require a second verb in the sentence, as in the following examples:

Malago' yo' chumocho.
'I want to eat.'

Ya-hu tumaitai i lepblo-ku.
'I like to read my book.'

Maleffa yo' chumule' i lepblo-ku.
'I forgot to bring my book.'

On the other hand, the verbs *malago'*, *ya-*, and *maleffa* all occur without second verbs in the sentence, as in the following examples:

Malago' yo' setbesa.
'I want a beer.'

Ya-hu setbesa.
'I like beer.'

Maleffa yo' ni lepblo.
'I forgot the book.'

In the examples cited above where there are two verbs in the sentence—and there are probably many similar examples—it is better *not* to consider the first verb an auxiliary. This type of construction can be analyzed more meaningfully on the syntactic level. We can say that the sentences with two verbs are actually *complex sentences*. That is, each sentence consists of two sentences that have been joined together.

For example, we might say that the first sentence above— *Malago' yo' chumocho*—comes from the following two sentences:

> Malago' yo' este.
> Chumocho yo'.

By a process of grammatical transformations we can then join the two sentences together to form a complex sentence. This process will be discussed in detail in the section on Complex Sentences.

It might prove helpful at this point to try to think of additional examples of auxiliary verbs in Chamorro—verbs, or verb-like words, that require a second verb in the sentence.

Base Form of Verbs. Before leaving the present discussion of verbs, there is one additional problem that should be considered. That is the problem of determining the *base form* of certain verbs.

A base form of a word is that form from which other forms of the same word can be derived. In English, for example, we say that the past tense form *walked* is derived from *walk*. Hence, we can posit *walk* as the base form for that verb. For irregular verbs such as *went,* we can say that the past tense form *went* is derived from *go*. Thus, *go* is the base form for that verb.

The determination of the base form in Chamorro becomes a problem only with one group of words. Certain verbs in Chamorro are pronounced with an initial m when used in the non-future tense and with an initial f when used in other constructions, such as future tense, imperative, and causative. Notice the alternation in the form of the verb in the following sentences: (The verb is underlined.)

> Malagu yo'.
> 'I ran.'

> Para bai hu falagu.
> 'I will run.'

> Falagu!
> 'Run!'

> Hu na'falagu si Juan.
> 'I caused Juan to run.'

The question is: Does *falagu* come from *malagu*, or vice versa? Which one is the base form from which the other is derived?

One argument might be that since *falagu* occurs in more instances than *malagu*, then we should say that *falagu* is the base form. *Malagu* would then be derived from it.

Another example of this alternation can be seen in the following set of sentences:

> Mata'chong yo'.
> 'I sat down.'
>
> Para bai hu fata'chong.
> 'I will sit down.'
>
> Fata'chong!
> 'Sit down!'
>
> Hu na'fata'chong si Juan.
> 'I caused Juan to sit down.'

Once again, the verb with initial m is used in the non-future tense form; initial f occurs elsewhere.

It would be desirable if all the verbs of the language conformed to this pattern. Such a situation would enable us to make general rules that would take care of the alternation between initial m in the non-future constructions and the initial f in the other instances. Unfortunately not all verbs follow this pattern. Note the following set of sentences:

> Ma'udai yo' i kareta.
> 'I rode in the car.'
>
> Para bai hu ma'udai i kareta.
> 'I will ride in the car.'
>
> Ma'udai!
> 'Ride!'
>
> Hu na'ma'udai si Juan ni kareta.
> 'I made Juan ride in the car.'

As can be seen in the above examples, the verb *ma'udai* does not change its form. There are several other verbs like *ma'udai* that do not change.

It should also be pointed out that all of the verbs which show this m-f alternation begin with *ma-* in the non-future form, e.g. *malagu, mata'chong, matto, macho'cho',* and *maloffan.* This is probably related to the problem of *ma-* discussed in section 3.5.3.

In view of the unpredictable nature of this alternation between m and f in some words but not in others, it seems advisable to consider the future form of verbs as the base form. We can then formulate a rule as follows: Verbs which have an initial f̲ in future tense will show a change to initial m̲ in non-future tense when used with *yo'*-type subject pronouns. The following examples showing some future and non-future forms will illustrate:

Future	Non-future
Para bai hu falagu.	Malagu yo'.
'I will run.'	'I ran.'
Para bai hu fatto.	Matto yo'.
'I will come.'	'I came.'
Para bai hu faloffan.	Maloffan yo'.
'I will pass by.'	'I passed by.'
Para bai hu maigo'.	Maigo' yo'.
'I will sleep.'	'I slept.'
Para bai hu mumu.	Mumu yo'.
'I will fight.'	'I fought.'

Notice that the last two examples have an initial m̲ in both future and non-future forms.

The base form for verbs will be that which is used in future tense. Thus, we can say that *malagu* is derived from *falagu, mata' chong* is derived from *fata'chong*, and so on. The great majority of Chamorro verbs have the same form in both future and non-future tenses.

Nouns

3.3.3   Among the Class II words there is a subclass that should be considered primarily as *nouns*. They are considered nouns for the following reasons: (1) In their base form they normally occupy a position in the sentence that can be designated "subject of sentence" or "object of sentence"; (2) They generally correspond in meaning to nouns in other languages such as English, where they designate or name a person, living being, object, thing, etc.

It must be remembered that other parts of speech—verbs, modifiers, location words, and even prepositions—may also function as subjects or objects of sentences. They can be converted to nouns, by a process called *nominalization*, by adding certain affixes. This process of nominalization will be discussed in a later section. (Cf. section 4.3.)

At the present time we are concerned only with words which in their base form (no affixes) can be considered nouns. Some examples of words that should be subclassed (under Class II) as nouns are the following:

lamasa	'table'	Pedro
guma'	'house'	Maria
hanom	'water'	Saipan
odda'	'soil'	Guam
ga'lagu	'dog'	
mannok	'chicken'	
lahi	'man'	
patgon	'child'	
ha'ani	'day'	
sakkan	'year'	

How do we know that all of the above words are nouns? We mentioned two methods for determining if words are nouns or not. One of the methods—probably the weaker one—is to check for the meaning of the word. For example, if the word 'man' in English is a noun, then the Chamorro word *lahi* is probably also a noun. By extension, the word meaning 'man' is probably a noun in all languages. The same test for meaning could be applied to all of the words in the above list.

The other method is to determine whether the word in question can substitute for another noun in a given phrase or sentence. For example, in the sentence

Maolek i lahi.   'The man is good.'

the noun *lahi* functions as the subject of the sentence. Can the other words in the list substitute for *lahi* in this same sentence? Look at the following series of substitutions:

Maolek i lamasa.
Maolek i gima'.
Maolek i hanom.
Maolek i edda'.
Maolek i ga'lagu.
Maolek i mannok
Maolek i lahi.
Maolek i patgon.
Maolek i ha'ani.
Maolek i sakkan
Maolek si Pedro.
Maolek si Maria.
Maolek iya Saipan.
Maolek iya Guam.

Since all of the words in the list can substitute for one another in the same slot, then they must all belong to the same class. We have designated this subclass of Class II words as nouns.

Notice that the last four nouns in the list require a different article. *Pedro* and *Maria* require the article *si*, while *Saipan* and *Guam* require the article *iya*. This would suggest that even a further subclassification of nouns is required.

Indeed, a formal grammar of Chamorro would require an elaborate system for subclassifying all of the parts of speech. Since this is not a formal grammar, we will not get involved with a detailed system for the *subclassification of nouns*. It may prove interesting to subclassify the few nouns in the foregoing list to suggest how the system of subclassification might work.

The most convenient way to approach the subclassification of nouns is to use a system that might be called a *binary system of semantic features*. For example, a word like *lamasa* is countable; that is to say, we can count *dos na lamasa, tres na lamasa,* and so on. A word like *hanom* is not countable. Using the binary feature system we can say that all nouns are either countable (+ count), or not countable (− count). We could say that *lamasa* has the feature < +count> while *hanom* has the feature < −count>. NOTE: Semantic features of words are customarily put within angle brackets <   >.

What are some of the other semantic features that are needed to subclassify the nouns listed above? In addition to knowing whether or not the nouns can be counted, we need to know whether they are animate or not. The feature notation for this is < +animate> or < −animate>. Other features that should be specified for the above nouns are as follows:

<+concrete>   <−concrete>
<+human >   <−human >
<+proper >   <−proper >

As stated earlier, a formal grammar would need to include these features (and probably others) in order to specify the rules for forming correct sentences. Such feature specifications are needed to prevent the rules of the grammar from producing such unacceptable sentences as the following:

*Chumocho i lamasa.
*Kumuentos i ha'ani.

*Maolek i Pedro.
*Mamokkat iya Guam.

Let us look at some of the nouns listed above to determine what semantic features they contain.

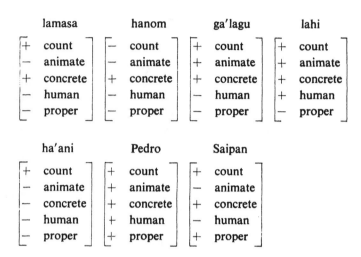

Later in this grammar we will need to subclassify nouns on the basis of < ±proper> and < ±human>, but we will not get much more specific than that.

Modifiers

3.3.4   Among the Class II words is another subclass that should be considered primarily as *modifiers*. They are called modifiers because they serve primarily to modify either verbs or nouns. There appears to be no reason for further subclassifying the modifiers as adjectives and adverbs.

Again it must be remembered that verbs and nouns can also function as modifers. And, on the other hand, modifiers sometimes function as a subject or predicate. There remains, however, a sizable group of root words whose primary function is that of modification.

Some examples of words that could be subclassed as modifiers are given here:

dánkolo	'big'	yommok	'fat'
díkike'	'small'	dalalai	'skinny'
maipe	'hot'	chaddek	'quick'

manengheng	'cold'	despasio	'slow'
ekklao	'crooked'	maolek	'good'
tunas	'straight'	baba	'bad'

Various types of modification will be taken up under that heading in the section on Syntax.

Changing Parts of Speech

3.3.5   In section 3.3 it was pointed out that a single word can often function as a verb, noun, or modifier. This is the main reason why it is difficult to put Chamorro words into a single category such as noun, verb, adjective, etc. Yet, we did establish the classes labeled I, II, and III for the major words in Chamorro. In addition, we examined subclasses of these classes, and we referred to them as verbs, nouns, and modifiers.

It is important to remember that only root words—words that contained no affixes—were assigned to one of these classes.

In this section we will look briefly at some of the processes involved when words in Chamorro change from one subclass to another. These processes are known generally as *affixation*. The several types of affixation will be discussed more fully in a later section. (Cf. section **3.5.2.**)

For the present discussion on how words change from one class to another we must establish some simple criteria for defining verbs, nouns, and modifiers.

A *verb* (for present purposes of classification) is a word that functions as the predicate of a sentence where some action is involved. (This excludes stative sentences, such as *Mediku si Juan* 'Juan is a doctor.') In the sentences below, the verb is underlined:

Ha <u>hatsa</u> si Juan i patgon.
'Juan <u>lifted</u> the child.'

<u>Mamaigo'</u> si Juan.
'Juan is <u>sleeping</u>.'

<u>Gumugupu</u> i paluma.
'The bird is <u>flying</u>.'

A *noun* (for present purposes) is a word that functions as the subject or object of a sentence. In the sentences below, the noun is underlined:

Ha gimen si Juan i <u>hanom</u>.
'Juan drank the <u>water</u>.'

Agaga' i haga'.
'The blood was red.'

Dankolo i lahi.
'The man is big.'

A modifier (for present purposes) is a word that modifies a verb or noun. In the sentences below the modifier is underlined:

Hu tungo' i baba na taotao.
'I know the bad man.'

Sumasaga yo' gi dánkolo na guma'.
'I live at the big house.'

There are basically four different types of grammatical processes that are involved when words are changed from one class to another. These grammatical processes all go under the general heading of *affixation*, which will be discussed in detail in section 3.5.2. The four types of affixes that will be illustrated here are 1) *infix*, 2) *reduplication*, 3) *prefix*, and 4) *suffix*.

Let us now see how these three types of affixes can change a word from one part of speech to another.

Verb to Noun. The transitive verb *hatsa* can be changed to a word that functions like a noun by all three types of affixes listed above. Look at the following examples in which the word *hatsa* has been transformed by affixes. For the resulting differences in meaning, look at the different glosses:

Infix:	Hu li'e' i hinatsa.
	'I saw the thing that was lifted.'
	Hu li'e' i humatsa yo'.
	'I saw the one who lifted me.'
Reduplication:	Hu li'e' i háhatsa.
	'I saw the one that was lifting.'
Prefix:	Hu li'e' i ga'manhatsa.
	'I saw the one who likes to lift.'

The prefix *ga'-* is used less often than the infixes or reduplication, and it is used more frequently with some verbs than with others. For example, from *kuentos* 'talk' we get *ga'kumuentos* 'one who talks a lot'; and from *maigo* 'to sleep' we get *ga'maigo'* 'sleepyhead'.

Intransitive verbs such as *gupu* 'to fly' can also be changed to words that function like nouns by some of the same affixes.

Infix:	Hu li'e' i gumupu.
	'I saw the one who flew.'

Reduplication: Hu li'e' i gigipu.
'I saw the flyer.'

(NOTE: As the result of certain morphophonemic processes and sound changes, the reduplicated form *gigipu* often comes out as *gekpo*, with the same meaning. This difference in forms can be explained as follows. The second vowel of *gigipu* was lost; the result of this loss is **gigpu*. Since the first vowel is now in a closed syllable (*gig-*), it is lowered to e (cf. 2.7.3 and 2.7.4). Now that the first vowel is the mid vowel e and is followed by two consonants and a vowel, the second vowel is lowered to o. At this stage the word is **gegpo*. Since voiced stops do not occur at the end of a syllable, g changes to k and we end up with the form *gekpo*. This process is very common in Chamorro and can be traced in scores of words.)

Verb to Modifier. Verbs can also be changed to modifiers through the process of reduplication, as in the following examples:

Reduplication: i háhatsa na taotao
'the lifting person'

i gigipu na paluma
'the flying bird'

Another way of converting a verb to a modifier is by adding the suffix -*on*, which might be compared to the English suffix '-able', as in 'lovable.' The Chamorro suffix has an allomorph -*yon* which occurs when the stem ends with a vowel. Some examples of this suffix are:

Verb	*Modifier*
atan 'look at'	atanon 'nice to look at' (lit. look at-able')
sangan 'to tell'	sanganon 'tellable'
guaiya 'to love'	guaiyayon 'lovable'
tulaika 'exchange'	tulaikayon 'exchangable'

Notice that the primary stress always shifts to the next to final syllable when this suffix is added.

Noun to Verb. Frequently nouns are changed to verb-like words through the use of the infix -*um*-. This can be illustrated in the following examples:

Infix: Humanom i leche. (from *hanom* 'water')
'The milk became water.'

Tumaotao i patgon. (from *taotao* 'person')
'The child became a person.'

Noun to Modifier. Nouns can be converted to modifiers by the use of certain prefixes and infixes, as the following examples will show:

Infix: Hinanom i leche. (*hanom* plus -in-)
'The milk is *watery*.'

Kinahet i kolot. (*kahet* plus -*in*-)
'The color is *orangeish*.'

Prefix: Míhaga' i litratu. (*mi*- plus *haga'*)
'The picture was *bloody*.'

Mípilu i lahi. (*mi*- plus *pulu*)
'The man is *hairy*.'

NOTE: Both *míhaga'* and *mipilu* have alternate forms which are *mehga'* and *mepplo* respectively. The formation of these shorter words is very much like the formation of *gekpo* from *gígipu* (described above). In the case of *mehga'* from *míhaga'*, the second vowel was lost, thereby producing *mihga'*. Since the first syllable became closed, the first vowel was lowered from i to e. The result was then *mehga'*. Can you describe the process whereby *mipilu* became *mepplo*?

Modifier to Verb. Modifiers can be converted to words that function like verbs by the addition of the infix -*um*-. For example:

Infix: Dumánkolo i palao'an.
'The woman became big.'

Dumíkike' i guihan.
'The fish became small.'

Umá'paka' i bihu.
'The old man became white.'

Modifier to Noun. Modifiers can function as noun-like words even without affixation. The position in the sentence and the use of the article i are sufficient.

Hu tungo' i dankolo.
'I know the big (one).'
Hu li'e' i agaga'.
'I saw the red (one).'
Hu guaiya i dikike'.
'I like the little (one).'

Modifiers may also be converted to noun-like words through adding the infix -*in*-. Look at the contrasting phrases that follow:

i baba na taotao
'the bad man'

Infix: i binaban taotao
'the man's badness'

Some words from the minor class (which are discussed in section 3.4.) can also change classes as a result of the processes described above. Two examples will illustrate how this happens:

Location word tatte 'behind'
With infix -um-: Tumatte yo'. 'I went behind.'
Reduplication: tátatte 'progeny, one left behind'

Location word halom 'inside'
With infix -um-: Humalom yo'. 'I went inside.'
With prefix mi- and infix -in-: mihinalom 'intelligence'

NOTE: The last word in the above example—*mihinalom*—is often pronounced *méhnalom*. Can this be explained according to processes that have been observed in other words?

In addition there are a fairly large number of verbs borrowed from Spanish which are converted to nouns by the same process that operates in Spanish. This process can be demonstrated by comparing the Spanish and Chamorro below:

Spanish   *aliviar* 'to relieve' becomes *alivio* 'relief'
Chamorro   *alibia* 'to relieve' becomes *alibiu* 'relief'

As can be seen from the preceding discussion, it is very common for words to change classes in Chamorro. This is one reason why it is difficult to claim that a particular word in Chamorro belongs to a particular part of speech or class. And this is the major reason why we chose to establish the major classes of words in Chamorro as Class I, II, and III.

MINOR WORD CLASS

3.4   The class of *minor words* in Chamorro contains a rather large but finite number of words that undergo limited or no affixation. The words of the minor class are a *closed set* because words are seldom added to or lost from this class. The minor class of words includes such categories as pronouns, prepositions, question words, and negatives, all of which will be discussed below. The affixes of Chamorro, of which there are many, will be considered separately from the minor word class.

Pronouns

3.4.1. The *pronoun* in Chamorro is generally similar to the pronoun of other languages. No special definition for this category is required. There are four sets of pronouns in Chamorro, each of which has its own special function. These four types of pronouns are discused separately below and are presented together at the end of the discussion in the form of a chart.

The first set of pronouns are called *hu-type pronouns*. The name of this set comes from the first person singular form, which is *hu*. The complete set of *hu*-type pronouns is as follows:

	1st	hu	'I'
Singular	2nd	un	'you'
	3rd	ha	'he, she, it'
	1st incl.	ta	'we inclusive'
Plural	1st excl.	in	'we exclusive'
	2nd	en	'you—2 or more'
	3rd	ma	'they'

The *hu*-type pronouns function as subject markers and always precede the verb. In transitive statements with Class I words, these pronoun subject markers must occur, even when a noun subject also occurs. Notice in the following examples that the first sentence has a subject noun plus the subject marking pronoun. The second example contains a pronominal subject only:

Si Juan ha li'e' i palao'an.
'Juan saw the woman.'

Ha li'e' i palao'an.
'He saw the woman.'

NOTE: The word order of the sentence in the first example could also be *Ha li'e' si Juan i palao'an* with no change in meaning. When this word order is used, the noun immediately following the verb is the subject noun.

The pronouns *ta* and *in* are both glossed as "we," with the additional specification "inclusive" or "exclusive." All of the Chamorro pronouns show this same distinction between the two pronouns meaning "we." The term *inclusive* means simply that the speaker is including the person he is talking to; *exclusive* means "we, but not you," or "we" excluding the person spoken to.

Both inclusive and exclusive forms of the pronoun may be

dual (referring to "we two") or plural (referring to three or more). Plurality as opposed to duality is indicated by the form of the verb used with the pronoun. This will be discussed later.

The second set of pronouns are called *yo'-type pronouns*. The name of this set comes from the first person singular form which is *yo'*. (The pronoun *yo'* was in all probability borrowed from Spanish. It is the only "non-native" pronoun in the language.) The complete set of the *yo'*-type pronouns is as follows:

	1st	yo'	'I, me'
Singular	2nd	hao	'you'
	3rd	gue'	'he, she, him, her, it'
	1st incl.	hit	'we inclusive, us'
Plural	1st excl.	ham	'we exclusive, us'
	2nd	hamyo	'you—2 or more'
	3rd	siha	'they, them'

The *yo'*-type pronouns function as both subject and object pronouns, and in both cases they always follow the verb. They should be considered subject pronouns under the following conditions:

1. When used with any Class II word:
   Gumupu yo'.
   'I flew.'

   Maolek yo'.
   'I am good.'

   Lahi yo'.
   'I am a man.'

2. when used with a Class I (transitive) word with an indefinite object:
   Manhatsa yo' lamasa.
   'I lifted a table.'

   Manli'e' yo' lahi.
   'I saw a man.'

   Manaitai yo' lepblo.
   'I read a book.'

The *yo'*-type pronouns should be considered object pronouns when they occur with a Class I (transitive) word as a specific object. See the following examples:

Si Juan ha li'e' yo'.
'Juan saw me.'

Si Maria ha hatsa gue'.
'Maria lifted him.'

I lahi ha sangani ham.
'The man told us.'

Like the other pronouns, the plural pronouns of the *yo'*-type can be either dual or plural depending on the form of the verb.

The *possessive pronouns* usually have the function that the name suggests; that is, they usually indicate possession of the noun to which they are attached. The possessive pronouns are listed here:

	1st	-hu	'my'
Singular	2nd	-mu	'your'
	3rd	-ña	'his, hers'
	1st incl.	-ta	'our inclusive'
Plural	1st excl.	-mami	'our exclusive'
	2nd	-miyu	'your—2 or more'
	3rd	-ñiha	'their—2 or more'

All of the possessive pronouns are written here with hyphens preceding them. This is a writing device to show that the possessive pronouns are bound morphemes—they must always be attached to the preceding word.

In section 2.6.2. on Phrase Stress, it was pointed out that the favored stress pattern in Chamorro was penultimate—on the next to final syllable. The addition of the possessive pronoun to a Chamorro word nearly always causes a shift in the primary stress to the penultimate syllable. For this reason, the possessive pronouns are sometimes referred to as *enclitics,* which are words that are pronounced as forming a phonetic unit with the stressed word preceding it.

Notice how the primary stress shifts to the penultimate syllable in the following examples:

karéta	'car'	karetá-hu	'my car'
karéta	'car'	karetá-ta	'our car'
karéta	'car'	karetan-mámi	'our car'
karéta	'car'	karetan-ñíha	'their car'

It will also be noticed that all of the disyllabic possessive pronouns (those with two syllables) require the *excrescent* consonant n before they are joined to a vowel-final stem. (Cf. 2.7.2.)

The possessive pronouns do not always show possession. With certain verbs and in certain grammatical constructions they appear to function more like subject pronouns. For example, the words of Class IIIc (cf. 3.3.2) must always take the possessive pronoun as the subject:

Ilek-hu "never."
'I said "never".'

Ga'o-mu este.
'You prefer this.'

Ya-hu humanao.
'I want to go.'

The possessive pronouns also occur as subject pronouns in certain question constructions which use the question words *hafa* 'what' and *hayi* 'who'. Notice the following examples:

Hafa malago'-mu?
'What do you want?'

Hafa lini'e'-ña?
'What did he see?'

Hayi malago'-mu?
'Whom do you want?'

Hayi lini'e'-ña?
'Whom did he see?'

It might be possible to translate the above sentences as 'What is your want?' and 'What was his thing-seen?' and so forth. This would preserve the possessive nature of the pronoun, but it would give us very clumsy translations. It seems preferable to say that the possessive pronouns also function as subject pronouns under certain conditions.

The possessive pronouns have another special function when they occur with location words. In this situation they seem to function as a kind of object of the location word, similar to an object of a preposition in English. The examples below will illustrate this special function:

hulo'	'above'	i hilo'-mami	'above us'
mo'na	'in front'	i me'nan-ñiha	'in front of them'
tatte	'behind'	i tatte-ku	'behind me'
fi'on	'near'	i fi'on-mu	'near you'
agapa'	'right side'	i agapa'-ña	'to the right of him'
akague	'left side'	i akague-ña	'to the left of him'

There is another important morphophonemic change in the
first person singular possessive pronoun. We have given the base
form of this pronoun as *-hu*. It also occurs as *-su, -tu,* and *-ku*
under the following conditions:

1. If the stem has a final s, the form of the pronoun is *-su*:
lássas 'skin;' *lassás-su* 'my skin.'
2. If the stem has a final t, the form of the pronoun is *-tu*: *páchot*
'mouth;' *pachót-tu* 'my mouth.'
3. If the stem has a medial consonant cluster, then the form of
the pronoun is *-ku*: *lépblo* 'book;' *lepbló-ku* 'my book'.

Under all other conditions, the form of the pronoun is *-hu*.

For purposes of writing, only *-hu* and *-ku* will be written.

The last set of pronouns to be discussed are the *emphatic
pronouns*. They usually function as subject pronouns and are used
in situations where the subject is emphasized. The full set of
emphatic pronouns is given here:

	1st	guahu	'I'
Singular	2nd	hagu	'you'
	3rd	guiya	'he, she, it'
	1st incl.	hita	'we inclusive'
	1st excl.	hami	'we exclusive'
Plural	2nd	hamyo	'you—2 or more'
	3rd	siha	'they—2 or more'

Some examples of the emphatic pronouns as subject pronouns are:

Guahu lumi'e' i palao'an.
'I am the one who saw the woman.'

Guiya humatsa i lamasa.
'He is the one who lifted the table.'

NOTE: When the emphatic pronouns are used as subject pronouns, the verb must take a special affix. In the above examples
the affix is *-um-*. This is part of the *focus system* of Chamorro
which will be discussed in section 4.10 below.

The emphatic pronouns may also be found in other types of
contructions where they should not be described as subject
pronouns. For example, in answer to the question *Hayi chumo'-
gue?* 'Who did it?', one could say *Guiya* 'Him.'

The emphatic pronouns are also found in such expressions
as *guatu giya guiya* 'towards him'. In addition, the emphatic
pronouns are used very commonly to mean 'at someone's house'

as in *giya hami* 'at our house' or *giya hamyo* 'at your place'. They may also occur as emphasized object pronouns in transitive constructions, as in *Guiya hu li'e'*. 'I see HIM.'

For purposes of comparison, a complete listing of all the pronouns in Chamorro is given in the following chart. It is interesting to notice the similarity of the pronouns of the various classes which refer to the same person. In some instances the pronouns are identical in form.

CHAMORRO PRONOUNS

hu-type Pronouns

	First Person		Second Person	Third Person
	Inclusive	Exclusive		
Singular	hu		un	ha
Plural	ta	in	en	ma

yo'-type Pronouns

	First Person		Second Person	Third Person
	Inclusive	Exclusive		
Singular	yo'		hao	gue'
Plural	hit	ham	hamyo	siha

Possessive Pronouns

	First Person		Second Person	Third Person
	Inclusive	Exclusive		
Singular	-hu∼-ku		-mu	-ña
Plural	-ta	-mami	-miyu	-ñiha

Emphatic Pronouns

	First Person		Second Person	Third Person
	Inclusive	Exclusive		
Singular	guahu		hagu	guiya
Plural	hita	hami	hamyo	siha

Demonstratives

3.4.2   In grammar books written for English one can find the terms "demonstrative pronoun" and "demonstrative adjective" used to refer to the words 'this, that, these, etc.' For Chamorro we can use the same term *demonstrative* to refer to the group of words that point out something specific.

Chamorro has a three-way demonstrative system. The most commonly used words that form this system are:

este	'this, close to speaker'
enao	'that, close to listener'
ayu	'that, away from speaker and listener'

Este 'this' was borrowed from Spanish, and has almost completely replaced the original Chamorro demonstrative which, according to Safford (41) was *ayen* "if placed before the predicate," and *yini* or *ini* "if placed after the predicate of a sentence." Safford reported in 1903 that the Spanish loanword *este* was "fast taking the place of *ayen* and *ini.*" While I have never heard these older Chamorro forms used in daily conversation, I have recorded *ini* in some folk tales as they were told by present-day Chamorro speakers. It is probably safe to conclude that the Spanish demonstrative *este* is now used far more frequently than *ini* or *yini* and that *ayen* is not used at all.

(Incidentally, *ini* occurs in modern Malay for 'this', and it parallels the modern Chamorro locative word *guini* in the same way that the demonstrative *enao* is related to the locative word *guenao.*)

The word *enao* has an alternate form *yenao* which is sometimes heard, especially in the speech of older persons or in folk tales. Although the word *yenao* does not occur in any of the texts on which this grammar is based, its occurrence in the language has been attested by several informants.

The word *ayu* is frequently heard as *eyu*. While both *ayu* and *eyu* are currently in use, it is possible that *eyu* will ultimately replace *ayu*. If this happens, then all three of the demonstratives will share the common feature of beginning with the same sound e. This apparent change in the language that is taking place can be described as a sort of *leveling,* a process by which the three demonstratives will share a common feature.

There is still another word *yuhi* that shares some of the same features as *ayu* and *eyu*. In some situations it may be used in place of *ayu* or *eyu* as a demonstrative. In other cases, it functions like a "relative pronoun." When *yuhi* is used as a demonstrative, it is understood that a prior reference to something has already been made or is understood, or that the feature of location is also included, as in 'that there'. Notice the following examples:

    a. Hu taitai <u>ayu</u> na lepblo.
        'I read that book.'

    b. Hu taitai <u>yuhi</u> na lepblo.
        'I read that there book.'

    c. <u>Ayu</u> na lepblo hu taitai.
        'That book I read.'

But not:

    d. *<u>Yuhi</u> na lepblo hu taitai.

Sentences a and b are not entirely synonymous. In sentence b the demonstrative *yuhi* suggests that the reference to "that book" is more specific, visible, or that its existence is known to both the speaker and listener. A closer translation of *yuhi* in sentence b might be 'that there'. Sentence d is considered ungrammatical.

    In other situations *ayu, eyu,* and *yuhi* appear to be interchangeable, as the following examples will show:

    Para   *ayu* siha na mañe'lu-hu i taotao i distritu kuatro.
           eyu
           yuhi
    'For those my brothers the people of the fourth district.'

The status of *yuhi* as a demonstrative is not entirely clear. The following sample sentence shows that all of the demonstratives except *yuhi* are acceptable:

    <u>Este</u> ha' manmacho'guen-mímiyu pa'go.
    <u>Ini</u>
    'This is how you are being treated now.'

    <u>Enao</u> ha' manmacho'guen-mímiyu pa'go.
    <u>Yenao</u>
    'That is how you are being treated now.'

    <u>Ayu</u> ha' manmacho'guen-mímiyu pa'go.
    <u>Eyu</u>
    'That is how you are being treated now.'

But not:

    *<u>Yuhi</u> ha' manmacho'guen-mímiyu pa'go.

Some further examples illustrating the use of demonstratives are given here:

Hafa este?	'What's this?'
Hafa ini?	
Hafa enao?	'What's that (towards listener)?'
Hafa yenao?	
Hafa ayu?	'What's that (away from both)?'
Hafa eyu?	
Hafa yuhi?	'What's that (you said, did, etc.)?'
Kao lepblo-mu este?	'Is this your book?'
ini?	
yini?	
Kao lepblo-mu enao?	'Is that your book (near you)?'
yenao?	
Kao lepblo-mu ayu?	'Is that your book (away from us)?'
eyu?	
Kao lepblo-mu yuhi?	'Is that your book (over there)?'

Locatives

3.4.3   Parallel to the set of demonstratives described above, Chamorro has a 3-way set of words relating to location. These words are called *locatives* and can be divided into two sub-classes: static locatives and motion locatives.

Static Locatives. The *static locatives* are used to refer to static or stationary locations; that is to say, there is no motion involved either towards or away from the location that is specified. The static locatives are listed here with sample sentences:

guini	'here'
guenao	'there (where listener is)'
guihi	'there (away from speaker and listener)'

Kao bula guihan guini?
'Are there many fish here?'

Mata'chong yo' guenao.
'I sat there (where you are).'

Gaige i se'se' guihi.
'The knife is over there.'

Motion Locatives. The *motion locatives* are used to refer to locations when verbs of direction or motion are involved. There are only two forms of the motion locatives. They are listed here with sample sentences:

> *magi*   'here—in direction of speaker'
> *guatu* 'there—away from speaker'
>
> Matto gue' <u>magi</u>.
> 'He came here.'
>
> Humanao gue' <u>guatu</u>.
> 'He went there.'

The last sentence above is somewhat ambiguous in that the locative word *guatu* could mean towards the listener or away from both speaker and listener. If one wishes to be more specific he can use the static locative *guenao* in combination with *guatu* as follows:

> Humanao gue' <u>guatu guenao</u>.
> 'He went there towards you.'

Locatives in Combination. Combinations of the locatives are frequently used in Chamorro where they form a consistent pattern. If the static locative occurs first, then the locational concept is primarily static; if the motion locative occurs first, then the locational concept is primarily one of motion. The following list with approximate English glosses may help to illustrate. (The more commonly used demonstratives are included in the list to show how the demonstratives and locatives form parallel systems.)

DEMONSTRATIVES AND LOCATIVES

Speaker		Listener		Somebody Else (away from speaker and listener)	
este	'this'	enao	'that'	ayu	'that'
guini	'here in this place'	guenao	'there towards you, in that place'	guihi	'there, that place'
*magi	'towards me'	*guatu	'there in that direction'	*guatu	'there in that direction'

Speaker		Listener		Somebody Else	
guini		guenao		guihi	
magi	'here at me'	guatu	'at you'	guatu	'over there, in that place'
*magi					
guini	'here towards me'	*guatu		*guatu	
		guenao	'towards you'	guihi	'away from us, in that direction'

*Forms marked by an asterisk may be considered *directionals*; that is, they are used in expressions where movement is involved.

In addition to the forms listed in the chart, the expression *gi guatu* should be added. This form is very common and is a contracted form of *guihi guatu*.

Location Words

3.4.4   In addition to the locatives discussed above, there are two other types of words in Chamorro that are related to the rather extensive system of expressing concepts of direction and location in Chamorro. They are the *location words* and some of the prepositions. The location words actually form a subclass of Class II words because they can take the affixes of other Class II words. However, since the location words have some special features that other Class II words do not have, they will be treated separately here.

The location words of Chamorro are:

halom	'in, inside'
huyong	'out, outside'
papa'	'down, under'
tatte	'behind, in back of'
fi'on	'next to, beside'
fo'na	'ahead, in front of'
hulo'	'above, on top of'

All of the location words occur with the preposition *gi* to form the relational part of a *locative phrase*. In other words, the preposition *gi* plus the following location word serve to relate the entire locative phrase to the rest of the sentence. The entire locative phrase, including the preposition and the location word, describes the location of something. In the following sample sentences, the entire locative phrase is underlined:

a. Gaige gue' <u>gi halom guma'</u>.   'He is inside the house.'
b. Gaige gue' <u>gi hiyong guma'</u>.   'He is outside the house.'
c. Gaige gue' <u>gi papa' guma'</u>.   'He is under the house.'
d. Gaige gue' <u>gi tatten guma'</u>.   'He is behind the house.'
e. Gaige gue' <u>gi fi'on guma'</u>.   'He is next to the house.'
f. Gaige gue' <u>gi me'nan guma</u>.   'He is in front of the house.'
g. Gaige gue' <u>gi hilo' guma'</u>.   'He is on top of the house.'

Notes on the sentences: *Huyong* changes to *hiyong, mo'na* to *me'na,* and *hulo'* to *hilo'* following *gi.* This change is explained by the vowel harmony rule (cf. 2.7.3). The final <u>n</u> of *tatte* and *me'na* (sentences d and f) is an excrescent consonant (cf. 2.6.2). It occurs when either *tatte* or *mo'na* is followed by a noun phrase.

The location words (with the exception of *hulo'*) can also form predicates of sentences by simply adding the affix *-um-* or *man-* and a subject. In most cases the meaning is predictable. There are, however, some special meanings for some of the affixed forms. In the examples below notice the relationship of the glosses given for the word given in isolation and in the sentences:

a. *halom* 'inside' Humalom gue' gi gima'.   'He went inside the house.'
   Manhalom siha gi gima'.   'They went inside the house.'

b. *huyong* 'outside' Humuyong gue' gi gima'.   'He went out of the house.'
   Manhuyong siha gi gima'.   'They went out of the house.

c. *papa'* 'down, under' Pumapa' sasatge gue'.   'He is going under the floor.'

d. *tatte* 'behind' Tumatatte gue' magi.   'He is coming here later.'

e. *fi'on* 'next to' Fumifi'on gue' gi gima'.   'He is nearing the house.'

f. *fo'na* 'ahead' Fumofo'na gue'.   'He is going ahead.'

It will be noticed in number c that the place (*satge* 'floor') precedes the subject pronoun.

The word *hulo'* is not included in the above list because it is irregular. In order to form a sentence with *hulo'* as the predicate, it is necessary to add the directional prefix *ka-* to get *kahulo'* 'to go up'. The infix *-um-* can then be added to this stem to form a predicate.

> Kumahulo' gue' gi ekso'. 'He went up the hill.'

> (NOTE: The directional prefix *ka-* found in the stem *kahulo'* is no longer productive. It is found in the word *káma'gas* 'to become a boss' from *ma'gas* 'boss', and perhaps in some other uncommon words. In view of the limited use of the prefix *ka-*, an alternative analysis of *kahulo'* is to consider it as a single morpheme which is related somehow to *hulo'*. Chamorro has several 'directional particles' similar to *ka-* which will be discussed later.)

It should also be noted that the word *hulo'* can take the infix *-um-* in the expression *Humulo'papa' yo'* 'I went up and down.' In this case the two words *hulo'* and *papa'* have come together to form a compound word *hulo'papa'*. This compound word can take the infix *-um-* to form a predicate. The word *hulo'* by itself requires the prefix ka- when it forms a predicate.

There are two words in Chamorro whose translations might suggest that they be considered location words. They are *hihot* 'near' and *chago'* 'far'. They are similar to the location words discussed above, since they can take the infix *-um-* and function as the predicate of a sentence:

Humihot yo' gi gima'. 'I was near the house.'

Chumago' yo' gi gima'. 'I was far from the house.'

However, unlike the other location words, *hihot* and *chago'* cannot form a *locative phrase* with the preposition *gi.* Note the following examples:

> Gaige yo' gi halom guma'.
> 'I am in the house.'

> Gaige yo' gi hiyong guma'.
> 'I am outside the house.'

> Gaige yo' gi papa' guma'.
> 'I am under the house.'

> Gaige yo' gi fi'on guma'.
> 'I am next to the house.'

But not:

> *Gaige yo' gi hihot guma'.
> for 'I am near the house.'

*Gaige yo' gi chago' guma',
for 'I am far from the house.'

In order to express the concept 'near the house' or 'far from the house' a different syntactic pattern is used:

Gaige yo' hihot gi gima'.
'I am near the house.'

Gaige yo' chago' gi gima'.
'I am far from the house.'

It appears that all of the location words include a "directional" element. What this means is that the concept of direction is included in such words as *halom, huyong, papa'*, etc., but is not included in the words *hihot* and *chago'*. These latter two words belong to the large group that have been termed Class II words.

Prepositions

3.4.5　　*Prepositions* in Chamorro can be divided into two types: Spanish and non-Spanish. Judging from the larger number of Spanish prepositions as opposed to the non-Spanish prepositions, we must conclude that before Spanish contact Chamorro had its own distinct way of expressing relational concepts which did not utilize prepositions.

　　Prepositions in Chamorro are words that precede other words or phrases and perform the function of relating the following word or phrase to the rest of the sentence. These phrases are called *prepositional phrases*. Usually the concepts of space or time are involved in the relationship.

　　The non-Spanish, or Chamorro, *prepositions* are presented first. They are *gi, giya, para, ginen,* and *as*.

　　The most frequently used Chamorro preposition is *gi*. It carries a very heavy functional load, i.e., it is used frequently with a noticeable variety of meanings. The English translation of this preposition is variable, depending on what follows *gi*. This preposition can be used with words indicating place, as in the following examples:

Gaige gue' <u>gi gipot.</u>
'He is <u>at the party.</u>'

Machocho'cho' gue' <u>gi tenda.</u>
'He works <u>at the store.</u>'

Pumipiknik siha gi tasi.
'They are picknicking at the beach (by the sea).'

Una patte gi tano'.
'One part of the land.'

Gi is used with other "concrete nouns" that do not refer to place.

Sen adahi mañaina-hu na en fanggaddon gi lasu.
'Be careful my parents that you don't become trapped by the lasso.'

Taya' ni unu ti ha kontra gi manmaga'lahi.
'There isn't one that he didn't oppose among the high-ranking people.'

Gi is also used with "abstract nouns" with slightly different translations from the previous ones already given.

Mayoria gi publiku manmalago' na u daña'.
'The majority of the public want to unite.'

Pues enaogue' sasaonao gi planu.
'That is included in the plan.'

Gi is also used with words pertaining to time. In some cases, it is not translatable at all.

Matto gue' gi painge.
'He came last night.'

Para bai hu fatto gi ega'an.
'I will come in the morning.'

Kasi gi oran alas sais.
'Around six o'clock.'

Finally, *gi* is used with all location words to form a *prepositional phrase*. In the previous section we used the term *locative phrase* for phrases which included the preposition *gi* plus location words. When any phrase is introduced by a preposition, we may also use the term *prepositional phrase*. Some examples of prepositional (and locative) phrases are given here:

I lepblo gaige gi hilo' i lamasa.
'The book is on top of the table.'

I lepblo gaige gi papa' i lamasa.
'The book is under the table.'

I lepblo gaige gi fi'on i lapes.
'The book is next to the pencil.'

I salape' gaige gi halom i lepblo.
'The money is in the book.'

I salape' gaige gi sanhalom i balakbak.
'The money is inside the purse.'

As stated earlier, the preposition *gi* carries a very heavy functional load in Chamorro. It covers the range of meaning of several English prepositions, and in some instances it is simply not possible to translate *gi*.

Another Chamorro preposition, more restricted in usage, is *giya*. It is used only with names of places and with the emphatic pronouns. The place name may be a proper noun—such as Guam, Saipan, Merizo—or it may be one of the emphatic pronouns, *hami* 'we, exclusive'. (Cf. 3.4.1.) When *giya* is used with the pronoun *hami*, it means 'at my house'; when used with *hamyo* it means 'at your house;' when used with any of the other emphatic pronouns, it means 'belonging to', 'to', 'from', or some other related meaning. Examples showing the use of *giya* are given here:

Sumasaga yo' giya Agaña.
'I live in Agaña.'

Manmatto siha giya Saipan.
'They came to Saipan.'

Hu li'e' gue' giya Toto.
'I saw him at Toto.'

Machocho'cho' gue' giya sanlagu.*
'He works in the United States.'

Gaige gue' giya hami.
'He is at my house.'

Alternate analysis of gi *and* giya

The statements above about the prepositions *gi* and *giya* assume that they are single morphemes that cannot be broken down into any smaller units. There is some fairly strong evidence to suggest that both *gi* and *giya* are actually two morphemes.

William Safford, for example, analyzes *giya* as consisting of the preposition *gi* and the article *iya* (used with place names only) (1909:112). When spoken in rapid speech, the two morphemes elide into the single word *giya*. If this interpretation is accepted, then the word *gi*, as described above, should also be analyzed

---

Sanlagu is an idiomatic form meaning "The United States."

as consisting of two morphemes, namely the preposition *gi* and
the article *i*. Like the word *giya,* when *gi i* is spoken in rapid
speech the two morphemes elide into the single word *gi*. Thus,
one might find the following alternate ways of expressing prepositional phrases:

Formal	*Informal (Rapid Speech)*
Sumasaga yo' gi iya Agaña.	Sumasaga yo' giya Agaña.
Sumasaga yo' gi i gima'-ña.	Sumasaga yo' gi gima'-ña.

Additional evidence that suggests that *gi* and *giya* are actually
made up of two morphemes can be seen in the following pairs of
sentences:

Iya Agaña nai sumasaga yo'. ∼	Sumasaga yo' giya Agaña.
I gima'-ña nai sumasaga yo'. ∼	Sumasaga yo' gi gima'-ña.

In the first sentence of each pair the location is given first in the
form of a noun phrase followed by a predicate. Notice that the
noun phrase is introduced by the simple article and the following
predicate is introduced by the particle *nai*. In the second pair the
location is given in the form of a prepositional phrase introduced
by *gi* and *giya*. The above examples suggest that the prepositions
written as *gi* and *giya* are actually contracted forms of *gi i* and
gi iya.

For purposes of agreement on how to write Chamorro, it is
probably better to think of *gi* and *giya* as single morphemes.

Para bai hu fatto giya hagu.
'I will come to you.'

Gaige i magagu-mu giya guahu.
'Your clothes are in my possession.'

Umeyak gue' giya guahu.
'He learned from me.'

Guaha tailayi giya guiya.
'There is something bad about him.'

The two prepositions that are used to indicate "to" and
"from" a location are *para* and *ginen*. The first of these prepositions, *para* (pronounced [pǽra]), presents somewhat of a puzzle
for Chamorro and for many Philippine languages. The puzzle is
in trying to determine whether there was an original Chamorro
word *para* before Spanish contact, or whether the Spanish word
para was borrowed into Chamorro and given different non-Span-

ish meanings. Since it appears impossible to find a solution to this puzzle, we will assume for the time being that there was a pre-Spanish Chamorro word *para* and that the meaning of the Spanish word *para* was simply added to the Chamorro vocabulary. The present discussion of *para* is restricted to its use as a preposition. Other meanings of *para* will be taken up elsewhere in the grammar It should also be noted that there is another word with the same spelling but with a different pronunciation and meaning. That word is pronounced /pára/ and it means 'stop.'

The preposition *para* is used most frequently as the counterpart of the preposition *ginen*. The following examples will illustrate their usage:

> Mamokkat gue' para i eskuela.
> 'He walked to the school.'
>
> Matto gue' ginen i eskuela.
> 'He came from the school.'
>
> Malagu gue' para i tenda.
> 'He ran to the store.'
>
> Malalagu gue' ginen i tenda.
> 'He is running from the store.'
>
> Humanao gue' para Agaña.
> 'He went to Agaña.'
>
> Matto gue' ginen Agaña.
> 'He came from Agaña.'

Ginen and *para* are frequently used in the same sentence, as in the following examples:

> Humanao gue' ginen Guam para Saipan.
> 'He went from Guam to Saipan.'
>
> Mamokkat yo' ginen Susupe para Chalan Kanoa.
> 'I walked from Susupe to Chalan Kanoa.'

Para is also used prepositionally with the meaning of 'for', in the benefactive sense; i.e., to do something for someone. In all probability this usage of *para* was borrowed from the Spanish, because there are now alternate ways of expressing the same benefactive concept; one of these might be called the "pure Chamorro" way while the other could be considered the Spanish way. Both of these methods of expressing the benefactive are illustrated below.

Chamorro form: Ha hatsayi si Pedro ni acho'.
'He lifted the stone for Pedro.'

Spanish form: Ha hatsa i acho' para si Pedro.
'He lifted the stone for Pedro.'

The Chamorro form involves a suffix for the verb combined with the use of the particles *si* and *ni*. (This form will be taken up in more detail in the section of focus constructions.) Other examples contrasting the Chamorro and Spanish forms are:

Chamorro form: Ha na'gasgasi si nana-ña ni gima'.
'He cleaned the house for his mother.'

Spanish form: Ha na'gasgas i gima' para si nana-ña.
'He cleaned the house for his mother.'

It is interesting to note that both methods of expressing the concept of benefactive are still used in modern Chamorro. However, there is strong evidence to suggest that the Spanish form (using *para*) is replacing the Chamorro form, at least with some verbs. For example, in order to express the concept of writing a letter "for" someone, the Spanish form is nearly always used. One might be able to use the following Chamorro form:

Ha tugi'iyi si Maria ni katta.
'He wrote the letter for Maria.'

But the more common form would be:

Ha tuge' i katta para si Maria.
'He wrote the letter for Maria.'

The fact that the Spanish form follows the structure of English grammar very closely has probably helped to establish the form using *para* as the more common form used by younger Chamorro speakers who learn English at a very early age.

Some additional examples of the co-existent forms are as follows:

Chamorro: Ha sanganiyi yo' ni estoria.
'He told the story for me.'

Spanish: Ha sangan i estoria para guahu.
'He told the story for me.'

Chamorro: Ha fa'tinasi i patgon ni chinina.
'She made the shirt for the child.'

Spanish: Ha fa'tinas i chinina para i patgon.
'She made the shirt for the child.'

The preposition *ginen* has an alternate form, *gini*, which is used very often in rapid conversational speech, as in the expression *Gini manu hao?* 'Where are you from?'

The prepositions *ginen* 'from' and *para* 'to' have parallel Spanish forms *desde* and *asta*. There is some overlapping in the use of these forms. This will be discussed in the following section on Spanish prepositions.

There is one additional non-Spanish word, *as*, which seems to fit partially into the category of Chamorro prepositions. Its status is not as clear as that of *gi, giya, para,* and *ginen* because it also seems to function as an article in Chamorro. Probably the best analysis is that there are two words in Chamorro that are pronounced the same but are actually different words. These are known as *homonyms*. Hence, we can think in terms of the preposition *as* and the article *as*. They are simply two words that are pronounced the same but have different functions and meanings.

The preposition *as* 'at a place' does not follow the exact same grammatical pattern as the other Chamorro prepositions do. It always precedes the name of a person—either a given name, surname or nickname. The preposition *as* is usually preceded by the preposition *gi*, as in the following examples:

> Sumasaga gue' gi as Bernardo.
> 'He lives at Bernardo's (place).'
>
> Mannangga si Juan gi as Guerrero.
> 'Juan waited at Guerrero's (place).'
>
> Machocho'cho' si tata-hu gi As-ñamu.
> 'My father is working at As-ñamu.' (Asñamu is a place named after someone's nickname 'Ñamu'.)

The preposition *gi* is not used when the verb (such as *falak*) includes the directional element or when the directional element is not specific:

> Malak as Camacho yo'.
> 'I went to Camacho's (place).'
>
> Hu bende i sine'so'-hu as Camacho.
> 'I sold my copra at Camacho's (place).'

Spanish Prepositions. The *Spanish prepositions* used in Chamorro can be divided into two groups, those that are used freely in combination with Chamorro words to form new expressions (Group I) and those that are used exclusively or primarily in idiomatic expressions (Group II). The Spanish prepositions that can be used freely in Chamorro will be called Group I, and they will be discussed first. These Group I prepositions are as follows:

desde
asta   (Sp. hasta)
sin
pot   (Sp. por)
kontra   (Sp. contra)

As mentioned earlier, the prepositions *desde* and *asta* are used in place of the Chamorro prepositions *ginen* and *para* in some cases. For example, one might hear any one of the following phrases. Notice the different possible combinations of prepositions.

desde Guam asta Saipan   'from Guam to Saipan'
desde Guam para Saipan   'from Guam to Saipan'
ginen Guam asta Saipan   'from Guam to Saipan'
ginen Guam para Saipan   'from Guam to Saipan'

Of course, not all speakers of Chamorro would use all of the above combinations of Spanish and Chamorro prepositions. A general rule is that *ginen* and *para* are used more frequently for referring to space relations while *desde* and *asta* are used for time. One might hear, for example, *desde nigap asta agupa'* 'from yesterday to tomorrow', but one never hears **ginen nigap para agupa'*.

We might conclude then that *desde* and *asta* are sometimes used to express relationships of space, but *ginen* and *para* are never used to express relationships of time.

Further examples of the use of *desde* and *asta* are as follows:

Maigo' gue' desde i painge asta pa'go.
'He slept from last night to now.'

Manmangge' yo' desde i ega'an asta pa'go.
'I have been writing from morning to now.'

Desde i ma'pos na simana
'Since last week'

Ti para u ta fanáli'e' asta i Lunes.
'We will not see each other until Monday.'

Asta agupa'.
'Until tomrorow.'

Desde nigap matto yo'.
'I came since yesterday (and am still here).'

Mata'chong yo' guihi asta i oran alas tres.
'I sat there until three o'clock.'

The Spanish preposition *asta* also occurs in Chamorro as
esta, especially in informal speech. (This is not to be confused
with another Chamorro word *esta* meaning 'O.K.' or 'good-bye'.)
In any of the above sentences *esta* may be used in place of *asta*
without changing the meaning at all. One may hear, for example,
either of the following very common expressions:

Asta agupa'.
'Until tomorrow.'

Esta agupa'.
Until tomorrow.'

No doubt some Chamorro speakers prefer either *esta* or *asta*, but
both are used very commonly throughout the Chamorro speaking
community.

The Spanish preposition *sin* is used in Chamorro very much
like it is used in Spanish to mean 'without'. Although Chamorro
has other ways of expressing the concept 'to be without' (cf. *tai*),
this Spanish form is used very often in everyday Chamorro speech.
The following examples will illustrate how the preposition *sin* is
used:

Hu li'e' i lahi sin sapatos.
'I saw the man with no shoes.'

Ti siña hao humanao sin guahu.
'You can't go without me.'

Maolek ha' yo' sin hagu.
'I'm O.K. without you.'

The preposition *pot* (from Spanish *por*) functions like other
Chamorro prepositions. The meaning of *pot* is rather broad, as
the following examples will illustrate:

Hu tungo' pot makina.
'I know about machines.'

Hu cho'gue pot hagu.
'I did it on account of you.'

Pot enao na rason na ya-hu hao.
'For that reason I like you.'

Pot hafa?
'For what?' ~ 'Why?'

The above examples show the Spanish preposition *pot* used in Chamorro constructions with Chamorro words. Several complete expressions using *pot* were borrowed from Spanish. Notice the following Chamorrocized examples of Spanish expressions:

> Chule' magi <u>pot fabot</u>. (from Sp. <u>por favor</u>)
> 'Bring it here <u>please</u>.'

> Pot fin.
> 'Finally.'

> Pot i hemplo.
> 'For example.'

> Pot uttimu.
> 'Ultimately.'

> Unu pot unu.
> 'One by one.'

Pot also functions as a type of conjunction. This will be discussed later in the section on conjunctions.

The preposition *kontra* has retained its original Spanish meaning 'against'. Like many Chamorro prepositions, it can also be used as a verb, as in the expression *Hu kontra i lahi* 'I challenged the man.' Examples of *kontra* as a preposition are:

> Umapo' yo' <u>kontra i liga</u>.
> 'I leaned <u>against the wall</u>.'

> <u>Kontra i lai</u> bumulachu.
> 'Being drunk is <u>against the law</u>.'

> Baba bida-ña <u>kontra i taotao</u>.
> 'His work is bad <u>against the people</u>.'

The Spanish prepositions that cannot be used freely in combination with Chamorro words will be called Group II prepositions. The most common prepositions of this group are as follows:

> di   (Sp. de)
> kon   (Sp. con)

The preposition *di* is used very often in Chamorro speech. In the majority of cases it is used in fixed idiomatic expressions that are of Spanish origin. Most of these expressions function more like conjunctions and subordinators, and will be discussed under those headings. For some examples of *di* as a preposition, or 'preposition like', see the following:

Basta di mama'baba.
'Stop fooling around.'

Sigi hao di mama'baba fan ta'lo.
'You are continuing to fool around again.'

Humanao gue' en lugat di guahu.
'He went instead of me.'

The preposition *kon* is used very often in Chamorro speech. Like *di*, it is often used like a conjunction or subordinator. Most of the time it is used in fixed idiomatic expressions which were borrowed from Spanish. In such cases the meaning is often not the same in Chamorro as in Spanish, as the following examples will show:

Sangani yo' kon tiempo.
'Tell me ahead of time.'

Kon petmisu.
'With permission.'

Na'i yo' ni i papet-mu kon todu i salape'-mu.
'Give me your paper together with your money.'

Humanao si Jose kon todu si Juan.
'Jose left and so did Juan.'

Humanao yo' yan i lalahi kon todu si Juan.
'I went with the boys, including Juan.'

Kon is occasionally used in combination with Chamorro words to form expressions that should probably be considered idiomatic. An example of this type of combination is:

Kon sigi gi hinanao-mu.
'Keep on going.'

The Spanish prepositions that were adopted by the Chamorro speakers raise interesting linguistic questions which can not be answered. The most important question is: Why were some Spanish prepositions borrowed while others were not? The pre-Spanish Chamorro language had ways of expressing all of the concepts that are expressed by Spanish prepositions in the above examples. Even in modern Chamorro it is possible, but not easy, to avoid using all of the Spanish prepositions.

It is also interesting to note the changes in meaning that the prepositions have undergone through borrowing. In several cases (e.g., *kon todu*) the primary Spanish meaning of 'however' has been completely lost.

Some of the Spanish prepositions discussed here will be taken up again in the discussion of conjunctions and subordinators.

Articles

3.4.6   There is a set of "little" words in Chamorro that will be called *articles*. Even though they are little (or small) words, they form a very important part of the grammar of Chamorro. In some cases they seem similar to the articles in English, but in many cases the use of the Chamorro articles is unique to Chamorro, and have no parallel to the use of articles in English or Spanish.

There are some Spanish articles used in Modern Chamorro, but their use is very limited. We will first look at the Chamorro articles and then take a brief look at the few Spanish loan articles.

The *Chamorro articles* can be subclassed into two types. There are *common articles* and *proper articles*. The proper articles are used with proper names of people or places; the common articles are used elsewhere. It should be remembered that the Chamorro articles can not always be translated into English.

The *proper articles* in Chamorro are *si, as,* and *iya*. Articles *si* and *as* are used with names of people; *iya* is used with names of places. Notice the use of the articles in the following examples:

Si

Si Juan.	'Juan.'
Si Nana.	'Mother.'
Si Maga'lahi.	'The Governor.'
Si Yu'us.	'God.'
Mangge si Rita?	'Where is Rita?'
Si Ben yo'.	'I am Ben.'
Si Juan ha chiku si Maria.	'Juan kissed Maria.'

It will be noticed that the article *si* never translates into anything in English. It is, however, obligatory in Chamorro.

It should also be noticed that when the article *si* is used with nouns such as *nana* 'mother', *tata* 'father', *pale'* 'priest', and *maga'lahi* 'governor', then the nouns are considered proper nouns and they refer to specific people.

As

The article *as* is also used with names of people. Its use is quite different from *si,* and it has various translations in English. Note the following examples of the article *as*:

Mangge si Jose? Gi as Juan.
'Where is Jose? At Juan's.'

Chiniku si Maria as Juan.
'Maria was kissed by Juan.'

Asñamu.
A place name (lit. 'at the mosquito's').

Ha bende i kinenne'-ña as Pedro.
'He sold his catch at Pedro's.'

Lini'e' yo' as Tomas.
'Tomas saw me.'

I gima' as Pale'.
'At Father's house.'

The rules governing the use of *si* and *as* are not easy to state without making reference to certain features of the syntax which will be discussed later under the heading of Focus System of Chamorro (section 4.10). For the time being we can say that the articles *si* and *as* are used with proper names of animate beings, usually people. Even though *as* often translates as a preposition in English, it should not be considered only a preposition. It has all the grammatical features of an article in Chamorro. *As* is always used with a proper name when the meaning is 'at someone's place', as in *As Juan* 'At Juan's place', and it is usually preceded by the preposition *gi.*

Iya

The article *iya* is used with place names, as in the following examples.

Iya Umatac dikike' na songsong.
'Umatac is a small town.'

Para bai hu falak iya Honolulu.
'I will go to Honlulu.'

Lokka' iya Lamlam.
'Lamlam (mountain) is high.'

When the article *iya* is used with a location or directional word, it has the effect of converting the word to a proper place name. Notice the following examples:

Iya kattan.
'The East.'

Iya hami.
'Our place, our land.'

Nihi ta falak iya hulo'.
'Let's go up (to someone's place).'

In the last example above, the expression *iya hulo'* suggests some-one's house or place because the article *iya* is used. The same general idea could be expressed by the following sentence:

Nihi ta falak hulo' gi gima'.

When *iya* is used, the concept of *gima'* is implicit and does not need to be expressed.

The *common articles* of Chamorro are *i, ni,* and *nu.* A com-plete explanation of their usage will not be possible without going into the Focus System which will be discussed in a later section under Syntax. The present discussion will be a preliminary one.

The article *i* is very similar in both usage and meaning to the English article *the,* although it is not always translated. The Chamorro article *i* could be considered a "definite" article be-cause it marks a definite or specific noun. Some examples of the article *i* are:

Hu li'e' i patgon.
'I saw the child.'

I patgon ha hatsa i lamasa.
'The child lifted the table.'

Magof i korason-hu.
'My heart is happy.'

Si Don Jose umásagua yan i palao'an.
'Don Jose married the woman.'

I dádalak i babui
'The pig's tail'

Notice that the Chamorro article *i* is not always translated into English.

The article *i* sometimes functions as a *nominalizer,* which means that it can cause a verb or modifier to function like a noun. See the following examples:

munhayan	'to finish'	i munhayan	'the finished thing'
ma'pos	'past'	i ma'pos	'the departed (one)'
sasaga	'staying'	i sasaga	'the stayer'
gumugupu	'flying'	i gumugupu	'the flyer'

NOTE: The vowels of *munhayan* and *gumugupu* are not fronted when preceded by i; vowel fronting (cf. 2.7.3) occurs only with vowels of the stem. The u of both *munhayan* and *gumugupu* is part of an affix, and therefore does not get fronted.

The article *ni* is much more difficult to account for than the articles discussed above. There are several problems involved.

In the first place, there is disagreement among native speakers of Chamorro as to whether it is pronounced *ni* or *ni'*. Some speakers feel that they are two separate words. Since I have not been able to find a clear contrast between *ni* and *ni'*, I am taking the position that there is only one basic form which may be pronounced differently by different speakers. In this grammar the article will be written as *ni* without the glottal stop, and may be pronounced as either *ni* or *ni'*.

There is, of course, a homonym (a word which sounds exactly the same as *ni*) which is not an article. This is the negative particle *ni* which occurs in expressions such as the following:

Ni hayiyi
'No matter who'

Ni hafafa
'No matter what'

Ni manu ya-hu na lugat.
'I don't like any place.'

Ni ngai'an na hu guaiya hao.
'I will never love you.'

In addition to the above problems, it is probable that *ni* is actually a contracted form of *nu* plus *i*. And it is possible to get the combination of *ni i*. Notice in the following examples that *nu, ni, nu i*, and *ni i* all occur in the same position. *Nu* occurs when followed by an emphatic pronoun; *ni, nu i*, and *ni i* occur when followed by a common noun:

Lini'e' yo' nu guiya.
'I was seen by him.'

Lini'e' yo' ni patgon.
'I was seen by the child.'

Lini'e' yo' nu i patgon.
'I was seen by the child.'

Lini'e' yo' ni i patgon.
'I was seen by the child.'

To complicate the picture further, the article *ni* is often translated by an English preposition, as in the following examples:

Hu puno' i panglao ni machette.
'I killed the crab with a machete.'

Ha utot i lapes ni kannai-ña.
'He snapped the pencil with his hand.'

Ngininge' i lahi ni ga'lagu.
'The boy was smelled by the dog.'

The article *ni* also seems to function like a *relative pronoun,* as in the following complex sentences:

I kareta ni poddong gi saddok iyo-ku.
'The car that fell in the river is mine.'

I galaide' ni sime' mafondo.
'The canoe which leaks sank.'

Si Pete ni primu-hu humanao para Guam.
'Pete, who is my cousin, went to Guam.'

And, at other times, it is not translated at all but appears to function like an article, as in the following examples:

Maleffa yo' ni lepblo-ku.
'I forgot my book.'

Malago' yo' ni lepblo-ku.
'I want my book.'

Mahalang yo' ni patgon-hu.
'I miss my child.'

As can be seen from the above discussion, there are a number of problems involved in presenting an adequate description of the article *ni*. It is possible, however, to offer some rules which are generally agreed upon.

1. There are at least two and possibly three different morphemes that are pronounced *ni*. They are:

    a. *ni* 'negative particle' as in *ni hayiyi* 'no matter who'
    b. *ni* 'relative pronoun' as in *guahu ni metgot* 'I who am strong'
    c. *ni* 'article' as in *lini'e' si Pete ni patgon* 'Pete was seen by the child.'

It is possible that the *ni* of sentences b and c above is the same morpheme. For present purposes it will be more convenient to consider them as different.

2. *Ni* is probably a contracted form of *nu i*, as is shown in the following examples:

> Lini'e' si Pete n̲i patgon.   'Pete was seen
> Lini'e' si Pete n̲u̲ ̲i̲ patgon.   by the child.'

As a result of this contraction, one often hears the sequence *ni i* as in *Lini'e' si Pete n̲i̲ ̲i̲ patgon.*

3. There are two pronunciations; some speakers pronounce it *ni'* while others pronounce it *ni*. There appears to be no difference in meaning.

4. The article *ni* is often translated by prepositions in English and other European languages, as in the following examples:

> Hu tuge' i katta n̲i̲ lapes.
> 'I wrote the letter with a pencil.'

> Hu achayi i amigu-hu n̲i̲ lilok n̲i̲ mattiyu.
> 'I pounded the nail with the hammer for my friend.'

Further discussion of the use of the article *ni* will be presented in the section on syntax under the heading of Focus Constructions.

Nu

The article *nu* presents certain problems, but its usage seems more clearly defined than *ni*. Safford describes *nu* as a preposition; it seems to follow more closely the pattern of articles.

As stated above, the article *ni* is probably a contracted form of *nu i;* this possibility is suggested since both of the sentences below are acceptable and have the same meaning.

> Lini'e' i lahi n̲i̲ patgon.   'The man was seen by the child.'
> Lini'e' i lahi n̲u̲ ̲i̲ patgon.

However, if we substitute an emphatic pronoun in the place of the noun *patgon,* then only *nu* occurs.

> Lini'e' i lahi n̲u̲ guiya.
> 'The child was seen by him.'

> Kuatro na nasion manmanmanda n̲u̲ hita.
> 'Four nations have administered us.'

> Manmaleffa siha n̲u̲ hamyo.
> 'They forgot you.'

Notice in the following set of sentences how *nu, as,* and *ni* (or *nu i*) fill the same position:

Ti piniti hao nu hami.
'You don't feel pity for us.'

Ti piniti hao as Pedro.
'You don't feel pity for Pedro.'

Ti piniti hao ni patgon.
'You don't feel pity for the child.'

Ti piniti hao nu i patgon.
'You don't feel pity for the child.'

Nu is also found before demonstratives:

Ti hu tungo' hafa bai hu cho'gue nu enao siha.
'I don't know what I will do about those.'

Ti manmalago' siha nu este.
'They don't want any of this.'

Esta ilek-hu sufisiente nu enao i tres na'an ni hu mente.
'I have already said those three names I have mentioned are sufficient.'

The word *nu* is also used as a *pause particle,* or filler. When used in this way it is not an article, but rather a sort of empty word . . . something to fill space while the speaker is thinking of what to say next. The sentence below was recorded during a conversation between two college students on Guam:

Kuantos años hao ni fine'ne'na un tutuhon nu humalom umeskuela?
'How old were you when you first started to go to school?'

Of course, *nu* used in this way is a stylistic device and will vary considerably from speaker to speaker. The point here is that not every occurrence of *nu* is the article *nu.*

Spanish Articles. The *Spanish articles* that are found in modern Chamorro are *un, la,* and *las.* They are very limited in their use and usually occur in fixed idiomatic expressions.

The article *un* is used with countable nouns when the noun is both indefinite and singular. It is used when the speaker wishes to emphasize the "oneness" of the noun. In some cases it might be translated as 'one':

Un lahi humanao.
'A man went' or 'one man went.'

Sumasaga un palao'an gi gima'.
'A woman lived at the house.'

Anai hu e'egga' i litratu hu li'e' un guaka, un kabayu, un paluma, un katu gi hilo' tronkon hayu, ya un ga'lagu ha hahaohao i katu.
'When I am looking at the picture I see a cow, a horse, a bird, a cat up in a tree, and a dog barking at the cat.'

Notice the following pair of sentences for the use of *un*:

Malago' yo' niyok.
'I want a coconut.'

Malago' yo' un niyok.
'I want one coconut (not two).'

In the second sentence above, the article *un* is used to emphasize oneness. (The numeral *unu* is used when actually counting.)

The article *un* occurs most frequently in fixed idiomatic expressions such as *Un dia* which means 'Once upon a time' or 'One day', and is used for beginning stories.

The article *la* is not used in Chamorro except in certain words where it has become a part of the word, in family names, and in telling time.

An example of a word in which the Spanish article *la* has become a part of the Chamorro word is *lamasa* 'table', which comes from Spanish *la mesa* 'the table', where *la* is the definite feminine article. In the process of being borrowed into Chamorro, the Spanish article *la* simply became part of the word. Another borrowed word in which the article became fused to the noun is *la'uya* 'pot' from Spanish *la olla*.

The article *la* is found in family names such as De la Cruz and De la Rosa, both of which have various spellings, such as De La Cruz, De la Cruz, and Dela Cruz.

La is also used in telling time. In this case it has become fused with the Spanish preposition *a*. The Chamorro form is *ala* as in *Oran ala una* 'one o'clock'.

The Spanish article *las* is used in Chamorro only when telling time, and it is fused with the Spanish preposition *a* when it is preceded by *oran*.

Oran alas dos	'Two o'clock'
Oran alas sinko	'Five o'clock'
Dies para las tres	'Ten before three'
Dies pasao las tres	'Ten past three'

In summary, three of the Spanish articles were borrowed into Chamorro, but their usage is restricted to those situations described above.

Particles

3.4.7　In addition to the articles described above, Chamorro has some additional "little words" that are called *particles*. In a sense they are the glue that holds the language together. Although they are small and almost never receive primary stress, they form a very important part of the grammatical system of Chamorro. Because they are "little words" and seldom receive primary stress, they are very difficult for the person who is trying to learn something about the rules of the language.

The particles that will be discussed here are *na* and *nai*. In many instances in rapid speech they sound alike. This makes any clear statements about their use even more difficult.

Na

The particle *na* might be called a *linking particle* since it serves to link together different words in a phrase and certain types of clauses. Each of these functions will be described below.

The particle *na* is used in noun phrases to link a modifier with a following noun, as in the following examples:

i yemmok na palao'an	'the fat woman'
i díkike' na patgon	'the small child'
i dánkolo na taotao	'the big man'
i kákati na palao'an	'the crying woman'

When *na* follows a modifier which ends in a vowel, it is frequently contracted to *-n*. Hence, one might hear either of the following sets of phrases:

Formal Speech	Fast Speech	English
i dánkolo na taotao	i dánkolon taotao	'the big man'
i kákati na palao'an	i kákaten palao'an	'the crying woman'
i betde na kareta	i betden kareta	'the green car'
i bunita na palao'an	i bunitan palao'an	'the pretty girl'

When the modifier follows the headword of the phrase, and when the headword ends with a vowel, the final *-n* always occurs. If the headword ends with a consonant, then there is no linking particle. Note the following examples:

i tendan Filipino	'the Filipino store'
i karetan Japanese	'the Japanese car'
i relos Japanese	'the Japanese watch'
i sapatos Amerikanu	'the American shoes'

It should also be pointed out that the use of *na* in modification structures is optional when *guaha* is used:

Kao guaha maolek na relos-mu?	'Do you have a good
Kao guaha maolek relos-mu?	watch?'

Na is also used to link demonstratives (cf. 3.4.2) with the nouns or noun phrases that follow:

Este na guma'	'this house'
Guini na tiempo	'at this time'
Enao na taotao	'that man'
Ayu na lepblo	'that book'
Ayu na sen ma'lak na ha'ani	'that very bright day'

In the last example above the first occurrence of *na* links the demonstrative *ayu* with the following noun phrase; the second *na* links the modifier *ma'lak* with the following noun.

The demonstrative may also be plural, as in the following examples:

Enao gue' siha na kandidaton Japanese
'those Japanese candidates'

Todu este siha na kongresu
'all those congressmen'

Na may also be used to connect the numbers beyond the number one with the following noun:

un patgon	'one child'
dos na patgon	'two children'
tres na paluma	'three birds'
katotse na chada'	'fourteen eggs'

Another use of *na* is to link certain question words with following nouns:

Manu na lepblo malago'-mu?
'Which book do you want?'

Hafa na klassen guihan este?
'What kind of fish is this?'

Kuanto na lapes ha fahan?
'How many pencils did he buy?'

Hayi na palao'an un tungo'?
'Which woman do you know?'

Notice how the linking particle *na* falls in the same position before the noun when preceded by modifier, demonstrative, number, and question word:

i dankolo na patgon   'the big child'
este na patgon   'this child'
dos na patgon   'two children'
manu na patgon   'which child?'

The particle *na* is also used to connect a *complement clause* to a main clause. (A more complete discussion of clause types will be taken up in the discussion of syntax.) In this situation it also performs a linking operation in that it links two clauses together. One might also think of it as the *complementizer*, since it is the particle that introduces the complement clause. Some examples of sentences in which *na* is used as a complementizer are as follows:

Hu tungo' na machocho'cho' i lahi.
'I know that the man is working.'

Ilek-ña na u fatto.
'He said that he would come.'

Manmalago' siha na bai hu hanao.
'They want me to go.'

Ilek-hu na ahe'.
'I said no.'

Sen adahi mañaina-hu na en fanggaddon gi lasu.
'Be careful my parents that you (don't) get caught in the trap.

Ti bai in sedi na en fanmafa'ga'ga'.
'We won't allow that you be treated as animals.'

Notice in the following example how the particle *na* is used to introduce two complement clauses in the same sentence:

Ilek-ñiñiha na ti ha nisisita na u adelanta mo'na mas i tano'-ñiha.

They are saying that it is not necessary to advance forward their land.'

In some cases the main clause does not appear to be a complete clause, as in the following examples:

Hafa na un cho'gue?
'Why did you do it?'

Taya' na pikatdiha bidada-hu.
'Never have I done anything wrong.'

Hafa mohon na pa'go ma chocho'gue enao?
'Why do they do those things now?'

For the time being we will consider *hafa* and *taya'* in sentences like the above to be clauses.

To summarize, the particle *na* acts as a linking particle. In some cases it links together two parts of a phrase; in other cases it links together two clauses, one of which is a complement clause.

Nai

The particle *nai* presents certain difficulties in describing how it functions. It is sometimes used as a reduced form of the subordinator *anai* 'when'; it can be used in place of the linking particle *na* in some cases; sometimes native speakers of Chamorro are not really certain whether they are saying *nai, anai,* or *na.*

In spite of the apparent confusion, there are some rules that may be given concerning the use of the particle *nai.*

It appears that there are actually two homonyms pronounced *nai,* or that they may be the same word used in different ways. For present purposes it seems better to claim that there are two particles pronounced *nai.* We will call one of them the *linking particle nai;* the other we will call the *emphatic particle nai.*

The linking particle *nai* has certain specific functions and some that are not quite so specific. The specific functions will be considered first.

As a linking particle, *nai* usually refers to 'place where' as in the following:

I sanhiyong nai ta maigo'.
'Outside is where we will sleep.'

Giya Tanapag nai mafañagu yo'.
'It was at Tanapag where I was born.'

NOTE: In the two sentences above, *nai* could also be considered a *complementizer.* This will be taken up again in the discussion of complement and relative clauses.

The linking particle *nai* is usually used with the following words when followed by a clause structure: *manu, ngai'an, taya', guaha, taimanu,* and *taiguini.* Again, the concept of place is often included. Safford calls *nai* a 'locative particle', which suggests that it usually refers to place (1909:108).

> Manu nai sumasaga hao?
> 'Where do you live?'
>
> Ngai'an nai mafañagu hao?
> 'When were you born?'
>
> Taimanu nai masasangan enao gi fino'-miyu?
> 'How is that said in your language?'
>
> Taiguini nai un sangan.
> 'You say it like this.'
>
> Guaha nai sumasaga yo' giya Susupe.
> 'There is a place where I live in Susupe.'
>
> Taya' nai humanao gue' gi plasa.
> 'He never went to the plaza.'

In the last two sentences above it would perhaps be better to consider *nai* a complementizer rather than a linking particle.

The use of *nai* becomes a little less clear as we examine further examples. The expressions *guaha nai* and *taya' nai* usually mean 'sometimes' and 'never', as in the following sentences:

> Guaha nai gumimen yo' setbesa.
> 'Sometimes I drink beer.'
>
> Taya' nai macho'cho'.
> 'He never works.'
>
> NOTE: *Taya' nai* is often contracted to *tatnai* meaning 'never'. In addition, according to some speakers, one could substitute the particle *na* in place of *nai* in all of the above examples with little or no difference in meaning. For example, the following sentences might be heard:
>
> Manu na sumasaga hao?
> 'Where do you live?'
>
> Ngai'an na mafañagu hao?
> 'When were you born?'

And it is possible to use both particles, as in the following:

> Manu nai na sumasaga hao?
> 'Where is it that you live?'
>
> Ngai'an nai na mafañagu hao?
> 'When was it that you were born?'

If this substitution of *na* for *nai* is permissible, are they really separate particles?

Some additional examples will perhaps help to answer this question. The following two sentences were taken from a tape recording of a political speech given in 1966 in Saipan. The two sentences were spoken one after the other just as they are given here:

Kao guaha na hu traiduti hamyo ni publiku?
'Have I ever betrayed you, the public?'

Hamyo ni publiku, kao guaha nai hu traiduti hamyo?
'You the public, have I ever betrayed you?'

Notice that in the second sentence the particle *nai* is substituted in place of *na*. The effect of using *nai* in the second sentence is one of emphasis. *Nai* is used in the second sentence because the statement has already been made in the preceding sentence using *na*. This appears to be an instance of using the *emphatic particle nai*.

The *emphatic particle nai* usually carries primary stress. It can be added to a simple phrase or clause to give it a kind of emphasis. The use of the emphatic particle *nai* also implies that a previous reference to the object under discussion has already been made. *Nai* can be used along with *na* under these conditions when emphasis is intended. Note the following contrasting examples:

i dikike' na patgon	'the small child'
i dikike' nai na patgon	'that small child (that we know about)'
Dikike' i patgon.	'The child is small.'
Dikike' nai i patgon.	'The child (that we know of) is really small.'
dos na lepblo	'two books'
dos nai na lepblo	'only two books (that we know of)'
Ilek-hu na ahe'	'I said no.'
Ilek-hu nai ahe'.	'Like I said, no.'
Ilek-hu nai na ahe'.	'What I said was *no*!'
Kuanto na lepblo guinaha-mu?	'How many books do you have?'
Kuanto nai na lepblo guinaha-mu?	'I asked how many books do you have?'

In all of the above sentences which illustrate *nai* as the emphatic particle, one could use *na* in place of *nai*, according to some speakers of Chamorro. Most, however, would use *nai*. The use of *nai* makes the sentence more emphatic. Even more emphasis can be achieved by using the combination of particles *nai na*, as in:

Manu nái na sumasaga hao?
'Where are you really living?'

Since either *nai* or *na* can be used in the sentences above and since both can be used together, it is difficult to know the precise function of *nai* as an emphatic particle.

It seems fairly clear, though, that *nai* conveys the concept of 'place where' in such sentences as the following:

Guaha nai sumasaga yo' giya Susupe.
'There is a place where I live in Susupe.'

Taya' nai humanao gue' gi plasa.
'At no place did he go at the plaza.'

Perhaps in the two sentences above it would be better to consider *nai* a complementizer rather than a linking particle.

Fan

Chamorro has a particle which is used for giving a tone of politeness to statements. It is called the *polite particle fan*. Since it can be moved around very freely in a sentence, it is considered a particle rather than an affix. It might be translated as 'please'. Notice in the following sentences how the polite particle *fan* can be moved around from one position to another without really changing the meaning of the sentence:

Na'i yo' magi un granu.
'Give me a piece.'

Na'i fan yo' magi un granu.
'Please give me a piece.'

Na'i yo' fan magi un granu.
'Please give me a piece.'

Na'i yo' magi fan un granu.
'Please give me a piece.'

Na'i yo' magi un granu fan.
'Please give me a piece.'

Hun

Another particle in Chamorro that can be moved around freely in the sentence is the *quotative particle hun*. The inclusion of *hun* in a sentence tells the listener that the information is simply reported and is not necessarily a fact. The following sentences illustrate the meaning and mobility of *hun*:

> Humanao gue' para i gipot.
> 'He went to the party.'
>
> Humanao hun gue' para i gipot.
> 'He said he went to the party' or 'It was said that he went to the party.'
>
> Humanao gue' hun para i gipot.
> 'He said he went to the party.'
>
> Humanao gue' para i gipot hun.
> 'He said he went to the party.'
>
> Humanao gue' para hun i gipot.
> 'He said he went to the party.'

The position of *hun* in the sentence is probably less random than the position of the polite particle *fan*. The sentences above illustrate, successively, the most preferred to the least preferred position.

Humanao hun gue' is considered more common than *Humanao gue' hun*, which in turn is more common than *Humanao gue' para i gipot hun*, and so forth. We might say that the most preferred position for *hun* is close to the verb.

Of course, there is a more formal way of making an indirect quotation, e.g.,

> Ilek-ña na humanao gue' para i gipot.
> 'He said that he went to the party.'

Connectors

3.4.8   Chamorro has a fairly large number of minor words that fall under the general heading of *connectors*, which serve to link words, phrases, and sentences. In addition to the fairly extensive set of native Chamorro connectors, there are more than a dozen that have been borrowed from Spanish. The Chamorro connectors will be treated first.

The Chamorro connectors can be subclassified into the following categories: Conjunctions, Subordinators, Relativizers, and Complementizers. Each of these will be discussed separately.

Conjunctions. Chamorro has four conjunctions. They are *yan* 'and', *ya* 'and', *pat* 'or', and *lao* 'but'.

Two of these conjunctions, *yan* and *pat*, are used to connect any two structures that are alike or that share something common to both parts of the longer structure. For example, they may connect two subjects of a single verb:

Ma'pos si Juan yan si Maria.
'Juan and Maria left.'

Kao ma'pos si Juan pat si Maria?
'Did Juan or Maria leave?'

Or, they may connect two objects of a single verb:

Hu li'e' i lahi yan i palao'an.
'I saw the man and the woman.'

Kao un li'e' i lahi pat i palao'an?
'Did you see the man or the woman?'

Or, they may connect two verbs in a sentence:

Kumakati yan chumachalek i palao'an.
'The woman is crying and laughing.'

Kao kumakati pat chumachalek i palao'an?
'Is the woman crying or laughing?'

The conjunction *yan* is also used in certain types of constructions where comparison or accompaniment is expressed:

Achálokka' ham yan i che'lu-hu.
'I am the same height as (with) my brother.'

Humanao yo' yan i che'lu-hu.
'I went with my brother.'

Humanao ham yan si Pedro.
'We went—Pedro and I.'

Notice that in the above examples the conjunction *yan* can be translated as 'with'. This translation should not affect our classification of *yan* as a conjunction.

The conjunctions *ya*, *pat*, and *lao* may be used to connect clauses. They express a relationship between the clauses that is conveyed by the meaning of the conjunctions. The following sentences will illustrate:

Malago' yo' ni lepblo ya hu fahan.
'I wanted the book and I bought it.'

Enaogue' mañaina-hu mampos na'manman ya ti hu hulat
kumomprende.

'That, my parents, is really amazing, and I cannot possibly understand.'

Ta fanmaigo' pat ta fanpasehu.
'We will sleep or we will go around.'

Para bai hu facho'cho' pat bai falak iya hami.
I will work or go home.'

Ya-hu hao lao ti ya-mu yo'.
'I like you but you don't like me.'

Ti bumaila gue' nigap lao bumabaila gue' pa'go.
'He didn't dance yesterday, but he is dancing now.'

The conjunction *lao* is often pronounced *lu*, especially in fast speech. There is no difference in meaning.

Both *lao* and *ya* are used to begin sentences which have a close semantic relationship with a preceding sentence.

Subordinators. There are five subordinators in Chamorro (not counting the Spanish subordinators which will be discussed separately). They are *yanggen* 'if, when', *anai* 'when', *gigon* 'as soon as', *achok* 'although, even though', and *sa'* 'because'.

These *subordinators* are always used to connect clauses. The clause that the subordinator introduces is always subordinate to the other clause.

The first four of the subordinators listed above may occur at the beginning of the sentence or somewhere in the middle. The subordinator *sa'* usually occurs following another clause. The following sentences will illustrate how these subordinators are used:

Yanggen

Yanggen humanao yo' bai hu espia hao.
'If I go, I will look for you.'

Bai hu li'e' hao yanggen humanao yo'.
'I will see you if I go.'

The subordinator *yanggen* has several allomorphs (variant forms) that are commonly used. Some of the allomorphs are *anggen, yang, yan, an, yagen.*

Anai

Chumocho yo' anai humanao yo' para i gima'-hu.
'I ate when I went to my house.'

> Anai humanao yo' para i gima'-hu, chumocho yo'.
> 'When I went to my house, I ate.'

Anai is sometimes shortened to *nai* and even *na*, especially in rapid speech. *Anai* also may occur initially or between two sentences.

Gigon

> Despues gigon ha' hu bira tatalo'-hu, un dulok ha' yo'.
> 'Then as soon as I turn my back you stab me.'

> Humanao gue' gigon matto hao.
> 'He left as soon as you came.'

Achok

The subordinator occurs as *achok*, but it is usually followed by the intensifier *ha'*. This has resulted in a fused form which is written as *achok ha'* and *achokka'*:

> Hanao para i lancho achok malangu hao.
> 'Go to the ranch even though you are sick.'

> Achokka' si Maria ti kumonfotme fatto ha' magi.
> 'Although Maria doesn't agree, just come here.'

In many instances *achok* is used along with the conjunction *lao*, as in the following examples:

> Ti mangganna yo' lao achok i amigu-hu.
> 'I didn't win, but at least my friend did.'

> Achokka' malago' yo' humanao lao taya' salape'-hu.
> 'Although I wanted to go, (but) I had no money.'

Sa'

The subordinator *sa'* has an alternate form *sis*. They can be freely substituted for each other. *Sa'* usually occurs in the middle of a sentence, as in the following examples:

> Ti hu konne' gue' $\begin{Bmatrix} \text{sa'} \\ \text{sis} \end{Bmatrix}$ kamten.
> 'I didn't take him because he was rowdy.'

> Humanao yo' para Saipan $\begin{Bmatrix} \text{sa'} \\ \text{sis} \end{Bmatrix}$ mañasaga siha i mañaina-hu.
> 'I am going to Saipan because my parents are living there.'

If *sa'* occurs at the beginning of a sentence, then we know it is related in a subordinate way to the preceding sentence:

Si Yu'us ma'ase' ni todu i atension-mu. <u>Sa'</u> hu tungo' ha' na un hahasso yo'.
'Thank you for all of your attention. Because I know that you are thinking of me.'

Complementizer na. Chamorro has a connector that introduces complement clauses. (These will be discussed in some detail later in the section on Complex Sentences, 4.19). This connector is called a *complementizer*. The complementizer that is used in Chamorro is *na,* and the rough English meaning is 'that' or 'which'.

The word *na* has already appeared in this grammar with a different label. It was described as a "linking particle" in section 3.4.7. We could continue to use the same label for *na,* or we could consider that we have *homophonous morphemes* (morphemes which sound alike but have different meanings), each of which serves a different function. It seems preferable to consider them separate morphemes and to give them different names. We will therefore distinguish between the linking Particle *na* and the Complementizer *na.*

In the following sample sentences, the complementizer and the complement clause are underlined:

na

Hu tungo' <u>na mafana'an i lahi</u> si Jose.
'I know that the man was named Jose.'

Hu tungo' <u>na macho'cho' i lahi gi J and G.</u>
'I know that the man worked at J and G.'

Hu hasso <u>na ha tattiyi i palao'an.</u>
'I remember that he followed the woman.'

Relativizers. The particles *ni* and *nai,* which have already been designated "linking particles," can also be called *relativizers* because they introduce relative clauses. (A more detailed discussion of relative clauses will be given in the discussion of complex sentences in section 4.19.) Examples of how these relativizers are used are given here.

When the relativizer *ni* is used, it replaces either the subject or the object of the relative clause. In the following sentences illustrating the relativizer *ni* the relative clause is underlined:

I taotao <u>ni tata-hu</u> humanao para Guam.
'The man who is my father went to Guam.'

Si Pedro ni hu li'e' humanao para Guam.
Pedro who I saw went to Guam.'

I mannok ni hu konne' malagu.
'The chicken that I caught ran away.'

As mentioned earlier, there are homonyms of *ni*. Indeed, they might be interpreted as one and the same morpheme. It seems preferable at this time to distinguish between the relativizer *ni* and the article *ni*.

When the relativizer *nai* is used, it usually replaces the locative NP of the relative clause. The following sentences will illustrate the use of the relativizer *nai*:

Humanao gue' para i lancho nai machocho'cho' i amigu-ña.
'He went to the ranch where his friend is working.'

Malak iya Guam yo' nai mafañagu yo'.
'I went to Guam where I was born.'

Manmalagu ham para i eskuela nai manestudia ham.
'We ran to the school where we studied.'

The relativizers *ni* and *nai* will be discussed in connection with relative clauses in section 4.19.

Probably due to their similarity in pronunciation, there appears to be some confusion about the relationships and differences in the words *anai*, *nai*, and *na*.

The following sentences will perhaps illustrate the use of the subordinator *anai*, the complementizer *na*, the emphatic particle *nai*, and the reasons for the apparent confusion about the use of them.

Hafa malago'-mu anai matto hao?
'What did you want when you came?'

In sentences such as the above, *anai* is often reduced to *nai*, thus resulting in something like the following:

Hafa malago'-mu nai matto hao?
'What did you want when you came?'

We also find the subordinator *na* in this position, but with a slightly different meaning, as in the following sentence:

Hafa malago'-mu na matto hao?
'What did you want that you came here for?'

The above sentence can also take the emphatic particle *nai*:

Hafa malago'-mu <u>nai na</u> matto hao?
'What did you want that you really came here for?'

Even though the words *anai, nai,* and *na* each has a different primary function, there are times, as can be seen in the above examples, when there is some apparent overlap. The differences in meaning, however, are still there and should not be confused.

Spanish Subordinators. Among the sentence connectors of modern Chamorro are several that were borrowed from Spanish. Some of these have undergone some sound changes to conform to the Chamorro sound system. Most, if not all, of the Spanish sentence connectors are subordinators. Listed below are most of the *Spanish subordinators.* The list is probably not complete. It is followed by a set of sample sentences.

antes ki	'before'	konto ki	'in spite of'
antes di	'before'	kosa ki	'so that'
asta ki	'until'	maskesea	'although'
desde ki	'since'	mientras ki	'while'
despues di	'after'	para ki	'so that'
fuera di	'besides, except for'	siakasu	'in case'
komo	'if'	sinó	'or else'

Sample Sentences

Maolek mohon na un fafamaisen <u>antes ki</u> un hanao.
'It is good if you ask permission before you go.'

Debidi un chocho <u>antes di</u> un hanao para i eskuela.
'You must eat before you go to school.'

<u>Asta ki</u> hu danche todu este na bai hu para.
'Until I can hit all of these then I will stop.'

<u>Desde ki</u> un li'e' i palao'an kaduku hao.
'Since you saw the woman, you have been crazy.'

<u>Fuera di</u> Guam, Saipan mas dankolo na isla giya Marianas.
'Except for Guam, Saipan is the biggest island in the Marianas.'

<u>Komo</u> maolek bida-mu gi che'cho'-mu, bai hu fa'mannge'- hu hao.
'If you do your work well, I will make you my sweetheart.'

Debidi un o'mak <u>despues di</u> munhayan hao macho'cho'.
'You should bathe after you finish work.'

<u>Konto ki</u> hu sangani na baba, ha cho'gue ha'.
'In spite of what I told him of its badness, he did it anyway.'

Pumara i taotao macho'cho' kosa ki siña gue'maigo'.
'The man stopped working so that he could sleep.'

Maskesea ti bunita lao ya-hu.
'Although she isn't pretty, I like her.'

NOTE: *maskesea* has an alternate form, pronounced *masea*.

Masea ti sen chume'lu siha, gof umafa'maolek.
'Although they are not real siblings, they get along with each other well.'

Mientras ki umo'o'mak yo', papaine hao.
'While I am taking a bath, be combing your hair.'

Para ki ti un matmas, usa i floater.
'So that you won't drown, use the floater.'

Siakasu na matai yo', gof adahi i lahi-ta.
In case I die, take good care of our son.'

Chiku yo' sinó bai hu kati.
'Kiss me or else I will cry.'

Sentence Modifiers. There are a few words and phrases in Chamorro that usually function as *sentence modifiers.* They are similar in some respects to subordinators; that is to say, they modify the entire sentence rather than any particular part of it. They usually introduce the sentence, since they usually (but not always) occur at the beginning of the sentence. Most of the sentence modifiers are Spanish loan words.

It is difficult to establish a clear definition for sentence modifiers. Some of them seem to follow the pattern of subordinators. Some of them could be classed as *adverbial modifiers.* (In a Spanish dictionary, most of the Spanish words that occur in the sentence modifiers of Chamorro are classed as adverbs.) Since we have avoided the term "adverb" for classifying parts of speech in Chamorro, we will use the term *sentence modifier* for this group of words and phrases.

A partial listing of the sentence modifiers is given here. Any other words or phrases that can be substituted for the ones listed below could be considered sentence modifiers.

buente ~ *siña (ha') buente* 'maybe, perhaps'

Buente gi dos pat tres oras.
'Maybe in two or three hours.'

Siña buente asta despues.
'Maybe later.'

despues ~ *pues* 'then'

> Despues i nana ha' sopbla yan i dos sotterita.
> 'Then the mother was left with the two young girls.'

> Bai hu o'mak; pues, bai hu minagagu.
> 'I will bathe; then I will get dressed.'

NOTE: *pues* is used to join two clauses that are closely related in meaning; otherwise *despues* is used.

entonses 'then, well then (implying 'Do you mean to say?')'

> Entonses na munga hao?
> 'Then, you don't want it?'

> Entonses na para un tattiyi yo'?
> 'Then, you are going to follow me?'

estaba 'used to be' (This word was classed as an Irregular Verb in section 3.3.2. It also appears to function as a sentence modifier.)

> Estaba guaha iyo-ku kareta.
> 'It used to be that I had a car' or 'I used to have a car.'

guaña 'really' (This word is often, but certainly not always, used to preface a question when asking for verification of a statement made by someone else.)

> Guaña ilek-ña na para ta fanhanao?
> 'Really, did he say that we will go?'

agon 'really, is it so?' (This word is similar to *guaña*, except that it is used to address someone directly when asking for verification.)

> Agon ilek-mu na para ta fanhanao?
> 'Really, did you say that we will go?'

kasi 'probably, perhaps' (often used with *buente*)

> Kasi si Pedro humanao nigap asta i espitat.
> 'Probably Pedro went to the hospital yesterday.'

naya 'yet, for a while' (*Naya* probably occurs at the end of sentences more often than at the beginning. It may be better to consider it an adverb of time or a "time modifier." It can also be classed as a "sentence modifier."

> Naya cha'-mu humanao.
> 'Don't go yet.'

puede 'hopefully, perhaps' (from Spanish *poder*)

> Puede humanao yo' agupa' asta Guam.
> 'Hopefully I will go to Guam tomorrow.'

tieneki 'surely, certainly' (from Spanish *tener que*)

> Tieneki ma li'e' hao gi gipot.
> 'Surely they will see you at the party.'

Tieneki ti bumola yo' sa' appleng i kannai-hu.
'Certainly I won't play ball because my hand is sprained.'

The *phrase-type sentence modifiers* listed here all refer to time and include the Spanish loan word *tiempo*. In some of the phrases (e.g., *apmam na tiempo, ma'pos na tiempo*) we find Chamorro words combining with the Spanish loan *tiempo*. In some other phrases (e.g., *todu i tiempo*) the two content words are Spanish, but are linked by the Chamorro article *i*.

apmam na tiempo 'in times past' (also pronounced *atman*)

Apmam na tiempo sumasaga un bihu gi lancho-ku.
'A long time ago an old man was staying at my ranch.'

hagas na tiempo 'for a long time' (*hagas* comes from a form of the Spanish verb *hacer*.)

Hagas na tiempo para bai hu hanao para Japan.
'For a long time I have been planning to go to Japan.'

Hagas is also used by itself as a predicate of a sentence which functions as a sentence modifier. In the following examples the sentence modifier including *hagas* is underlined. (Notice that *hagas* has its own subject pronoun.)

Hagas ha' gue' sumaga giya Hawaii.
'He stayed in Hawaii for a long time.'

Hagas ha' yo' mannangga desde Huebes.
'I have waited for a long time since Thursday.'

gi manma'pos na tiempo 'in past time' (*Ma'pos* suggests a more recent past than *apmam*.)

Gi manma'pos na tiempo humanao gue' para Guam.
'In the recent past he went to Guam.'

Like *hagas*, *ma'pos* also functions by itself as a predicate:

Ma'pos gue' para Guam.
'He left for Guam.'

gi mamamaila' na tiempo 'in the time to come' (From the word *maila'* 'to come'.)

Gi mamamaila' na tiempo para ta fanhanao para Saipan.
'In the time to come we will go to Saipan.'

todu i tiempo 'all the time'

Todu i tiempo machocho'cho' gue' duru.
'All the time he works hard.'

As stated earlier, many of these *sentence modifiers* could also occur at the end of the sentence, or even in the middle. When they occur at the beginning, they seem to modify the entire sentence that follows. This is why they are called sentence modifiers. There are no doubt a number of additional words and phrases that could be added to the list.

Question Words

3.4.9   Question words are used to signal that the following clause asks a question. They are often called *interrogative* pronouns, adverbs, and such. In this grammar any word that introduces a question will be called a *question word*.

The question words of Chamorro are as follows:

kao	general question word
hafa	'what'
hayi	'who'
manu	'where, which'
ngai'an	'when'
taimanu	'how'
kuanto	'how much, how many'

Notice that all of the question words except *kuanto* are native Chamorro words. Each of these words will be discussed briefly.

Kao. The question word *kao* converts any Chamorro statement into a "yes-no" question. In other words the question can be answered by either *hunggan* 'yes' or *ahe'* 'no'. Notice the following pairs of sentences:

Mediku gue'.	Kao mediku gue'?
'He is a doctor.'	'Is he a doctor?'
Lokka' i tronkon hayu.	Kao lokka' i tronkon hayu?
'The tree is tall.'	'Is the tree tall?'
Manmacho'cho' duru i famalao'an.	Kao manmacho'cho' duru i famalao'an?
'The women worked hard.'	'Did the women work hard?'
Gumugupu i páharu.	Kao gumugupu i páharu?
'The bird is flying.'	'Is the bird flying?'
Guaha tenda giya Tanapag.	Kao guaha tenda giya Tanapag?
'There is a store at Tanapag.'	'Is there a store at Tanapag?'
Un tungo' mama'tinas kelaguen.	Kao un tungo' mama'tinas kelaguen?
'You know how to make kelaguen.'	'Do you know how to make kelaguen?'

When questions are formed from statements using the question word *kao*, there is also a change in the intonation of the sentence. Generally speaking, the pitch level of the voice always tends to go higher at the end of a question. Compare the marking (below) of the intonation on the last pair of sentences. (The line represents the relative highness and lowness of pitch levels.)

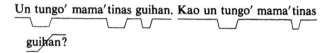

Un tungo' mama'tinas guihan. Kao un tungo' mama'tinas

guihan?

The pronunciation of *kao* usually varys somewhere between pronunciation of the full diphthong /kao/ and a simple vowel, as in /ko/.

Hafa. The translation given for *hafa* is 'what'. Actually, the question word *hafa* has a broader range of meaning than that. The real meaning of *hafa* depends on what follows. The following examples will help illustrate.

When *hafa* is followed immediately by a demonstrative or sentence, then it usually means 'what?'.

Hafa este?
'What is this?'

Hafa enao?
'What is that (near you)?'

Hafa un cho'gue?
'What did you do?'

Hafa bidada-mu?
'What are you doing?'

Hafa un li'e' gi tenda?
'What did you see at the store?'

When used in greetings the question word *hafa* is usually translated as 'how'.

Hafa, ga'chong?
'How is it, friend?'

Hafa dei.
'Greetings.'

Hafa tatatmanu hao?
'How are you?'

NOTE: The common written form for the popular Chamorro greeting is *Hafa adai*. I have never heard it pronounced this way by native speakers of Chamorro. The real meaning of these greetings is also a matter of some speculation. One theory that I have heard for *hafa adai* is that the original form was *hafa ádahi*, which might translate as 'what, watch out for each other.' It has been suggested that *tatatmanu* is a slightly distorted reduplicated form of *taimanu* 'how', which, according to the formal rules for reduplication, should come out as *tataimanu*. Reconstructing the formal history for common greetings in any language is usually difficult.

Hafa na. The question word *hafa* means 'why' when it is connected to a following clause by the *linking particle na*. Notice the following pairs of questions:

Hafa un cho′gue?
'What did you do?'

Hafa na un cho′gue?
'Why did you do it?'

Hafa un fahan?
'What did you buy?'

Hafa na un fahan i kareta?
'Why did you buy the car?'

Hafa ha ayao?
'What did he borrow?'

Hafa na ha ayao i lepblo?
'Why did he borrow the book?'

When *hafa* is used to mean 'why', it can always be preceded by *sa′*.

Hafa na un cho′gue?
'Why did you do it?'

Sa′ hafa na un cho′gue?
'Why did you do it?'

And when it stands alone as a question in response to another statement, it is always preceded by *sa′*.

Ti ya-hu i ma′estro-ku.
'I don't like my teacher.'

Sa′ hafa?
'Why?'

Hafa is frequently reduced to *haf* in rapid speech, as in

Haf taimanu mafa′tinas-ña?
'How is it made?'

Hafkao. Another form that is derived from *hafa* is *hafkao*, which is actually a contracted form of the phrase *hafa ha′ hao*. *Hafkao* could be considered a separate (and stronger) question word from *hafa* and may be used when the subject of the question is second person, as in the following examples:

Hafkao bidada-mu guenao?
'What in the world are you doing?'

Hafkao malago′-mu?
'What is it that you want?'

The question word *hafa* is also used to introduce subordinate clauses, in which case it requires different kinds of syntactic constructions. These matters will be taken up later in the discussion of Chamorro syntax.

Hayi. The question word *hayi* is used when referring to people and is usually translated as 'who'.

> Hayi lumi'e' i palao'an?
> 'Who saw the woman?'
>
> Hayi lini'e'-mu?
> 'Whom did you see?'
>
> Hayi na'an-mu?
> 'What (who) is your name?'
>
> Hayi na palao'an?
> 'Which woman?'
>
> Notice that in the last two sentences the English glosses for the question word are 'what' and 'which.' In Chamorro, the question word *hayi* is used whenever the reference is to a human being.

The question word *hayi* is frequently reduced to *hai,* particularly in rapid speech, as in:

> Hai lumi'e' i palao'an?
> 'Who saw the woman?'

Manu. The question word *manu* has two different meanings, 'which' and 'where'. The meaning is determined usually by what follows. If what follows is linked by the particle *nai* or if there is a reference to location, then the meaning of *manu* is 'where.'

> Para manu hao?
> 'Where are you going?'
>
> Ginen manu hao?
> 'Where are you from?'
>
> Manu nai sumasaga hao?
> 'Where do you stay?'
>
> Manu nai un po'lo?
> 'Where did you put it?'
>
> Manu nai gaige i asagua-mu?
> 'Where is your wife?'

If what follows is linked by *na,* or if it does not refer to location or people, then the meaning of *manu* is 'which'.

Manu na lepblo malago'-mu?
'Which book do you want?'

Manu i para guahu?
'Which one is for me?'

Manu na mannok i ga'-mu?
'Which chicken is yours?'

Manu gi ayu siha na lepblo finahan-mu?
'Which of those books did you buy?'

When there are only two objects in question, the prefix *a-* is attached to *manu*.

Amanu malago'-mu?
'Which of the two do you want?'

Amanu na mannok i ga'-mu?
'Which of the two chickens is yours?'

Mangge. The question word *mangge* (also pronounced *mungge*) is a contracted form of *manu nai gaige*. It is used in existential constructions (cf. 4.6) and is followed by a noun or pronoun. *Mangge* and *manu nai gaige* are often used freely in place of one another, but with the following difference in meaning. When the subject is very specific, the longer form is used. When the subject is non-specific, either form may be used.

Manu nai gaige i kareta-hu?   'Where is my car?'
Mangge i kareta?   'Where is the car?'

Manu nai gaige si Pedro?   'Where is Pedro?'
Mangge si Pedro?

Manu nai gaige i asagua-mu?   'Where is your wife?'
Mangge i asagua-mu?

Manu nai gaige gue'?   'Where is he?'
Mangge gue'?

When the subject is plural, the plural prefix *man-* must be used as follows:

Manu nai manggaige i manestudiante?   'Where are the
Manmangge i manestudiante?   students?'

Manu nai manggaige i famalao'an?   'Where are the
Manmangge i famalao'an?   women?'

Ngai'an. The question word *ngai'an* is used with reference to time and is usually translated as 'when'. It is followed by *nai* plus a clause, or by some sort of noun phrase:

Ngai'an nai mafañgu hao?
'When were you born?'

Ngai'an nai humanao hao?
'When did you go?'

Ngai'an nai para un hanao?
'When will you go?'

Ngai'an na ha'ani anai un ta'lo magi?
'Which day will you come back?'

Ngai'an i gipot?
'When is the party?'

Ngai'an na sakkan anai matai gue'?
'Which year did he die?'

Taimanu. The question word *taimanu* is apparently a combined form of the prefix *tai-* (as in *taiguini* 'like this') plus *manu* 'where, which'. When put together they form the question word *taimanu* which can be translated as 'how' or 'in what manner'. In questions, *taimanu* is often preceded by the question word *hafa*.

Taimanu bumaila hao?
'How do you dance?'

Taimanu agang-mu ni patgon?
'How did you call the child?'

Taimanu kumahulo'?
'How does one go up?'

Taimanu yinemmok-ña?
'How fat is it?'

Taimanu minalangu-ña?
'How sick is he?

Hafa taimanu masangan "pencil" gi fino' Chamorro?
'How is pencil said in the Chamorro language?'

The question word *taimanu* is often pronounced *tatmanu* with no change in meaning:

Tatmanu bumaila hao?   'How do you dance?'
Tatmanu kumahulo'?   'How does one go up?'

When it is followed by a possessed form, the question word *taimanu* 'how' means something like 'to what extent'. Notice the following examples:

Taimanu dinankolo-ña?   'How big is it?'
Taimanu ina'paka'-ña?   'How white is it?'
Taimanu minaolek-ña?   'How good is it?'

Kuanto(s). The only Spanish question word that occurs in modern Chamorro is *kuanto* 'how much, how many'.

Kuanto bali-ña?
'How much is it?'   (Lit. 'How much is its value?')

Kuanto malago'-mu?
'How much (many) do you want?'

When *kuanto* is used with the plural form of a Spanish noun, the plural form *kuantos* is used:

Kuantos años hao?
'How old are you?'   (Lit. 'how many years you?')

Kuantos minutos mamaigo' gue'?
'How many minutes did he sleep?'

This Spanish question word has replaced the Chamorro form described by Safford (43-44) as follows:

> 5. Fia, fafia, fiiyai?—These forms, signifying 'how many', are used according to the nature of the nouns they modify. They are etymologically identical with the Samoan *fia* and the Hawaiian *e-hia, a-hia* (how many). *Fia* is used in reckoning time; as *Fia puenge?* 'How many days?' (literally 'How many nights?'). *Fafia* is used for asking the number of persons and living things; as *Fafia na taotao?* 'How many people?' *Fiiyai* is used with inanimate objects; as *Fiiyai na guma'*? 'How many houses?' Other derived interrogatives are *takfia*, used in asking measurements; as, *Takfian yini na sagman*? 'How many (fathoms long) is this boat?' and *Fahafa?* 'How many times?'
>
> Each of these forms requires a particular form of numeral in reply.... Both the interrogatives and the numerals have become obsolete in Guam, being replaced by the Spanish *cuanto* (how much) and *cuantos* (how many) and by the Spanish numerals.

Safford's claim that the old Chamorro interrogatives listed above "have become obsolete in Guam" is not entirely true. The one exception is the question word *takfiha* (also pronounced *takfia*). It is used in the sense of 'guess' or 'estimate' in asking measurements. It is sometimes used with *kuanto*. In the following examples, the parentheses indicate that *kuanto* is optional:

Takfiha (kuanto) dinankolo-ña i tronkon hayu.
'Guess how big the tree is.'

When a suffix is added, the h is pronounced distinctly:

Takfihayi yo' ni dinankolo-ña i tronkon hayu.
'Guess (estimate) for me how big the tree is.'

It is worth noting that Costenoble (228) lists the same words as Safford, but with the following spellings: *fi'a, fafi'a,* and *fihjay* (where j = y and ay = ai).

The old sytem of Chamorro numerals and question words was obviously tied in with a complex system of semantic and grammatical classification, most of which has been completely lost.

Kuanto occurs as *kuantos* with certain words which refer to units of time. Most of these time words are Spanish and most of them reflect the Spanish plural form. The words occuring frequently with *kuantos* are *minutos, oras, dias, simana, meses, años,* and *sakkan.* (Only the last of the above words is not Spanish; *simana* never occurs with the Spanish plural suffix).

Kuantos minutos mannangga hao?
'How many minutes did you wait?'

Kuantos oras maigo' hao?
'How many hours did you sleep?'

Kuantos simana sumaga hao?
'How many weeks did you stay?'

Kuantos meses gue' sumaga guini?
'How many months did he stay here?'

Kuantos años hao?
'How old are you?'

Kuantos tiempo maigo' hao?
'How long did you sleep?'

Kuanto is followed by the linking particle *na* plus a noun, or it is followed immediately by a possessed noun. Notice that *simana* and *sakkan* occur with *kuantos* and *kuanto na:*

Kuanto na simana sumaga hao giya Saipan?
'How many weeks did you stay in Saipan?'

Kuanto na sakkan un nisisita?
'How many years do you need?'

Kuanto na famagu'on un li'e'?
'How many children did you see?'

Kuanto bali-ña?
'How much is it?'

<u>Kuanto</u> salape'-mu?
'How much money do you have?'

<u>Kuanto</u> chinago'-ña i gima'-mu?
'How far is your house?'

<u>Kuanto</u> mineggai-ña na famalao'an?
'How many women are there?'

Other Question Markers. In addition to the formal overt question words discussed above, there are two very common ways of marking questions in Chamorro.

Probably the most common way of marking a "yes-no" question in Chamorro is through intonation. If the speaker wishes to convert a statement to a "yes-no" question he can either use the question marker *kao* or he can simply use the question intonation pattern. The main characteristic of question intonation is a marked rise in pitch level at the end of the question. Contrast the following three sentences. The pitch level is marked by a line in all three sentences as they would be spoken under ordinary circumstances.

Statement: Sumasaga gue' giya Susupe.
'He lives in Susupe.'

Question: Kao sumasaga gue' giya Susupé?
'Does he live in Susupe?'

Question: Sumasaga gue' giya Susupé?
'Does he live in Susupe?'

The final rise in pitch level signifies a question. It is used whether the question word *kao* is present or not.

The following brief exchange was recorded in Guam in 1962. The two speakers were discussing the days catch of fish.

1st Speaker: Manggaige meggai na guihan.
'There were many fish.'

2nd Speaker: Saksak?
'Saksak?'

1st Speaker: Saksak.
'Saksak.'

2nd Speaker: Kinenne'-mu?
'Your catch?'

1st Speaker: Kinenne'-hu.
'My catch.'

The questions are simply marked by a higher level of pitch at the end of the sentence.

Tag Questions. Tag questions are used very commonly in all languages when the speaker anticipates an answer. An example of a tag question in English would be, "This is a book about Chamorro, isn't it?" or "He read the book, didn't he?"

In Chamorro *tag questions* are formed by simply adding the word *no* to the end of a statement, as in the following examples:

> Ya-mu manestudia, no?
> 'You like to study, don't you?'
>
> Machocho'cho' hao duru, no?
> 'You are working hard, aren't you?'
>
> Para un fatto giya siha, no?
> 'You are going to his place, aren't you?'

Classifiers

3.5.0   Many of the languages of Asia and the Pacific area have a grammatical feature generally known as *classifiers*. In a language with a fully operative classifier system each concrete noun belongs to a certain class and is marked by the use of that classifier. In a language such as Trukese this system of classifiers is found in the counting system and the possessives.

The Chamorro system of classifiers was probably much more elaborate in the past than it is now. The system of counting described by Safford (1909: 47–50) and by Costenoble (1940: 259–265) suggests that Chamorro once had a system of classifying nouns that has been lost. Only vestiges of the classifier system are still in use.

In modern Chamorro the classifiers are used in possessive constructions only. The classifiers and the categories they mark are as follows:

> na'   'edible things'
> ga'   'non-human animals'
> iyo   'inanimate objects'
> gimen   'drinkable things'

Of the four classifiers, the first three are commonly used. The last one, *gimen*, is frequently omitted. *Iyo* is used metaphorically with human objects, as in *Iyo-ku hao*, 'You belong to me.'

Following are some examples showing the use of the Chamorro classifiers:

na'

> Guaha na'-hu guihan.
> 'I have a fish to eat.'
>
> Guaha dos mannok na'-ña.
> 'He has two chickens to eat.'
>
> Guaha na'-hu nenkanno'.
> 'I have food.'

ga'

> Guaha ga'-hu guihan.
> 'I have a (pet) fish.'
>
> Malingu i ga'-ña ga'lagu.
> 'His dog was lost.'
>
> I patgon estaba humugagandu gi kanton tasi yan i ga'-ña
>   haguihi.
> 'The child was playing at the beach with his crab.'

> NOTE: The word *ga'lagu* 'dog' is a compound word made up of
> the morphemes *ga'* 'animal classifier' and *lagu* 'north'. Literally
> translated *ga'lagu* means 'animal from the north', which suggests
> that it was introduced by a foreign group.

The classifier *ga'* is also used with verbs to mean 'one who
loves to' do something, as in the following examples. (Primary
stress usually falls on gá'-.)

ga' + kuentos	'talk'	→	ga'kumuentos 'talker'
ga' + gimen	'drink'	→	ga'gumimen 'drinker' or 'a drunk'
ga' + taitai	'read'	→	ga'manaitai 'one who reads (or prays) a lot'
ga' + e + palao'an		→	ga'umepalao'an 'woman chaser'

iyo

> Estaba guaha iyo-ku Evinrude.
> 'I used to have an Evinrude.'
>
> Guaha iyo-ña kareta si Pedro.
> 'Pedro has a car.'
>
> Guaha iyon-ñiha kareta i famalao'an.
> 'The women have a car.'

In the last three sentences above the use of the classifier *iyo* could
have easily been avoided by phrasing the statements differently.

Estaba guaha Evinrude-hu.
'I used to have an Evinrude.'

Guaha kareta-ña si Pedro.
'Pedro has a car.'

Guaha karetan-ñiha i famalao'an.
'The women have a car.'

These alternate forms would suggest that the classifier *iyo* may be declining in use in modern Chamorro. The word is still used, however, in the sense of 'belonging to' as in:

iyon tasi	'belonging to the sea'
iyon lahi	'belonging to the man'
Iyo-ku i kareta.	'The car belongs to me.'

It will be noticed that all of the classifiers are followed immediately by a possessive pronoun.

gimen

Maila' i gimen-hu setbesa.
'Bring me my beer.'

Ha apasiyi yo' ni gimen-hu kafe.
'He paid for my coffee for me.'

Numbers

3.5.1   The Chamorro system of numbers was replaced by the Spanish system a good many years ago. Safford, whose work was first published in 1903, claims that "the Chamorro numeral system is no longer used in Guam, but a few of the numerals are retained in derived words" (p. 49). Costenoble, whose work is based on the period 1905–1913, claims that the Chamorro numerals were used only by the older generation on the island of Rota (1940:260). Von Preissing claims that the old Chamorro numeral system is "now obsolete" (1918:15). I have never met any Chamorro speaker with any knowledge of the pre-Spanish numeral system.

Chamorro Numbers. According to Safford, Chamorro "has a purely decimal system." He lists the first ten basic numerals as follows:

hacha	'one'
hu-gua	'two'
tulu, tulo	'three'
fatfat	'four'

lima	'five'
gunum	'six'
fiti	'seven'
gualu	'eight'
sigua	'nine'
manot	'ten'

For a more detailed discussion of the pre-Spanish Chamorro numerals see Safford, 1909, pp. 48–56.

Spanish Numbers. Chamorro has borrowed the complete system of Spanish numbers, with certain sound changes to conform to Chamorro pronunciation. Some representative cardinal numbers are listed here:

un, unu	(1)	dies i siete	(17)
dos	(2)	dies i ocho	(18)
tres	(3)	dies i nuebe	(19)
kuatro	(4)	bente	(20)
sinko	(5)	bente i unu	(21)
sais	(6)	trenta	(30)
siete	(7)	kuarenta	(40)
ocho	(8)	sinkuenta	(50)
nuebe	(9)	sisenta	(60)
dies	(10)	sitenta	(70)
onse	(11)	ochenta	(80)
dosse	(12)	nubenta	(90)
trese	(13)	siento (s)	(100)
katotse	(14)	kinientos	(500)
kinse	(15)	mit	(1000)
dies i sais	(16)		

In rapid speech the particle *i* (from Spanish *y*) is usually not pronounced clearly. Very often it elides with the preceding vowel to form a diphthong, as in *kuarentai sais* '46'.

Siento '100' is pluralized when used with numbers other than *unu*:

dos sientos	'200'
tres sientos	'300'

For numbers higher than *tres*, the linking particle *na* is used to connect the number with the following noun, except when the noun is a Spanish loan word, such as *pesos, años, oras,* etc.:

tres mangga	kuatro na mangga
'3 mangoes'	'4 mangoes'
tres pesos	kuatro pesos
'3 pesos'	'4 pesos'

Ordinal Numbers. There are two sets of *ordinal numbers* in Chamorro up through the number five. Beyond five, the ordinal numbers are formed by combining a Chamorro prefix *mina'-* with Spanish numbers. The Chamorro word for 'first' is an exception. Following are some representative ordinal numbers in Chamorro:

fine'nana	'first'
primet, primeru	'first'
mina'dos, sigundo	'second'
mina'tres, tetseru	'third'
mina'kuatro, kuatto	'fourth'
mina'sinko, kento	'fifth'
mina'sais	'sixth'
mina'siete	'seventh'
mina'ocho	'eighth'

The word *fine'nana* is derived from *mo'na* 'at first, ahead'. All of the other ordinal numbers are either borrowed completely from Spanish or are formed by combining the prefix *mina'-* with the Spanish cardinal numbers.

It appears that the Spanish system of numbers is rapidly giving way to the English system, particularly when one is counting money.

Distributive Numbers. *Distributive numbers* are formed by adding the prefixes *man-* and *a-* plus reduplication of the cardinal number. The prefixes *man-* and *a-* wil be discussed in more detail in the section on affixation.

In forming the distributive numbers, we are actually converting numbers to verbs. (Cf. 3.3.5 on Changing Parts of Speech). Through affixation and reduplication, the number takes on the grammatical features of verbs, as the following examples will illustrate:

Manakuakuatro papa'.
'They were going down four-by-four.'

Manhanao manadodos.
'They went two-by-two.'

U fanasasais magi.
'They will come here six-by-six.'

NOTE: The prefix *man-* changes to *fan-* to indicate future tense.

Affixation

3.5.2   Chamorro might be described as a language that uses many affixes. Affixation is a very important part of the grammatical system. There are four types of affixes in Chamorro. Each type will be described here. In the following section a more complete presentation of the affixes will be given, and further examples will be given throughout the discussion of the grammar.

Stems and Affixes. Affix is a general term used to describe bound morphemes that are attached to something else. They may be attached to a *simple word*, as in *apasi* (*apas* plus -*i*), or they may be attached to a *complex word*, as in *manapasi* (*man-* plus *apas* plus -*i*). Whenever an affix is attached to a word (whether it is simple or complex), the word to which it is attached is called the *stem*. If the stem cannot be analyzed into smaller components, it is also known as a *root*. Thus, *apas* in the word *apasi* is both a stem and a root. *Apasi*, as in the word *manapasi* is a stem, but not a root because *apasi* can be further analyzed as *apas* plus -*i*.

A root, then, is a word which cannot be broken down into smaller meaningful parts. A stem is the word to which an affix is attached. Stems, if they cannot be broken down into smaller morphemes, are also roots.

There are four types of affixes in Chamorro. They are called prefix, suffix, infix, and reduplication, and it is possible for all four types of affixes to occur simultaneously with a single stem.

Prefixes. Prefixes are affixes that come before the stem. When they are attached, they become part of the word. An example of a prefix is the Indefinite Object Marker *man-*. (When affixes are written separately, a hyphen is used to indicate whether they are prefixes, suffixes, or infixes. The hyphen shows where the affix is attached to the stem.) An example of the prefix *man-* used with the word *hatsa* 'to lift' is *Manhasta yo' siya*. 'I lifted a chair.' (Cf. 2.7.1 for review of morphophonemic changes caused by the prefix *man-*.) An example of a prefix in English is *in-* 'not' as in the words *incapable, intolerant, indecent,* and so forth.

Suffixes. Suffixes are affixes that follow the stem. Like the prefixes, when they are attached they become part of the word. An example of a suffix in Chamorro is -*i* (Referential Suffix), as in *sangani* 'tell to' (from *sangan*) or *kuentusi* 'talk to' (from *kuentos*) as in *Ha kuentusi si Pedro*. 'He talked to Pete.' An example of a suffix in English is *-ing* as in *He was writing*.

Infixes. Infixes are affixes that occur within the stem. In Chamorro they always occur immediately before the first vowel of the stem. An example of an infix in Chamorro is the Nominalizing Infix *-in-*, as in *hinasso* 'thought, knowledge' (from *hasso* plus *-in-*). If the stem is spelled with an initial vowel, then the infix precedes the initial vowel, as in *inipe'* 'thing cut' (from *ipe'* plus *-in-*). It is important to remember that the initial *in-* of *inipe'* is not a prefix; it is the same morpheme that we have in *hinasso*. If phonetic data were brought to bear as proof, we would see that *ipe'* is actually ['ipe'] with an initial glottal consonant. The infixed form would then be ['inipe'], with the infix coming before the first vowel and after the initial consonant. English does not have infixes.

Notes to linguists

There are two infixes in Chamorro, *-um-* and *-in-*, both of which probably have more than one function. It is interesting that the canonical form of both of these affixes is just the opposite of what one would expect in a language that is basically CVCV. It is tempting to posit underlying prefixes *mu-* and *ni-* for these infixes with appropriate rules for metathesis. There appears to be some evidence to support such a hypothesis.

The argument based on canonical forms is not an isolated one.

Additional support comes from the frequent free variation between *mu-* and *-um-*, especially in the Chamorro spoken in Guam. One finds, for example, the forms *munangu* and *numangu* meaning 'swam', and the forms *mu'e'ekingok* and *ume'ekingok* meaning 'listening'.

When the infix *-um-* occurs with the prefix *na'-* plus a stem, the resultant form is always *muna'-*, as in *Guahu muna'chalek i patgon*. 'I am the one who caused the child to laugh.' When the infix *-in-* occurs with the causative prefix *na'* -the resultant form is *nina'-*. Given only this surface form, it is impossible to determine whether *nina'-* is prefix *ni-* plus *na'-* or whether it is prefix *na'-* plus infix *-in-*. If we follow the hypothesis that infixes in Chamorro are metathesized prefixes, then the form *nina'-* results from *ni-* plus *na'-*.

One final argument favoring the underlying prefix hypothesis can be drawn from an analysis of the Chamorro word *fanchinemma'*, meaning 'forbidden things'. The surface morphology of this word is as follows: *fan-* (plural marker), *chomma'* 'forbid,' and *-in-* (nominalizing infix). The change of the vowel from *o* to *e* (chomma'- chinemma') is accounted for by the vowel harmony rules. However, one would also expect the consonant assimilation-reduction rules also to apply to produce **fañinemma'* (cf. 2.7.1). How can we account for the fact that the consonant assimilation-reduction rules do not apply in this instance?

One reasonable explanation for this is the underlying prefix hypothesis. In the formation of the word *fanchinemma'* we can observe the following steps:

1. Root word *chomma'* plus prefix *ni-* → *nichomma'*.
2. Vowel harmony rule #1: *nichomma'* → *nichemma'*.
3. Prefix *fan-* is added: *nichemma'* → *fannichemma'*.
4. Infix metathesis rule: *fannichemma'* → *fanchinemma'*.

NOTE: Rule 2 above is unordered: details for formalizing the metathesis rule are not given here.

The above evidence suggests very strongly that infixes in Chamorro (and possibly other Philippine languages?) may actually have prefixes as their underlying forms.

Reduplication. Reduplication is the linguistic term used to describe a special type of affix which results from the repetition of the stressed vowel of the stem plus the preceding consonant if there is one present. The following pairs of words will illustrate how this affix works:

Stem		Reduplicated Form	
atan	'look at'	á'atan	'looking at'
li'e'	'see'	lili'e'	'seeing'
hatsa	'lift'	háhatsa	'lifting'
taotao	'people'	tátaotao	'human body'

Sometimes reduplication also causes a shift in the position of primary stress from the penultimate syllable to some other syllable in the word. The differences in types of reduplication will be discussed in chapter 4, which treats Chamorro syntax. The important thing to remember now about reduplication in Chamorro is that it is the stressed vowel and the preceding consonant of the stem that are repeated, *not the entire syllable*.

Ordering of Affixes. In languages which have as many types of affixes as Chamorro, it is usually necessary to specify an order in which the affixes must occur. We don't simply add several affixes to a stem simultaneously. For example, if a word contains an infix plus reduplication, is it possible to determine which affix came first? Is it possible to establish rules for determing which affix comes first, which one comes second, and so on?

Let us examine the word *sumasaga,* which contains an infix plus reduplication, to see if the ordering of affixes makes any difference.

We can start with the root word *saga.* If we add the infix first, we get *sumaga,* which is a perfectly acceptable form. If we now add the reduplication affix (remember that the rule for reduplication is to repeat the stressed vowel and preceding consonant of the stem), we get the unacceptable form **sumamaga,* which is often heard in the speech of young children. Obviously something is wrong in the ordering of affixes if the resulting word is **sumamaga.*

In this particular case we can see that it is necessary to apply the reduplication rule first: *saga* → *sásaga.* After this first step we can then apply the infix rule (the infix always goes immediately before the first vowel of the stem) to give us *sumásaga.*

Limited rules can be given for the ordering of verb affixes for Chamorro as follows:

1. Suffixation
2. Indefinite Object Marker *man* ~ *fan* - (IOM)
3. Reduplication
4. Infixation
5. Plural Subject Marker *man* ~ *fan* - (PSM)

Some examples will now be given to illustrate why the ordering of affixes is important.

From the root word *peska* 'to fish' we can derive *famepeska,* which consists of *peska,* the Plural Subject Marker (PSM) *fan-* and reduplication. What would be the result if we added the prefix before reduplication?

fan + *peska* → *faméska*

(The *n* of *fan-* changes to *m* and the *p* is lost—consonant assimilation and reduction rule.)

If we now try to reduplicate *faméska* we would get **famémeska,* which is an unacceptable form. Clearly, the ordering of affixes in the case of *famépeska* is as follows:

Root: péska
Reduplication: pépeska
PSM: fan + pépeska
Cons. Assimilation Rule: famépeska

Another example to illustrate ordering of affixes is *bidan-ñiñiha* 'their doing'. This form consists of the root *bida* plus the possessive suffix *ñiha* plus reduplication. If we put reduplication before suffixation the result would be **bibida-ñiha* because it is the stressed vowel and preceding consonant of the stem that is repeated. The ordering of affixes in the case of *bidan-ñiñiha* is as follows:

Root: bida
Suffixation: bidan-ñiha (Stress shifts to penultimate syll-able)
Reduplication: bidan-ñiñiha

Another example which illustrates suffixation and reduplica-tion is *kuentátayi* 'substituting for' which comes from the root *kuénta* plus the suffix *-yi* plus reduplication. The ordering of affixa-tion is as follows:

Root: kuénta
Suffixation: kuentáyi
Reduplication: kuentátayi

One more example will be given here to show that infixation must precede the prefixation of *man-* or *fan-*. The word *fanchiném-ma'* meaning 'forbidden things' has the following order of affixa-tion:

Root: chomma'
Infixation: chinémma' (*o* becomes *e* because of preceding *-in-*)
PSM: fanchinémma'

If the prefix had been added to the stem, the consonant assimila-tion and loss rules would have applied, thereby giving *fañomma'*, which does in fact occur. But, we cannot now apply the infixation rule to get **fañinemma'*. Since the infixation rule is applied first, the consonant assimilation rule is blocked; thus, we get *fan-chinemma'*. (For an alternate analysis of this form, see the pre-ceding Notes to Linguists section.)

The affixes of Chamorro will be discussed further in the following section.

It is important here to distinguish between the Indefinite Object Marker *man-* and the Plural Subject Marker *man-* because they follow different ordering rules. Notice the difference between the following two paradigms, one for an intransitive verb and the other for a transitive verb:

	Transitive Verb	*Intransitive Verb*
Root:	tókcha'	sága
IOM:	manókcha'	— — — —
Redup.:	manónokcha'	sásaga
PSM:	manmanónokcha'	mañásaga
Root:	pácha	póddong
IOM:	mamácha	— — — —
Redup.:	mamámacha	pópoddong
PSM:	manmamámacha	mamópoddong

If the distinction were not maintained between the homophonous morphemes *man-*, we would end up with unacceptable forms such as **manotokcha'*, **mamapacha*, **mañañaga*, and **mamomoddong*.

Affixes in Chamorro

3.5.3   Affixes are often divided by linguists into two classes, *derivational affixes* and *inflectional affixes*. The major difference between these two classes of affixes is as follows:

Derivational affixes usually change the meaning of a word and usually cause the word to change from one part of speech to another. They may be considered *semantic affixes*.

Inflectional affixes usually have no independent meaning; their primary function is to give pertinent grammatical information. They may be considered *grammatical affixes*.

Examples of each of these types of affixes will be presented and discussed below.

It should be pointed out that the classification of Chamorro affixes into one of these two classes is sometimes arbitrary. In some instances it is not entirely clear whether an affix is more like a derivational affix or an inflectional affix. This lack of precision simply emphasizes the fact that language does not always lend itself to a division into neat little categories.

Derivational Affixes. Listed below in alphabetical order are some of the derivational affixes of Chamorro. The names that have been chosen for them are arbitrary. Whenever possible the author has used traditional terminology. In some cases the prefix is given a name; in other cases a translation seems more appropriate.

Some of the affixes are more *productive* than others: that is to say, some affixes can be easily combined with new stems to form new words. Most of the affixes listed here are still very productive. There is no doubt that some affixes which were formerly productive have now become fossilized in a few words. For example, there is an obvious relationship between *papa* 'wing' and *palapa* 'to flap wings', but the meaning of *-la-* (if there ever was one) has been lost. We find it in a few other words such as *chalaochao* (from *chaochao*) 'shake, rattle,' *kalaskas* (from *kaskas*) 'rustling sound,' and *palangpang* (from *pangpang*) 'explosion.' Even in these words the meaning of the affix *-la-* is not clear.

á- Reciprocal Prefix. This prefix is always attached to a verb. It means 'to each other'. It may occur with other affixes, and it carries primary stress.

> Umátungo' i dos.
> 'The two know each other.'
>
> Umápacha i dos.
> 'The two touched each other.'
>
> Manápacha i famagu'on.
> 'The children touched each other.'

achá- Similative Prefix. This prefix may be attached to different types of words. It conveys the meaning of 'similarity', 'sameness', or 'equally'.

> Achálokka' i dos.
> 'The two are the same height.'
>
> Ma'acháguaiya i dos.
> 'The two were loved equally.'
>
> U fanma'acháguaiya i tres.
> 'The three of them will be loved equally.'

án- 'leftover'. This prefix is usually attached to noun-like words.

> Ha kanno' i ánkanno'.
> 'He ate the leftover food.'

Ha songge i ánsupiyu.
'He burned the wood-shavings (left-over from planing).'

chát- 'not very'

chátbunita	'not very pretty'
chátmetgot	'not very strong'

This prefix has taken on idiomatic meaning in the form *chatpa'go* 'ugly'. Translated literally *chatpa'go* might mean 'not very now'.

é- 'look for, hunt'. This prefix usually occurs with nounlike words that also have a verbalizing affix. It also has an alternate form *o-*, but it is seldom used. (cf. Inflectional Affixes below.)

Umépanglao yo'.	'I hunted (looked for) crabs.'
Manépanglao siha.	'They looked for crabs.'
Para bai hu épanglao.	'I will look for crabs.'

fa'- 'pretend, change to'. This prefix can be used with a variety of words. The meaning of the affixed forms can often not be predicted. The examples below will illustrate:

Root Word		Affixed Form
guaha	'have'	Hu fa'guaha kareta-hu. 'I pretended to have a car.'
bunita	'pretty'	Ha fa'bunita gue' i palao'an. 'The woman pretended to be pretty.'
bentana	'window'	Hu fa'bentana i petta. 'I changed the door into a window.'
ande'	'show off'	Hu fa'ande' i amigu-hu drumaiba. 'I coaxed my friend to drive.'
hanom	'water'	fa'hanom 'melt'
baba	'bad'	fa'baba 'to fool, dupe'
chada'	'egg'	fa'chada' 'flatter falsely'
donne'	'chili pepper'	fa'denne' 'make chili sauce'

The last form above is the word from which *fina'denne'*, the famous Chamorro hot sauce used for seasoning food, is derived.

As can be seen, the words derived by using the prefix *fa'-* are numerous, and their meanings are often unpredictable. In some Chamorro words this prefix has become fossilized. Some examples of words that contain the fossilized prefix are:

fa'aila'	'tell on'
fa'na'gue	'teach'
fa'nu'i	'show'
fa'tinas	'cook, make'

fama'- ~ *mama'-* 'change to.' The prefixes *fama'-* and *mama'-* are not really separate prefixes, even though Safford and Costenoble describe them as such. Actually, they are the result of the prefix *man-* (alternate form *fan-*) plus the prefix *fa'-*. The prefix *man-* is the indefinite object marker. (See below under Inflectional Affixes.) When the two occur together we find the expected consonant alternation discussed in 2.7.1.

man + fa'
    Rule 1. Consonant assimilation: *mamfa'-*
    Rule 2. Loss of voiceless consonant: *mama'-*

Since *man-* occurs as *fan-* in future and imperative forms, we find *fama'-*, as in:

Para bai hu fama'tinas nenkanno'.
'I will fix some food.'

Fama'taotao ya un mafa'taotao.
'Act like a man and you will be treated like a man.'

NOTE: The *ma-* in *mafa'taotao* is the Passive Voice prefix. See below under Inflectional Affixes for a description of the prefix *ma-*.

ga'- 'one who likes something very much'. This prefix is probably an extension of the use of the animal classifier described earlier.

gá'kumuentos 'one who talks a lot', 'a garrulous person'
Gá'salape' si Juan. 'Juan is a lover of money.'

gé'- Comparative Directional. This prefix is used with words of direction and location with the general meaning of 'more in that direction'.

gé'papa'	'further down'
gé'hilo'	'further up'
gé'magi	'closer'
gé'guatu	'farther'

gi- 'person from'. This prefix probably comes from the preposition *ginen*. When it is used with a place name, it means a 'person from' that place:

Gilita.	'a person from Rota'
Gisa'ipan	'Saipanese'
Gihagatña	'Guamanian' (as used by Saipanese)
Gilagu	'Caucasian'

The term *gilagu* has been almost completely replaced by other terms, such as 'statesider' and *Amerikanu*.

há- Adverb-forming Prefix. This prefix (also pronounced *háh-*) is often used to describe a condition of a person:

maleffa	'to forget'	hámaleffa	'forgetful'
malangu	'be sick'	hámalangu	'sickly'
makonne'	'be caught'	hámakonne'	'catchable'

Há- is often adverbial in nature when it modifies the predicate element of the sentence. It is considered a prefix rather than a separate word mainly because it carries the primary stress of the phrase:

Háguaha bisita gi gima'-ña.
'He usually has visitors at his house.'

Hámayulang i kareta-hu.
'My car is usually broken.'

ka- This prefix is no longer productive and is not easily labeled. It preserves a relationship between words as the examples will illustrate:

didok	'deep'	kadidok	'sharp'
laktos	'thorn'	kalaktos	'sharp'

(Notice that this prefix is not stressed.)

ká- 'having, exhibiting'. This is a productive prefix that can be used with a large number of nouns:

Káhaga' i sapatos-hu.
'There is blood on my shoe.'

Kálaña i chinina-ña.
'There is oil on her dress.'

ké- 'about to, try'

Hu kéhatsa i lamasa.
'I tried to lift the table.'

Hafa kumeké'ilek-ña?
'What is he trying to say?'

Kumekématai gue'.
'He is about to die.'

(The prefix *ke-* has been reduplicated in the last two sentences.)

lá- Comparative Degree. This prefix is not used when making comparisons between two things. The Comparative Suffix *-ña* is used for that. It might be translated as 'more'.

Stem		*Affixed Form*	
maolek	'good'	lámaolek	'better'
bunita	'pretty'	lábunita	'prettier'
metgot	'strong'	lámetgot	'stronger'

mi- 'have lots of'

Mísalape' gue'.
'He has lots of money.'

Mífamagu'on i palao'an.
'The woman has lots of children.'

Míchigo' i lemon.
'The lemon has lots of juice.'

The word *michigo'* in the sentence above is usually contracted to *mesgo'*. See section 2.7.4 on Chamorro Vowels and Syllable Structure for the process involved in this sort of contraction.

mina'- Ordinal Marker

| i mina'tres | 'the third |
| i mina'kuatro | 'the fourth' |

pinat- 'have more of'. There is some question as to whether this should be treated as a prefix or as a separate word. It is included here as a prefix.

Stem		*Affixed Form*	
lassas	'skin'	pinatlassas	having more skin'
mames	'sweet'	pinatmames	'having more sweet quality'
ma'asen	'salty'	pinatma'asen	'having more salt'

tai- 'like'

| taiguini | 'like this' |
| taiguenao | 'like that' |

fan. . . an(yan) 'place of'. This affix is part prefix and part suffix. It is known technically as a *discontinuous morpheme*. The allomorph *yan* occurs when the stem ends in a vowel.

fanbinaduyan	'place abounding in deer'
fañochuyan	'eating place'
fano'makan	'shower, bathing place'

-an Attributive Suffix. It is difficult to find an appropriate name for this suffix. It is usually added to nouns. The affixed form then describes something that has attributes or features of the stem. The following examples will illustrate. The stem usually, but not always, takes the infix *-in-*.

Stem		*Affixed Form*
bosbos	'skin rash'	binesbusan 'condition of having skin rash'
chugo'	'sap, juice'	chigu'an 'salty fish sauce'
mugo'	'secretion from eyes'	minigu'an 'having secretion from eyes'
mukos	'mucous'	minikusan 'condition of having mucous'
palao'an	'woman'	pinalao'anan 'effeminate male' or 'having attributes of woman'
pao	'odor'	paguan 'smelly'

NOTE: In the last item the glide *ao* in *pao* undergoes a morphophonemic change when the suffix is added. See section 2.7.4 on morphophonemic changes through Affixation.

-hun Quotative Suffix. Chamorro has a way of showing through affixation whether a statement is one of fact or whether it is information that has been reported to be true. There is really no strong argument for considering it a suffix rather than a free word. For our purposes it will be considered a suffix:

Si Pete gumupuhun.
'It was said that Pete flew.'

Notice, however, that *hun* can be shifted away from the verb, in which case it would not be written as a suffix:

Humanao gue' hun para i gipot.
'He said he went to the party.'

-on (-yon) 'capable of'. Like the preceding suffix, *-on* has an allomorph *-yon* when it follows a stem with a final vowel:

guasa'on	'can be sharpened' or 'sharpener'
falaguyon	'capable of running'
punu'on	'capable of being killed'

-ña Comparative Degree Suffix. This suffix differs from *la-* in that two things are usually compared. The structure word *ki* or *kinu* is also required in the statement, as is shown in the following examples:

Metgotña yo' kinu hagu.
'I am stronger than you.'

Dikike'ña si Rosa kinu si Rita.
'Rosa is smaller than Rita.'

Dankoloña i sapatos-hu kinu i sapatos-mu.
'My shoes are bigger than yours.'

-ñaihon 'for a while'. If the stem ends in a vowel, an extra *n* is inserted before the suffix is added:

sagannaihon	'stay for a while'
falagonñaihon	'run for a while'
asonñaihon	'lie down for a while'

-guan 'unintentionally, covertly'. This prefix covers a range of meaning that is difficult to translate into English:

pinalakse'guan	'slip of the tongue'	(from *palakse'*)
pineddongguan	'accidental fall'	(from *poddong*)
pachaiguan	'touch covertly'	(from *pacha*)
chikongguan	'steal a kiss'	(from *chiku*)

In addition to the derivational prefixes and suffixes, four types of *reduplication* should be included as derivational affixes. The first type serves to convert a verb-like word to a noun. The process is known as *nominalization*. The rule for reduplication for nominalization is to repeat the stressed vowel and preceding consonant (if one it present). The primary stress falls on the first vowel of the reduplicated form. If the vowel of the stem is back, then it gets fronted. The following examples will illustrate:

Root Word		*Reduplicated Form*	
gupu	'to fly'	gigipu	'flyer'

adda′	'mimic'	á′adda′	'mimicker'
kanno′	'eat'	kákanno′	'eater'
tuge′	'write'	títuge′	'writer'

Note to linguists

In the author's opinion, the stressed vowel of the reduplicated form is fronted because the nominalized form is usually preceded by the article *i*. It will be recalled that *i* causes vowel fronting, as in *guma′* 'house', *i gima′* 'the house'. It does not seem feasible to try to account for the vowel fronting as the result of reduplication.

Many of the nominalized forms undergo further reduction, especially when the words are very commonly used. Some examples from the above list will illustrate this process:

gígipu	→	gekpo
kákanno′	→	kakno′
títuge′	→	tekge′

The sequence of rules for this change is as follows:

1. Vowel deletion

gígipu	→	*gigpu
kákanno′	→	*kaknno′
títuge′	→	*titge′

2. Devoicing of voiced consonant at end of syllable
   (Voiced consonant becomes voiceless.)

   | *gigpu | → | *gikpu |

3. Lowering of high vowel in closed syllable

   | *gikpu | → | *gekpu |
   | *titge′ | → | *tetge′ |

4. Lowering of final vowel following CC

   | *gekpu | → | gekpo |

5. Consonant assimilation

   | *tetge′ | → | tekge′ |

The geminate *nn* of **kaknno′* is reduced to a single n̲ to produce *kakno′*.

It should be pointed out that an affixed form of a word can also be nominalized through reduplication. For example, the transitive verb *kanno′* 'to eat' can take the passive voice prefix *ma-*. The affixed form is then *makanno′* 'be eaten' or 'was eaten.'

*Indicates that this form does not occur, but is an intermediate step in the mophophonemic process.

This now forms the stem for reduplication of the initial CV (consonant-vowel). The reduplicated form is *mámakanno'* 'a thing capable of being eaten' or 'an edible.'

The second type of derivational reduplication is noticeably different in form and function. Its function is to intensify the quality of something; it can therefore be called *Intensifier Reduplication*. The rule for forming the intensifier reduplication is to repeat the final CV of the stem. The following examples will illustrate:

Stem		Reduplicated Form	
ñalang	'hungry'	ñálalang	'very hungry'
dánkolo	'big'	dánkololo	'very big'
metgot	'strong'	métgogot	'very strong'
bunita	'pretty'	bunítata	'very pretty'

The third type of derivational reduplication is found in the directional-locative system, and can be called *directional reduplication*. In form, it is like the type described above. The final CV of the stem are repeated. The directional word is always preceded by *giya*:

Root		Reduplicated Form
guatu	'there, in that direction'	guátutu
	Hanao giya guátutu na guma'.	
	'Go to the furthest house.'	
magi	'here, in this direction'	mágigi
	Hanao giya mágigi na guma'.	
	'Go to the nearest house.'	
hulo'	'up'	hululo'
	Gaige giya hululo'.	
	'It is at the very top.'	
kattan		káttatan
	Gaige giya kátatan.	
	'It is at the easternmost place.'	

The fourth type of reduplication is probably related to the previous type. It is called *emphatic reduplication*, and it is used with the negative particle *ni*. The final CV of the stem are repeated:

Ni háyiyi.	'No one else.'
Ni háfafa.	'What else—no other thing'
Ni guáhuhu.	'Not even me.'
Ni ngái'a'an.	'Not even when—never.'
Ni mánunu.	'No matter what place.'
Ni taimánunu.	'No matter how.'

Directional Prefixes. There is a sub-group of derivational affixes that are used exclusively with words of location and direction. They are tied in with the Chamorro directional system, the details of which are not completely understood at this time. These may be considered *directional prefixes.* They are listed below with sample phrases:

ge'-	+ papa'	'down'	→ gé'papa'	'further down'
hat-	+ halom	'in'	→ háttalom	'further in'
san-	+ lagu	'north'	→ sanlagu	'towards north' (or east)
tak-	+ hulo'	'up'	→ tákkilo'	'way up high'
talak	+ huyong	'outside'	→ talakkiyong	'look outside'
ya-	+ guatu	'over there'	→ yaguátutu	'furthest away'

The prefix listed here as *ya-* could very well be considered part of the preposition *giya.* If this is so, then it is probably also found in the article *iya.* The status of *ya* relative to *iya* and *giya* is not entirely clear.

It is possible to have two of these prefixes occurring together with the causative prefix *na'-*, as in the following examples:

na' + la + hat + hulo'	→ na'laháttilo'	'make it higher'
na' + la + ge' + hulo'	→ na'lagé'hilo'	'make it higher'
na' + la + tak + hulo'	→ na'latákkilo'	'make it higher'

Inflectional Affixes. As stated earlier, the primary function of the *inflectional affixes* is to carry pertinent grammatical information. Of course, they also change the meaning to some extent; but, their primary function is grammatical rather than semantic.

In this portion of the grammar the inflectional affixes will be listed, described, and illustrated. Most of them will be discussed further in the section on syntax. Costenoble's grammar gives a fairly long list of items that are labeled affixes. Many of those are not included here because they are not now considered to be true affixes.

-um- Actor Focus Infix. This infix is used when the focus of the sentence is on the actor. (A fuller explanation of the focus system is given in the section on syntax.)

Guahu lumi'e' i palao'an.
'I am the one who saw the woman.

Si Pedro humatsa i lamasa.
'Pedro lifted the table.'

Hayi humatsa i lamasa?
'Who lifted the table?'

-um- Verbalizing Infix. This infix is used with the majority of
Class II words when they function as the predicate. When it is
used it has the apparent effect of converting non-verbs to verbs.
It must also be used with most intransitive verbs when the subject
is singular:

gupu	'to fly'	Gumupu i páharu. 'The bird flew.'
tohge	'to stand'	Tumohge i lahi. 'The man stood up.'
dánkolo	'big'	Dumánkolo i patgon. 'The child became big.'
metgot	'strong'	Mumetgot i lahi. 'The man became strong.'
katpenteru	'carpenter'	Kumatpenteru yo'. 'I became a carpenter.'

This infix *-um-* is also used in constructions that might be described as 'infinitives', as in the following examples:

Malago' yo' lumi'of gi tasi.
'I want to dive in the ocean.'

Hu chagi humatsa i lamasa.
'I tried to lift the table.'

Ya-ña humanao para Saipan.
'He likes to go to Saipan.'

It is very probable that the two infixes listed above are actually one and the same. A very technical, detailed analysis of Chamorro grammar might lead to that conclusion. It is possible to consider both of the infixes an 'action' infix, or something like that,
because whenever it is used the emphasis is on the actor or the
action.

For present purposes we will continue to distinguish between
the Actor Focus infix and the Verbalizing infix *-um-*.

It should be mentioned that the infix *-um-* often appears as
a prefix *mu-* when the stem begins with n, ñ, or ng. Notice the
following examples:

ngelo'	'peep at'	+ -um-	→	mungelo'
nangu	'swim'	+ -um-	→	munangu
na'	'cause'	+ -um-	→	muna'-

Not all speakers follow this pattern which results from *metathesis* of the infix *-um-*. It appears to be more prevalent in Guam than elsewhere.

man- Indefinite Object Marker. This prefix is used in transitive statements when the object is non-specific, or indefinite. When it is prefixed to a stem it causes the morphophonemic change described in section 2.7.1.

> Manli'e' yo' palao'an.
> 'I saw a woman.'

> Mangonne' si Pete guihan.
> 'Pete caught fish.'

> Manokcha' gue' guihan.
> 'He speared fish.'

man- Plural Subject Marker. Although this prefix sounds exactly like the preceding one, it must be considered a different morpheme. It might be considered the plural counterpart of the Verbalizing Infix *-um-*. The prefix *man-* is used with intransitive verbs or verbs with non-specific objects when the subject is plural. This prefix causes the same morphophonemic changes as the preceding one:

> Manggupu i páharu siha.
> 'The birds flew.'

> Manohge i lalahi.
> 'The men stood up.'

> Mandankolo i famagu'on.
> 'The children became big.'

> Manmetgot i lalahi.
> 'The men became strong.'

> Mangatpenteru siha.
> 'They became carpenters.'

It is not uncommon at all for both of the prefixes above to occur together with a single stem when the subject is plural and the object is indefinite:

> Manmanli'e' siha guma'.
> 'They saw a house.'

Manmanokcha' i lalahi guihan.
'The men speared fish.'

-in- Goal Focus Infix. This infix is used in verb constructions that are called Goal Focus. This means that focus of the sentence is on the goal or object of the action. (This will be discussed more fully in the section on syntax.)

'Hafa lini'e'-mu?
'What did you see?'

Hinatsa i patgon ni lahi.
'The man lifted the child.'

Lini'e' i palao'an ni lahi.
'The man saw the woman.'

-in- Nominalizing Infix. This infix is probably the same as the preceding one. A technical grammer of Chamorro would probably show that they both serve the same function, namely to focus attention on the goal. The nominalizing infix is often used to convert verbs to nouns; hence its name. This can be illustrated by the examples below:

Verb		Nominalized Form	
hasso	'think'	i hinasso	'the thought'
faisen	'ask'	i finaisen	'the question'
konne'	'catch'	i kinenne'	'the thing caught'
sangan	'tell'	i sinangan	'the thing told'

In all of the nominalized forms above the noun is the result, or 'goal', of the action of the verb. This is good evidence that the two infixes *-in-* are really one and the same.

-in- Adjectivizing Infix. This infix is also probably related to the Goal Focus infix. When it is affixed to a noun, it converts a noun or verb to a type of modifier, In this respect, *-in-* should be classed as a derivational affix. It is included here because of its obvious relationship to the other infix *-in-*. Some examples of the Adjectivizing Infix are as follows:

Root Word		Infixed Form
palao'an	'woman'	i pinalao'an na lahi 'the womanish man' or 'the man who likes women'
a'paka'	'white'	i ina'paka' na magagu 'the whitish clothes'

poddong	'fall'	i pineddong somnak
		'the setting sun'
somnak	'sunlight'	i sinemnak na tinanom
		'the sunned plant'

The infix -*in*- has some additional functions which have not been described under the three categories of -*in*- listed above. These other functions are not easy to explain, due to a lack of complete understanding of the function of this infix. It appears that all of the forms which include the infix -*in*- are somehow related to its primary function which we are calling *Goal Focus*. This means that whenever the infix -*in*- is used, the "focus" of the statement is on that word which includes the infix: or if -*in*- occurs in the predicate, then the "focus" is on the goal of the action. (One might substitute the word "emphasis" for "focus," although the two do not mean exactly the same thing.)

Look at the following examples which contain the infix -*in*-:

Root Word		Affixed Form
magagu	'clothing'	Minagagu yo'. 'I got dressed.'
sapatos	'shoes'	Sinapatos yo'. 'I put on shoes.'
relós	'watch'	Rinelós yo'. 'I put on a watch.'

The concepts in the above sentences might also be expressed through translation as follows:

Minagagu yo'.
'I was clothed.'

Sinapatos yo'.
'I was shod.'

Rinelós yo'.
'I was wrist-watched.'

To an English speaker these translations seem rather strange. However, they do help show the concept of "goal focus" or "emphasis" on the word containing the infix -*in*-.

Perhaps some additional examples will help illustrate this use of -*in*-:

Root Word		*Affixed Form*
chupa	'tobacco'	Chinipa yo'. 'I smoked.'
guma'	'house'	Ginima' yo'. 'I was housed.'
kareta	'automobile'	Kinareta yo'. 'I went by car.'
batkon aire	'airplane'	Binatkon aire yo'. 'I went by plane.'

kabayu 'horse'   Kinabayu yo'. 'I rode a horse.'
menengheng 'cold'   Minanengheng yo'. 'I was chilled.'

As mentioned before, all of the forms containing the infix *-in-* seem to have something in common which might be loosely termed "goal focus." At the present time we are unable to give explicit rules to explain just how the process works. Perhaps the reason for the author's lack of comprehension is that the conceptualization in Chamorro is so different from conceptualization in English.

na'- Causative Prefix. This prefix is also part of the focus system of Chamorro. It is called Causative because the meaning of it is to cause or allow something to be done:

Na'la'la' i kandet.
'Turn on the light.' (Lit. 'Cause the light to live.')

Hu na'hatsa i lahi ni patgon.
'I caused the man to lift the child.'

Ha na'gasgas i lamasa.
'She cleaned (caused to be clean) the table.'

-i Referential Focus Marker. This suffix also forms part of the focus system of the language. It is called Referential for lack of a more precise term and because it may be translated in more than one way. Notice the following examples:

Sangani yo' ni estoria.
'Tell the story to me.'

Para bai hu apasi hao.
'I will pay you.'

Hu tugi'i si Maria ni katta.
'I wrote the letter to/for Maria.'

The suffix *-i* has two allomorphs, *-yi* and *-gui*. The allomorph *-yi* occurs following stems that end with a vowel or with the diphthong *-ai*:

Hu kantayi si Maria.
'I sang to/for Maria.'

Hu taitayi si Maria.
'I read to/for Maria.'

NOTE: In the last example the stem is *taitai* 'to read'. Before the suffix is added the final glide of the diphthong is deleted. (cf. section 2.1.4 Notes to Linguists, and Topping 1969a.)

The allomorph *-gui* occurs following some stems that end with the consonant ng̲, f̲ or the diphthong ao̲:

Hu huyonggui si Pedro.
'I went out for Pedro.'

Hu li'ofgui i patgon.
'I dived for the child.'

Hu hanagui si Maria.
'I went to Maria.'

NOTE: In the last example the stem is *hanao* 'to go'. Before the suffix is added, the final glide of the diphthong must be deleted. (cf. section 2.1.4 Notes to Linguists, and Topping 1969a.)

At least two verbs with a final nasal consonant take an h̲ before the nasal when this suffix is added. They are:

ason   'lie down'   asohni   'lie down with'
fata'chong 'sit down'   fata'chohngi 'sit down with'

There may be other such verbs which have not yet come to my attention.

-iyi Benefactive Focus Suffix. This suffix also forms part of the focus system in Chamorro. It is called Benefactive because it designates the benefactor of an action, or the person or thing for which the action is performed.

It appears as though this benefactive suffix *-iyi* is in a stage of transition and is not used as much as it once was to distinguish between referential and benefactive focus. The distinction is maintained with certain words, while with other words there appears to be no difference in meaning between the referential focus and the benefactive.

For example, the verb *tuge'* 'to write' takes only the referential focus suffix but could be translated as either referential or benefactive:

Hu tugi'i si Pete ni katta.
'I wrote the letter to Pete' or 'I wrote the letter for Pete.'

The verb kanta 'to sing' is the same.

Hu kantayi si Maria.
'I sang to Maria' or 'I sang for Maria.'

Other verbs, however, take the referential suffix and the benefactive suffix in order to show a rather clear distinction in meaning. Examples are *sangan* 'to tell' and *kuentos* 'to speak'

Hu sangani si Pete ni estoria.
'I told the story to Pete.'

Hu sanganiyi si Pete ni estoria.
'I told the story for Pete (in his stead).'

Hu kuentusi si Pete.
'I talked to Pete.'

Hu kuentusiyi si Pete.
'I talked for Pete (in his stead).'

The similarity of the referential and benefactive suffixes may contribute to the apparent ambiguity. The base forms for the two suffixes are:

-i   Referential
-iyi   Benefactive

The opinion of native speakers is somewhat divided on the use of the benefactive suffix with all verbs. The majority of those consulted seem to feel that the benefactive form is understandable when used with all verbs, but most Chamorro speakers would probably use the referential form *-i* unless there is a need to draw a specific contrast between the referential meaning and the benefactive meaning.

The suffix *-iyi* has the form *-guiyi* following the *ao* diphthong:

Hu hanaguiyi si Pedro.
'I went for Pedro.'

And there is at least one outstanding example of an unpredictable sound change, final *o* to *oi* before the suffix is added. From the word *fatto* 'to come' we get:

Hu fattoiguiyi si Pedro.
'I came for Pedro.'

Reduplication. In addition to the reduplication described under Derivational Affixes, there is another kind of reduplication that belongs under the heading of Inflectional Affix. The rules for its formation are basically the same as those given for the nominalizing reduplication: repeat the stressed vowel and preceding consonant (when there is one present). When inflectional reduplication occurs it changes the *aspect* of the verb to *continuative,* or *progressive.* Contrast the following pairs of sentences:

Sumaga yo' giya Susupe.
'I lived in Susupe.'

Sumásaga yo' giya Susupe.
'I am living in Susupe.'

NOTE: *Sumasaga* also contains the infix *-um-*. The root is *saga*.

Para bai hu saga giya guiya.
'I will stay at his place.'

Para bai hu sásaga giya guiya.
'I will be staying at his place.'

This type of reduplication will be taken up again during the discussion of *aspect*.

ma- Passive Voice Marker. This prefix is used to mark the true passive voice in Chamorro. It is possible that this prefix is the same as the pronoun *ma* 'they'. Notice that the following sentence could have two meanings:

Mali'e' i palao'an.   'They saw the woman.'
                         'The woman was seen.'

It is possible that in Chamorro the pronoun *ma* can be used as an impersonal pronoun, which could also be translated as passive voice. A similar situation is found in English. For example, the following two sentences are very similar in meaning:

They say that smoking is bad for your health.

It is said that smoking is bad for your health.

The first sentence uses the impersonal 'they'; the second uses the true passive construction, also called *extraposition*.

For purposes of clarity in the Chamorro writing system, the pronoun *ma* is written separately, and the passive voice marker is written as a prefix. Thus, we get the following in written Chamorro:

Ma li'e' i palao'an.
'They saw the woman.'

Mali'e' i palao'an.
'The woman was seen.'

ma- Verbalizer. This is possibly the least understood of all the Chamorro affixes, with the possible exception of *-in-*. It is probable that in earlier Chamorro it was a productive verb prefix and its distribution was clearly marked. In modern Chamorro its use is not quite so clear.

The peculiar thing about the verbalizer *ma-* is that it occurs only with certain words. There is no way to predict by general rules which Class II word will take *ma-* as the verbalizer rather than *-um-*. The great majority of Class II words take *-um-* when they occur as predicates. There are also some words—all of which begin with m̲—that take no verbalizing affix (e.g., *matai, magap, matto*). And there are some that simply take *ma-*. Some of these roots that take *ma-* and their affixed forms are given here:

Root Word		Affixed Form	
ta'chong	'seat'	mata'chong	'sit down'
fondo	'bottom'	mafondo	'sink'
haga'	'blood'	mahaga'	'be in heat'
pokkat	'walk'	mamokkat	'walk'
cho'cho'	'work'	macho'cho'	'to work'
udai	'ride'	ma'udai	'to ride'

It is possible that this Verbalizer *ma-* is actually the same morpheme as the Passive Marker *ma-*. One could think of *mata'-chong*, for example, as a form that means 'to be seated', in which case the *ma-* might be considered passive. Such an interpretation would not fit the prefix *ma-* on a word like *macho'cho'* 'to work', because it would be impossible to think of *macho'cho'* as a passive construction. It seems preferable at this point to consider *ma-* a Verbalizer which we would like to know more about.

Additional Problems of *ma-*. The prefix *ma-* appears to have become fossilized in a fairly large number of intransitive verbs and modifiers. That is to say, the *ma-* can no longer be separated and identified as a separate morpheme. The following words probably contain the fossilized prefix *ma-*.

malagu	'run'	makaka	'itch'
malangu	'get sick'	malayu	'wilted'
malago'	'want'	matuhok	'sleepy'
maleffa	'forget'		

Since the above words all have three syllables, and since they all begin with *ma-*, it is tempting to consider *ma-* a separate morpheme, as it is in the words *mata'chong* and *macho'cho'*. However, if we remove the *ma-* from the words listed above, then we are left with meaningless stems, as follows:

*lagu	*leffa	*tuhok
*langu	*kaka	
*lago'	*layu	

Of course, Chamorro does have the words *lagu* 'north, east' and *lago'* 'melt, tear', but these have no relationship in meaning to *malagu* 'run' and *malago'* 'want'. Therefore, we must conclude that they are different morphemes, and that the *ma-* of *malagu* and *malago'* cannot be separated.

There are quite a few words in Chamorro that begin with *ma-*. Many of these present a very interesting problem. The question is this: Is the initial *ma-* a fossilized prefix or not?

For several of the words that begin with *ma-* the answer to this question is probably *no*. We can assume that the word just happens to begin with the sounds represented by *ma-*. Some of these words are:

magap	'to yawn'
matto	'to come'
matai	'to die'
mata	'eye'
mata'	'raw'
maila'	'come'

The initial *ma-* of these words is neither the passive marker nor the verbalizer. It is simply part of the word.

However, there are several other words of two syllables that begin with *ma-* where the *ma-* is clearly a prefix, as in the case of *macho'cho'* and *mata'chong*. The problem is that the prefix is not easy to recognize because of the changes that have taken place in the word after the prefix was added. Look at the examples given below which show the prefix *ma-* plus the stem, followed by the affixed form after it has undergone the sound changes:

Prefix + Stem		Derived Form	
ma + upos	'pass'	ma'pos	'past, went'
ma + ungak	'cause to be off balance'	ma'ngak	'tilt, stagger'
ma + ipe'	'cut open'	ma'pe'	'cracked'
ma + iteng	'break off'	ma'teng	'broken off'

In the above examples, an excrescent glottal stop was inserted between the *ma* and the initial vowel of the stem. Then the initial vowel of the stem was lost. This is a fairly simple sound change.

The following examples will illustrate another type of vowel loss, namely the vowel following the stem-initial consonant:

ma + funot	'squeeze, tighten'	mafnot	'tight'
ma + funas	'erase'	mafnas	'erased'
ma + higef	'crush'	mahgef	'tired'
ma + hulok	'break'	mahlok	'broken'
ma + hulos	'make smooth'	mahlos	'smooth'
ma + pugao	'scatter'	mapgao	'scattered'
ma + tugan	'pick off'	matgan	'pop off, fall off'

There are still quite a few words that show even more drastic sound changes when the prefix is added. Some of these are listed below:

Prefix and Stem		Derived Form	
ma + huchom 'close'		machom	'closed'
(loss of h and u)			
ma + hihot 'near'		ma'i'ot	'narrow'
(loss of both h's)			

The following words show still more drastic sound changes. No attempt is made here to describe the processes involved in the changes, but the reader should be able to analyse the changes that the word has undergone:

ma + tife'	'break off'	mafte'	'broken off'
ma + luño'	'penetrate'	makño'	'sunk in'
ma + upong	'cut off point'	makpong	'blunted'
ma + la'ya	'float'	ma'ya	'floated'
ma + gutos	'break off'	maktos	'snap, break'
ma + lumos	'drown'	matmos	'drowned'

More Fossilized Prefixes. There are still more words in Chamorro that appear to contain a fossilized form of the prefix *ma-*. These words are suspicious because of their phonological structure. Most native Chamorro words have, or used to have, a structure that follows the pattern (C)VCV(C), which shows that most Chamorro root words originally contained two syllables. The first syllable contained a consonant and a vowel, or just a vowel, and the second syllable contained a consonant, vowel, and possibly a final consonant. If the word contained a double consonant in the middle—(C)VCCV(C)—then the double consonant was *geminate*. (cf. 2.4.3 and 2.5.)

When we see Chamorro words that do not follow this basic pattern of consonants and vowels, we have reason to suspect that the word has been derived from a combination of morphemes. For example, the word *mehto* 'lousy' violates the standard pattern because it has two medial consonants that are not geminate. Further analysis shows us that *mehto* is derived from the prefix *mi-* plus *hutu* 'louse'. All of the derived words listed above have been reconstructed. There still remain a number of words that appear to be derived from the prefix *ma-* plus a stem. At the present time, however, they cannot be reconstructed because the original stem has either been lost from the language or has been completely covered up by the sound changes that resulted from affixation.

We must conclude, then, that these words probably contain fossilized prefixes. Some of these words are listed below:

ma'gas	'boss'	ma'lak	'shiny, bright'
mahñao	'change mind'	mangto'	'pulverize'
maktan	'rain gutter'	matmo	'hard rain'
masga	'repentant'	matfos	'balding'
ma'son	'unripe coconut'		

It has been suggested that *mangto'* is derived from *ma-* plus *tutong* 'pound'. If this is so, the sound changes involved are difficult to account for.

It is more likely that all of the above words contain a *fossilized prefix.*

The word *maila'* 'to come' presents a special case by itself. In the imperative form it occurs as *maila'* and *mamaila'*. In the continuative form it is *mamamaila'*, as in *Mamamaila' gue'*. 'He is coming.' The initial *ma* of *mamaila'* is not a verbalizer, as in the case of *mata'chong*; if it were, it and it alone would be used in the imperative form. Neither is the initial *ma-* of *mamaila'* the reduplicated syllable; for the continuative aspect of *maila'*, we must say *mamamaila'* 'be coming'. At this time we must say that the initial *ma-* of *mamaila'* is simply a special case.

Other affixes can also become fossilized. For example, the word *hineksa'* 'cooked rice' probably contains the infix *-in-*, as in the word *nina'i* 'gift' (from *na'i* plus *-in-*). But, if we remove the *-in-* from *hineksa'* we are left with either **heksa'* or **hoksa'*, neither of which means anything in modern Chammorro.

The reconstruction of words with fossilized affixes is a very interesting endeavor. It would carry us into the area of etymology, which is beyond the scope of this book.

Sample Paradigms for Affixes

3.5.4   It might be interesting at this point to take three Chamorro words and show some of the various affixes that each can take. We have selected a transitive verb *sangan* 'to tell, say', an intransitive verb *li'of* 'to dive', and a modifier *lokka'* 'tall'. It may be necessary to put some of the derived forms in the proper context before they sound natural:

sangan

1. Reciprocal Prefix *á-*:	umásangan 'tell about each other'
2. Similative Prefix *achá-*:	achásangan 'tell at same time'
3. Prefix *chat-*:	chátsangan 'didn't tell well'
4. Prefix *fa'-*:	fa'sangan 'to libel'
5. Prefix *gá'-*:	gá' mañangan 'a teller, one who loves to tell'
6. Prefix *há-*:	hásangan 'usually tells'
7. Prefix *ké-*:	késangan 'about to tell'
8. Affix *fan...an*:	fañanganan 'place of telling'
9. Suffix *-on*:	sanganon 'tellable'
10. Suffix *-ñaihon*:	sangañaihon 'tell for a while' or 'gossip'
11. Suffix *-guan*:	sangangguan 'tell secretly'
12. Reduplication (Nom.):	i sásangan 'the teller' (reduces to *i sak- ngan*)
13. Actor Focus Infix *-um-*:	guahu sumangan 'I'm the one who told'

14. Infinitive Infix -*um*-:   sumangan
    'to tell'

15. Indefinite O.M. *man*-:   Mañangan yo' estoria.
    'I told a story.'

16. Plural Subject Marker   Manmañangan siha estoria.
    man-:   'They told a story.'

17. Goal Focus Infix -*in*-:   Sinangan ni lahi i estoria,
    'The man told the story.'

18. Nominalizing Infix -*in*-:   i sinangan
    'the story'

19. Causative Prefix *na'*-:   na'sangan
    'cause to tell'

20. Referential Suffix -*i*:   sangani
    'tell to'

21. Benefactive Suffix -*iyi*:   sanganiyi
    'tell for'

22. Reduplication (Aspect):   sasangan
    'telling'

23. Passive Prefix *ma*-:   masangan
    'was told'

li' of

1. Similative Prefix   acháli'of
    achá-:   'dive simultaneously'

2. Prefix *chat*-:   chátli'of
    'not a good dive'

3. Prefix *fa'*-:   fa'lumi'of
    'pretend a dive'

4. Prefix *ga'*-:   ga'lumi'of
    'one who loves to dive'

5. Prefix *há*-:   hálumi'of
    'usually dives'

6. Prefix *ké*-:   kéli'of
    'about to dive'

7. Prefix *lá*-:   láli'of
    'dive further'

8. Prefix *pinat*-:   pinatlumi'of
    'diving more than'

9. Affix *fan...an*:   fanli'ufan
    'diving place'

10. Suffix -*on*:   li'ufon
    'capable of diving'

11. Suffix -*ñaihon*:	li'ofñaihon 'dive for a while'
12. Suffix -*guan*:	li'ofguan 'diving covertly'
13. Reduplication (Nom.):	lili'of 'diver'
14. Actor Focus Infix -*um*-:	Guahu lumi'of. 'I am the one who dove.'
15. Verbalizing Infix -*um*-:	Lumi'of yo'. 'I dove.'
16. Plural Subject Marker *man*-:	Manli'of siha. 'They dove.'
17. Causative Prefix *na'*-:	na'li'of 'cause to dive'
18. Referential Suffix -*i*:	li'ofgui 'dive to'
19. Benefactive Suffix -*i*:	li'ufi 'dive for'
20. Reduplication (Aspect):	lili'of 'diving'

Lokka'

1. Similative Prefix *achà*-:	achálokka' 'of the same height'
2. Prefix *chát*-:	chátlokka' 'not very tall'
3. Prefix *fa'*-:	fa'lokka' 'pretend to be tall'
4. Prefix *gá'*-:	gá'lokka' 'lover of tall things'
5. Prefix *gé'*-:	gé'lokka' 'taller' (as in na'lage'lokka')
6. Prefix *há*-:	hálokka' 'usually tall'
7. Prefix *lá*-:	lálokka' 'taller'
`8. Prefix *pinat*-:	pinatlokka' 'more of tall things'
9. Suffix -*on*:	lokka'on 'capable of being tall'
10. Suffix -*ña*:	lokka'ña 'taller than'

11. Reduplication (Int.):	lokkaka' 'very tall'	
12. Verbalizer -*um*-:	lumokka' 'become tall'	
13. Plural Subject Marker *man*-:	Manlokka' hit. 'We are tall.'	
14. Nominalizing Infix -*in*-:	linekka' 'the tall thing'	
15. Causative Prefix *na'*-:	na'lokka' 'make tall'	
16. Reduplication (Aspect):	lólokka' 'being tall'	

Combinations of Affixes. Chamorro permits a variety of combinations of affixes with stems. Listed below are a few examples of "words" that have been derived from a single stem plus affixes:

Stem	Affixes	Derived Word
guaha	-in-	guinaha
saga	man-, Reduplication	mañasaga
hatsa	-um-, na'-, -i	muna'hatsayi
guaiya	man-, man-, Redup.	manmangguaguaiya
a'ñao	man-, achá-, ma-, Reduplication	manachachama'a'ñao
hulo'	-um-, na'-, la-, ge'-, -i	muna'lage'hilu'i

Various combinations of affixes with stems are possible in Chamorro. This is one very common method of making up new words in the language.

Other Minor Words.

3.5.5   In addition to the words and affixes discussed thus far, there are several that simply don't fit into any of the other categories. Some of them form single-word sentences; some might be considered *expletives;* some are simply idiomatic.

A partial listing of some of the "other" minor words is given here:

Hu'u	'Yes'
Hunggan	'Yes'
Hekkua'	'I don't know'
Ahe'	'No'

Munga	'Don't, no thanks'
Adahi	'Look out'
Cho	'Whoa'
O'la'~Ohla'	'Oh, hopefully...'
Ásaina	'Oh, Lord'
Si Yu'us Ma'ase'	'Thank you'
Nihi	'Let's'
Laña'	general expletive
Diahlo	'Never mind'
Basta	'Stop, enough, don't'
Naya	'In earlier times'
Ada	'Possible?'
Uhu	'Take it'
Ai di mi...	'Oh my...'

4   Syntax

A description of the syntax of a language is an attempt to describe the rules by which a native speaker makes up sentences from the words of his language. In his syntactic description. the linguist tries to present the syntactic rules of the language as he has observed them. In an ideal language situation the linguist would present a set of rules—perhaps as many as fifty or even a hundred —which would account for all of the ways to make up sentences in a language.

Unfortunately, this ideal goal has never been achieved for any language by any linguist. English has been studied for many, many years by linguists, who have written many, many books about English grammar. And yet there are still many perfectly good English sentences that have not yet been properly analyzed by the linguists.

The major reason for this situation is that language (especially syntax) is an extremely complicated phenomenon. Every human being who is fluent in any language frequently says new things in his language that he has never said or heard before. There are, of course, limits on the innovative things he can do with his language. But the limits are very broad. The linguist who tries to give all of the rules for all of the things that can be said in a language—all of the sentences that are grammatical—faces an impossible task.

In the following discussion of Chamorro syntax we will examine some of the basic syntactic structures and processes of the language. There will no doubt be exceptions to the rules presented here, and there are no doubt many additional rules that could be incorporated. Perhaps a Chamorro grammarian will take up that task some day soon.

202

In the presentation of the topics included in this chapter I have tried in general to proceed from simple grammatical structures to more complex ones as judged from a linguistic point of view. The reader—and especially the native speakers of Chamorro —may disagree with the order in which the topics are presented. In fact, the author has on several occasions been in disagreement with himself about what the most appropriate order would be. The reader should therefore feel free to skip around from one subsection to another to follow his own interests.

THE NOUN PHRASE

4.1   The *noun phrase* (NP) is probably a basic grammatical unit in all languages. The term noun phrase is used to define a structure that contains a noun or nounlike word as a *nucleus*. The nucleus may be considered the "center" or the "headword" of the NP. The headword may or may not have *attributes* or *modifiers*.

(The various terms such as nucleus, center, headword, attribute, and modifier are all used by various linguists. In this discussion of the NP we will use the terms *headword* for "nucleus" and *modifier* for "attribute.")

The NP in Chamorro may consist of any of the following:

$$
NP \;\rightarrow\; \begin{bmatrix} \text{Emphatic Pronoun} \\ \textit{hu}\text{-type Pronoun} \\ \textit{yo}'\text{-type Pronoun} \\ \text{Proper Noun} \\ \text{Common Noun + Modifiers} \\ \text{Other Nominals} \end{bmatrix}
$$

Some examples showing the above types of NP's are given here:

Emphatic Pronoun:	<u>Guahu</u> tumungo' i lahi. 'I am the one who knows the man.'
hu-type Pronoun:	<u>Hu</u> tungo' i lahi. 'I know the man.'
yo'-type Pronoun:	Manungo' <u>yo'</u> lahi. 'I know a man.'
Proper Noun:	<u>Si Maria</u> ha tungo' i lahi. 'Maria knows the man.'
Common Noun:	<u>I palao'an</u> ha tungo' i lahi. 'The woman knows the man.'

Common Noun plus Modifiers:	I bunita na palao'an ha tungo' i lahi. 'The pretty woman knows the man.'

I bunita na palao'an ni machocho'cho' gi banko ha tungo' i lahi.
'The pretty woman who works at the bank knows the man.'

I risuttan i kontrata humuyong dos na pattida.
'The result of the contract brought forth two parties.'

*Other Nominals: Ha na'triste yo' i yinamak-ñiha ni gima'.
'Their destruction of the house made me sad.'

I hinasso-ña muna'manman i pale'.
'His thoughts surprised the priest.'

Malagu i sásake.
'The thief ran.'

I manggaige gi Popular Party mayoria.
'The ones in the Popular Party are the majority.'

I lina'la' i tano'-ñiha
'The life of their land.'

The above examples illustrate types of NP's that have been defined according to their internal structure. We have tried, then, to define what a NP is in Chamorro by describing what it is composed of.

Another way of defining a NP is on the basis of its function. In Chamorro NP's can function as the subject of sentence, object of sentence, object of causative, object of preposition, benefactor, and instrument. Note the NP's in the following sentences:

NP as Subject: I dankolo na lahi ha tungo' i ma'estro-ku.
'The big man knows my teacher.'

Mata'chong i dankolo na lahi.
'The big man sat down.'

Object of
Sentence: Hu tungo' i dankolo na lahi.
'I know the big man.'

Si Maria ha li'e' i dankolo na lahi.
'Maria saw the big man.'

*The "other nominals" will be explained in some detail in Section 4.3.

Object of
   Causative: Hu na'hanao i dankolo na lahi.
                 'I made the big man go.'

                 Hu na'akka' i ga'lagu as Pete.
                 'I made the dog bite Pete.'

In the last sentence above there are two NP's: *i ga'lagu* and *as
Pete*. The first of these—*i ga'lagu*—is the object of the causative;
the second is the object of the sentence.

Object of
   Preposition: Humanao gue' para i tenda.
                 'He went to the store.'

                 Machocho'cho' gue' gi kanton tasi.
                 'He is working at the seashore.'

   Benefactor: Ha sangani yo' ni estoria.
                 'He told the story to me.'

                 Ha sanganiyi yo' ni estoria.
                 'He told the story for me.'

                 Ha sangani i dikike' na famagu'on ni estoria.
                 'He told the story to the little children.'

   Instrument: Ha chachak i kannai-ña ni se'se'.
                 'He cut his hand with a knife.'

                 Ha chachak i kannai-ña ni dankolo na se'se'.
                 'He cut his hand with a big knife.'

Subject Marker ha. In several of the above examples we can see
the subject NP followed by the word *ha*. It is difficult to decide
how this word should be classed. On the one hand, it belongs to
the set of pronouns called the "hu-type" pronouns. We have
said that "hu-type" pronouns can form a NP. On the other hand,
we see that *ha* must occur in addition to a subject NP when the
verb is transitive. The following pair of sentences will help
illustrate the problem: (The subject NP is underlined.)

  1. Ha li'e' i guaka.
     'He saw the cow.'

  2. I patgon ha li'e' i guaka.
     'The child saw the cow.'

In the first sentence *ha* has to function as the subject NP. In the
second sentence *i patgon* is obviously the subject NP. Where does
that leave *ha*? Does it belong to the NP with *i patgon*? If so, our
NP would be *i patgon ha*. Or, does *ha* belong to the *Verb Phrase*

with li'e'? If so, then our analysis of the sentence would be as follows: *ha* would be considered a *Subject Marker* (SM), and would belong to the verb phrase.

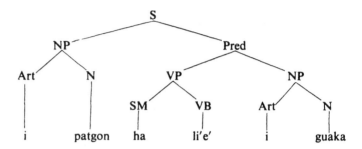

The alternate analysis in which *ha* would form part of the subject NP would be as follows:

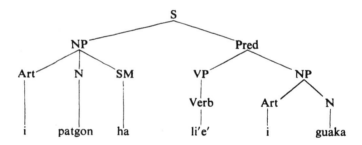

Either interpretation would be possible, but in both cases it seems advisable to give *ha* a special designation. I have chosen to call it a *subject marker*. When it occurs by itself, it should be considered a NP, as the following diagram will show:

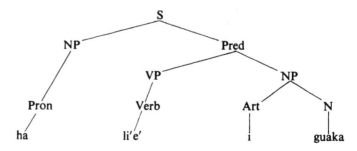

Further analysis of NP's which contain either common nouns or "other nominals" shows that they contain some additional elements such as articles, numerals, demonstratives, and various types of modifiers. Examples of each of these types are given below:

Articles:	i batkon aire	'the airplane'
	ni se'se'	'the knife'
	(as in *Hu na' i i patgon ni se' se'*.)	
Numerals:	un se'se'	'one knife'
	dos se'se'	'two knives'
	tres na se'se'	'three knives'

(Notice that the last example may include the linking particle *na*. Cf. section 3.5.1.)

Demonstratives:	este na lepblo	'this book'
	ayu na lepblo	'that book'
	enao na lepblo	'that book'
Modifiers:	meggai na bi'ahi	'many times'
	i bunita na palao'-an	'the pretty woman'
	i tres na mankon macheng	'the three crippled monkeys'

All NP's that contain proper nouns must include one of the proper articles, which are not translated into English:

Si Pedro	'Pedro'
As Pedro	'Pedro'
iya Saipan	'Saipan'

We might formalize the description of the NP in Chamorro by giving a rule used in modern linguistics:

$$
NP \rightarrow \left[\begin{array}{l} \text{Emphatic Pronoun} \\ \textit{hu}\text{-type Pronoun} \\ \textit{yo'}\text{-type Pronoun} \\ \text{Proper Article} + \text{Proper Noun} \\ \text{Common Article (Modifier} + \textit{na)} \text{ Common Noun} \\ \text{Common Article} + \text{Nominal Phrase} \end{array} \right]
$$

Even this description is not very explicit because we have left the details of the Nominal Phrase unspecified. These will be taken up in Section 4.3.

MODIFICATION

4.2   There are several different types of modification constructions
in Chamorro. Each of them involves a *modifier* and its relationship to its *head* (or nucleus). This aspect of Chamorro grammar
is introduced at this time because many noun phrases include
some type of modifier. Our discussion of modification will go
beyond the noun phrase in order to provide an overview of the
different types of modification in Chamorro.

Modification of Nouns. There are two very common types of
modification structures found in noun phrases. One very common
type can be seen in the following examples where the modifier
precedes the headword:

Modifier + Headword

i dánkolo na taotao	'the big man'
i dikike' na patgon	'the small child'
meggai na bi'ahi	'many times'
i betde na kareta	'the green car'

Notice that when the modifier precedes the headword, the two
words are joined by the *linking particle na*. The modifiers which
always precede the headword are Class II words, and their primary
function is that of a modifier. (It will be remembered from sections
3.3.1 and 3.3.5 that practically any word in Chamorro can function as modifier, noun, or verb. The words listed above are
primarily modifiers, but they may also function as nouns, as in
Matai i dikike' 'The little one died.')
       When the modifier has a final vowel, the linking particle *na*
may be reduced to *n* in rapid speech. Hence, one might hear
such phrases as *i dankolon taotao* or *i buniton kareta*. When this
happens, we can consider the final *-n* a reduced form of the linking particle *na*.
       The other very common modification construction is when
a noun headword is followed by a modifier. In most instances
the following modifier is another noun, but not always. In some
instances one has the choice of placing the modifier before the
headword or following it, as in the following example:

i ekonomia na kareta	'the economical car'
i karetan ekonomia	'the economical car'

Notice that when the modifier follows the headword that ends with a vowel an additional *n* is attached to the headword. The nature of this *n* is discussed in the paragraphs following.

When a headword is modified by another noun, the modifier always follows the headword. Notice the following examples:

Headword + Noun Modifier

i papet aseru	'the sandpaper (paper of steel)'
i gima' Filipino	'the Filipino house'
i relós Amerikanu	'the American watch'
i sapatos lahi	'the men's shoes'

When the headword of this type of modification construction ends with a vowel, *n* is added, as in the following examples:

Headword		*Headword + Noun Modifier*
tenda	'store'	tendan Filipino
		'Filipino store'
saga	'place'	sagan apu
		'ash tray' (place for ashes)
tronko	'tree'	tronkon hayu
		'tree' (of wood)
tommo	'knee'	tommon kannai
		'elbow' (knee of the arm)

The final *n* found in these modification constructions is probably not the same as the *n* found in a phrase such as *i danko-lon kareta*. The final *n* of the headword-noun constructions serves no grammatical function. On the other hand, the particle *na* in the modifier-headword constructions does serve a grammatical function. It links the two parts of the phrase together. In constructions where the headword comes first, no linking particle is required. Hence, the final *n* seems to serve the purpose of making the phrase "sound better." It is similar to the final *n* found in plural possessive constructions such as *lepblon-mami* 'our book', from *lepblo* 'book'. (See section 4.4. below.)

The two major types of modification constructions in which nouns occur as headwords might be described as: (1) modifier + *na* + headword, and (2) headword + noun modifier. In the second type, headwords whose base form ends with a vowel take a final *n*.

Sequence of Modifiers. It should also be noted that nouns can take more than one modifier at a time. When there are several modifiers for a single headword, they usually precede the headword, as in the following examples:

I bunita, guaiyayon yan ti tulaikayon na palao'an
'the beautiful, lovable, and not exchangable woman'

I bibu, bunitu yan guaguan na kareta
'the fast, pretty, and expensive car'

Theoretically there is no limit to the number of modifiers that can occur with a single headword. More than three modifiers would probably seem unusual, though not impossible, to most Chamorro speakers.

There are probably some semantic rules that govern the order of the modifiers. If such rules do exist, one order of modifiers should seem preferable to another. Look at the following four phrases and try to determine whether one of them sounds better than the others:

1. i guaguan, bunitu yan bibu na kareta
2. i bunitu, guaguan yan bibu na kareta
3. i bibu, bunitu yan guaguan na kareta
4. i bunitu, bibu yan guaguan na kareta

Which, if any, of the above phrases sounds most natural? Which sounds least natural? If there is any agreement among native speakers in their answers to the question of naturalness, then there are probably some rules of Chamorro that are functioning. Perhaps emphasis on one of the modifiers would determine which one comes first. No attempt will be made at this time to determine what the rules are.

Modification of Verbs. There are very few words in Chamorro that are strictly limited to the function of modification of verbs. All of the verb modifiers—or *adverbs*, to use the traditional term—also serve to modify sentences. As will be shown, there are certain structural differences when the modifier has a direct relationship to the verb.

Costenoble lists several different types of adverbs. I would classify most of his adverbs differently. For example, under the heading Adverbs of Direction (405) he lists such words as *haya* 'east',* *lagu* 'west', *magi* 'here', and *halom* 'in'. In the present analysis, these words are considered simply location words (cf. 3.4.4). Under Adverbs of Place Costenoble lists such words as *guini* 'here', *guenao* 'there', *hihot* 'near', and *este* 'here' (1940: 406). In the present analysis *guini* and *guenao* are classed as Loca-

*For a discussion of the differences in Chamorro directional terminology see Solenberger 1953.

tives (see 3.4.3), *hihot* as a Location Word (3.4.4), and *este* as a Demonstrative (3.4.2.)

Costenoble (408) lists under Adverbs of Time such words as *hagas* 'long time', *sesso* 'often', *nigap* 'yesterday', and *agupa'* 'tomorrow'. These probably come closer to being "adverbs," or modifiers of verbs, than the other adverbs that Costenoble lists. Since they are all time words, they are usually associated directly with the verb and therefore may be considered modifiers of Verbs.

Costenoble also lists Adverbs of Type and Manner and Adverbs of Modality (pp. 410, 412).

It seems unrealistic to set up a special class of words in Chamorro to be labeled "adverbs" because most of the words listed by Costenoble can function as predicates or modifiers of nouns. I prefer to examine some of the characteristic features of modification of verbs.

The word *chaddek* 'fast, quickly' is often used to modify a verb, as in the following sentence:

Kumuentos <u>chaddek</u> gue'. 'He talked fast.'

However, the modifier *chaddek* can be moved around so that it is at the beginning of the statement, as in:

<u>Chaddek</u> kumuentos gue'.

Or, it can occur at the end of the sentence:

Kumuentos gue' <u>chaddek</u>.

In addition, the modifier *chaddek* can be followed directly by the subject pronoun:

<u>Chaddek</u> gue' kumuentos.

All of the above sentences mean essentially the same thing. The movement of the modifier suggests a slight change in emphasis, but the basic meaning of the sentence remains unchanged.

If the verb (or predicate) ends with a vowel, then there is a significant change in the structure when the modifier immediately follows the verb. Notice the difference in the following set of sentences:

Malagu gue' chaddek.
'He ran fast.'

Malagón chaddek gue'.
'He ran fast.' or 'His running is fast.'

When the modifier immediately follows a verb that ends with a vowel, an *n* is added to the verb. This *n* serves no special grammatical function, but it must be added to the verb. This *n* (which can be called an *excrescent consonant*) serves the same purpose as the final *n* in plural possessive constructions (see 4.4 below) and in the modification constructions where the headword comes before the modifier.

Some additional examples of this final *n* are given here in the following pairs of sentences:

> Ha hatsa i lamasa chaddek.
> 'He lifted the table quickly.'
>
> Ha hatsan chaddek i lamasa.
> 'He quickly lifted the table' or 'His lifting the table was quick.'
>
> Ha pacha i feggon gi kubatde-ña.
> 'He touched the stove timorously.'
>
> Ha pachan kubatde i feggon.
> 'He touched the stove timorously' or 'His touching the stove
> was timorous.'

The alternate translations for the sentences in which the modifier immediately follows the verb suggest that there is a slight difference in meaning, a difference which is not easy to explain.

Modification of Sentences. Sometimes it is difficult to say whether a modifier modifies a single word in a sentence or the entire sentence. In the case of nouns it is pretty easy to see how a particular modifier relates directly to a specific noun, as in the following examples:

Modifier	*Headword*	
i bunita na	palao'an	'the pretty woman'
i dankolo na	ga'lagu	'the big dog'
i mannge' na	nenkanno'	'the delicious food'

Headword	*Modifier*	
i tendan	Filipino	'the Filipino store'
i sapatos	Japanese	'the Japanese shoes'
i tronkon	niyok	'the coconut tree'

However, when the headword is not a noun, the relationship of the modifier to the rest of the sentence is sometimes not easy to determine.

In the sentence *Malagu gue' chaddek* 'He ran fast' we might say that the modifier *chaddek* modifies the sentence *Malagu gue'*.

In the sentence *Malagon chaddek gue'* we might say that *chaddek* modifies the verb *malagu*. And in the sentence *Chaddek malagu gue'* we could say that *chaddek* modifies the following sentence.

Another instance where there is a close relationship between a modifier of a verb and a modifier of the sentence can be seen clearly in the modifier *chatta'* 'hardly, barely'. This modifier has another form *chat* that is used when it clearly modifies a verb. Notice the contrast in the following two sentences:

Verb Modifier: Hu chattokcha' i guihan.
            'I barely speared the fish.'

Sentence Modifier: Chatta' hu tokcha' i guihan.
            'I barely speared the fish.'

These examples, which show slightly different forms of the same word, show the extremely close relationship between modifiers of verbs and modifiers of sentences.

There are other cases where the modifier clearly modifies the sentence rather than any particular part of it. In the examples given below the sentence modifiers are underlined:

Matto gi gipot nigap.
'He came to the party yesterday.'

Todu i tiempo mamaigo' gue'.
'He is sleeping all the time.'

Ensigidas ineppe as Pedro.
'Right away Pedro answered.'

Guaha na bi'ahi na sin sapatos gue'.
'Sometimes he was without shoes.'

Guaha nai manegga' ham TV.
'Sometimes we watch TV.'

Taya' nai kumanta i ma'estra-ku.
'Never did my teacher sing.'

Despues nai hu li'e' i che'lu-hu.
'Then I saw my brother.'

Sentences sometimes function as modifiers of other sentences:

Anai ha li'e' si Taga' este, mama'tinas planu.
'When Taga' saw this, he made a plan.'

Despues anai munhayan este i planu-ña, ha agang i patgon ya
   ha puno'.
'Then when his plan was finished, he called the child and killed
   him.'

Anai matto si Ukudu ginen Guahan gi un galaide', ha sodda' si
Rai Taga'.
'When Ukudu came from Guam by canoe, he found King Taga'.'

The above examples show *complex sentences* which contain
subordinate clauses. In each of the sentences above the subordinate clause comes first and modifies the main clause. Complex
sentences in Chamorro will be discussed in more detail later in
this chapter.

This discussion of modification in Chamorro is not exhaus-
tive. The major types of modification have been illustrated. They
include the following:

Modifier + *na* + Headword
Headword + Modifier
Modifiers of Verbs
Modifiers of Sentences

It was shown in Section 3.3.5 that most words in Chamorro can
function as modifiers. It might be interesting to think of several
different types of modifiers for each of the types of modification
discussed above.

Intensifiers. The modification system of Chamorro includes the
intensifiers of the language. An intensifier strengthens or makes
more intensive the quality of a modifier or a verb. It is usually
translated as 'very' or 'really'.

The three types of intensifiers in Chamorro (which will be
illustrated separately) can be divided into (1) words that precede
the modifier, (2) reduplication, and (3) the particle *ha'*.

gof. The intensifier *gof* usually occurs before a modifier or a sentence as the following examples show:

Gof maolek i lepblo.
'The book is very good.'

Gof baba i gera.
'The war is very bad.'

Hu tungo' i gef malate' na lahi.
'I know the very intelligent man.'

Si Rosa gof malangu.
'Rosa is very sick.'

Gof ya-ña chumocho.
'He likes to eat very much.'

Notice in the third example above the form that occurs is *gef.*

This is an alternate form of *gof* that occurs when preceded by a front vowel (see 2.7.3 on Vowel Harmony).

There are also dialect variants of *gef* and *gof* which are *ges* and *gos.*

The intensifier *gof* (and its alternate *gef*) has combined with certain stems to form compound words whose meanings are not predictable. Some examples of this compounding are:

> gof + mata 'eye' = géfmata 'sharp-sighted'
> gof + saga 'stay' = géfsaga 'wealthy'
> gof + taotao 'person' = géftao 'unselfish'
> gof + li'e' 'see' = gófli'e' 'to like'
> gof + lamen 'injure' = góflamen 'agreeable'

(All of the above compound forms are pronounced with the stressed o and stressed e.)

sen. The intensifier *sen* is very similar in meaning to *gof*, and in some instances they may be used interchangeably, as in:

> Gof bunita i palao'an.   'The girl is very pretty.'
> Sen bunita i palao'an.

The major difference in the two words is that *sen* suggests a stronger degree of intensification.

Both *gof* and *sen* can take the verbal affixes *-um-* and *man-*. When this happens, the two words take on characteristics of a predicate, as in the following sentences:

> Gumof bunita i palao'an.
> 'The girl became very pretty.'
>
> Manggof magof siha.
> 'They became very happy.'
>
> Sumen bunita i palao'an.
> 'The girl became very pretty.'
>
> Mansen magof siha.
> 'They became very happy.'

NOTE: Ordinarily when the prefix *man-* is affixed to a stem with an initial s, consonant assimilation takes place, as in *man + saga→mañaga*. For some unexplainable reason the expected assimilation does not occur in the form *mansen*. One possible explanation is that *sen* is really a prefix and is therefore not subject to the morphophonemic rule of consonant assimilation (see section 2.7.1).

Reduplication. Another type of intensifier is the reduplication of the final consonant and vowel of a modifier. This can also be translated by 'very' or 'really.'

> Dánkololo i lahi.
> 'The man is really big.'

> Bunitata i palao'an.
> 'The woman is very pretty.'

If the stem ends with a consonant, it is not included in the reduplication:

> Dikikike' i patgon.
> 'The child is really small.'

> Ñalalang i ga'lagu.
> 'The dog is very hungry.'

For extra emphasis the final CV may be repeated more than once:

> Dikikikike' i patgon.
> 'The child is very, very small.'

The number of times a syllable can be repeated for emphasis is partly a matter of one's own speaking style.

ha'. The intensifier *ha'* has a slightly wider range of meaning than the preceding intensifiers, and it occurs immediately following the word or phrase to which it is related. The following sentences will illustrate the range of meaning of the intensifier *ha'*:

> Maolek ha' i che'cho'-ña.
> 'His work is o.k.'

> Hu tungo' ha' i planu.
> 'I already know the plan.'

> Si Juan ha' humanao para Guam.
> 'Juan alone went to Guam.'

> I che'lu-ña ha' hu tungo'.
> 'I know only his brother.'

> Hafa ha' un espipiha?
> 'Just what are you looking for?'

> Kao enao ha' malago'-mu?
> 'Is that all you want?'

> Hagas ha' hu tungo' hao.
> 'I've known you for a long time.'

maisa. The word *maisa* may not really belong to the group of words that we are calling intensifiers. It is included here because it seems to have a close semantic relationship to *ha'*. The primary meaning of *maisa* is 'alone' or 'oneself'. It can be used along with the intensifier *ha'*. The following examples will illustrate the use of *maisa*: (Incidentally, the word *masia* in Ilocano is the number 'one'.)

> Ha fa'tinas maisa gue'.
> 'It makes itself.'
>
> Hu li'e' yo' na maisa.
> 'I saw myself alone.'
>
> Humanao maisa gue'.
> 'He went alone.'
>
> Humanao gue' na maisa.
> 'He went alone.'
>
> Guiya ha' na maisa humanao.
> 'Only he alone went.'

Notice that the last sentence includes both *ha'* and *maisa*. The use of both of these words emphasizes the fact that the person was the only one who went.

Comparative. Another type of construction that should be included as a type of modification is the *comparative* structure. This is used when one of the things being compared possesses a certain quality to a greater extent than another thing. When the two things that are being compared are included in the statement there are two morphemes in the construction. They are the suffix *-ña* and the word *kinu* or *ki*. Since they do not occur together they are called *discontinuous morphemes*. The following sentences will illustrate:

> Metgotña yo' kinu hagu.
> 'I am stronger than you.'
>
> Dikike'ña si Rosa kinu si Rita.
> 'Rosa is smaller than Rita.'
>
> Chaddekña hao chumocho kinu guahu.
> 'You are faster at eating than I am.'

Quite often the second item in the comparative construction is omitted when the thing that is being compared is obvious. See the following examples:

> Ga'o-ña i Jeep sa' metgotña.
> 'He prefers the Jeep because it is stronger.'
>
> Ga'o-ku este na guma' sa' dankoloña.
> 'I prefer this house because it is bigger.'

NOMINALIZATION

4.3   The term *nominalization* is used to describe the process whereby
a word, a phrase, or even a sentence can be made to function like
a noun.

Earlier in the section on nouns (3.3.3) some general rules
were given on the identification of nouns. The first rule is that if
a word occupies a position in the sentence that can be designated
"subject of sentence" or "object of sentence," it can then be
classed as a noun. It is also possible, of course, to find a phrase
or even a sentence functioning as the subject or object of a sentence. When this happens, we can say that the phrase or sentence
has been *nominalized.*

We might also expand the functions of the nominalized forms
to include the following: indirect object of the verb, object of
preposition, and object complement.

In Section 3.3.5 on Changing Parts of Speech it was shown
how various types of words can be changed through affixation
to function like nouns. When a word has been changed to a noun,
we can say that if has been *nominalized.* These processes will be
reviewed briefly here. The root word used here is *konne'* 'to catch'.

> Infix: konne' + -in- → i kinenne'
>   'the thing that was caught'
>   konne' + -um-→ i kumonne'
>   'the one that caught'
>
> Reduplication: i kékenne'
>   'the catcher'
>
> Prefix: i gá'mangonne'
>   'the one that loves to catch'
>   i mámakonne'
>   'the catchable thing'

NOTE: In the two forms illustrating the prefix form of nominalization, more than one prefix has been included. In the first form
gá'mangonne' the Indefinite Object Marker *man-* has also been
prefixed to the root word *konne'*. In the second example *màma-
konne'* the passive marker *ma-* has been added to the stem word
konne' to form *makonne'* 'be caught'. The word *makonne'* now
forms the stem for reduplication of the initial CV. The reduplicated form is *mámakonne'* 'a thing capable of being caught'
or 'catchable thing.'

The examples above all show the nominalized form occurring
with the article *i.* This is not coincidental. In fact, it could be
argued that the affixes have nothing to do with the process of

nominalization. Another way to look at this phenomenon is that it is the article *i* that performs the function of nominalization, not the affix that is used.

It is also possible to nominalize sentences. When this happens, entire sentences are converted so that they function like nouns. The sentences become noun phrases. There are various ways by which sentences can be nominalized. Some of the processes will be examined here. We will not go into a detailed analysis of how every step in the process is made. Three types of nominalized sentences will be considered: stative sentences, intransitive sentences, and transitive sentences.

Nominalized Stative Sentence. A *stative sentence* is one which contains a comment and a topic, but no verb. The stative sentence used for illustration here is *Dankolo si Juan* 'Juan is big.' This sentence can be nominalized by one of the following processes:

Nominalized Phrase	*Nominalized Phrase in Sentence*
i dinankolon Juan	I <u>dinankolon Juan</u> ha na'manman yo'.
	'Juan's bigness surprised me.'
i dinankolo-ña si Juan	I <u>dinankolo-ña si Juan</u> ha na'-manman yo'.
	'Juan's bigness surprised me.'
i dumankolon Juan	I <u>dumankolon Juan</u> ha na'man-man yo'.
	'Juan's development (becoming big) surprised me.'
i dumankolo-ña si Juan	I <u>dumankolo-ña si Juan</u> ha na'-manman yo'.
	'Juan's state of development surprised me.'

There are slight differences of meaning among the various forms of the nominalized sentence that are not made clear in the English translation.

Each of the nominalized sentences contains an infix; two of them also contain the possessive pronoun *-ña*. When the modifier ends with a vowel (as in *dankolo*), an *n* is added. This is probably the same *n* that we saw in the discussion of modification.

Nominalized Intransitive Sentences. An *intransitive sentence* is one that contains an intransitive verb as the predicate. The intransitive sentence used for illustration here is *Maigo' si Juan* 'Juan slept.' This sentence can be nominalized in the same way that stative sentences can be nominalized:

Nominalized Phrase	*Nominalized Phrase in Sentence*
minaigo' Juan	Kao un tungo' pot <u>i minaigo' Juan</u>? 'Did you know about Juan's sleeping?'
i minaigo'-ña si Juan	Kao un tungo' pot <u>i minaigo'-ña si Juan</u>? 'Did you know about Juan's sleeping?'
i mumaigo' Juan	<u>I mumaigo' Juan</u> ha na'manman yo'. 'Juan's sleeping surprised me.'
i mumaigo'-ña si Juan	<u>I mumaigo'-ña si Juan</u> ha na'manman yo'. 'Juan's sleeping surprised me.'

The English translations do not convey the subtle differences in meaning of the different nominalized sentences.

Nominalized Transitive Sentences. A transitive sentence is one that contains a subject and an object. When a transitive sentence is nominalized the subject or the object may be omitted. For the purpose of illustrating the types of nominalization that can take place using transitive sentences, we will use the statement *Ha gimen i taotao i tiba* 'The man drank the tuba.'

Nominalized Phrase	*Nominalized Phrase in Sentence*
i gígimen na taotao	Hu tungo' <u>i gígimen na taotao.</u> 'I know the drinking man.'
i gumimen i tiba	Hu tungo' <u>i gumimen i tiba.</u> 'I know the one who drank the tuba.'
i magimen na tuba	Hu li'e' <u>i magimen na tuba.</u> 'I saw the tuba that was drunk.'
i magimen i tiba	<u>I magimen i tiba</u> ha na'magof yo'. 'The drinking of the tuba made me happy.'
i ginimen i taotao	Hu li'e' <u>i ginimen i taotao.</u> 'I saw the thing that was drunk by the man.'

| i ginimen-ña tuba i
taotao | <u>I ginimen-ña tuba i taotao</u> ha na'
magof i che'lu-ña.
'The man's drinking of the tuba made
his brother happy.' |

If we replace the subject *i taotao* with the proper name *Juan*, we can add still another example of nominalization:

| i ginimen Juan ni tiba | <u>I ginimen Juan ni tiba</u> ha na'triste
i che'lu-ña. 'Juan's drinking of the
tuba saddened his brother.' |

If you look closely at the nominalized phrases you will see such things as the infixes -*in*- and -*um*- reduplication, and the prefix *ma*-. A good question (which we will not try to answer here) is: When the affixes occur in nominalized phrases, do they have the same grammatical significance as they have when they occur in regular sentences?

There are possibly other types of nominalization that can be found in Chamorro. Any phrase that can function as the subject of a sentence is probably a nominalized sentence. The reader is invited to think of additional examples.

POSSESSION

4.4 Possession in Chamorro is highly regular and relatively simple. The *possessive pronouns*, which were discussed in section 3.4.1, are used in most possessive constructions. The possessive pronouns of Chamorro are listed again here:

	1st	-hu	'my'
Singular	2nd	-mu	'your'
	3rd	-ña	'his, her'
	1st incl.	-ta	'our inclusive'
	1st excl.	-mami	'our exclusive'
Plural	2nd	-miyu	'your-2 or more'
	3rd	-ñiha	'their-2 or more'

When one of these pronouns is affixed to a stem, the primary stress of the affixed form is moved to the penultimate syllable, as the following examples illustrate:

lápes	lapés-hu	'my pencil'
lamása	lamasá-ña	'his table'
gúma'	gima'-mámi	'our house'

If the stem has a medial consonant cluster and ends with a vowel the allomorph -*ku* occurs in place of -*hu*:

tommo	tommo-ku	'my knee'
lepblo	lepblo-ku	'my book'
katta	katta-ku	'my letter'

If the stem ends with a vowel, and if the possessive pronoun is -*mami*, -*miyu* or -*ñiha*, the excrescent consonant *n* must be added to the stem:

kareta	karetan-mami	'our car'
lepblo	lepblon-miyu	'your book'
tata	tatan-ñiha	'their father'

When the possessor can be expressed by a pronoun, the possessive pronoun is usually affixed directly to the noun. Notice the following sentences:

Si Juan ha sodda' i gima'-ña.
'Juan found his house.'

Si Maria ha taitai i lepblo-ña.
'Maria read her book.'

I famagu'on ma gimen i lechen-ñiha.
'The children drank their milk.'

Possessive Nouns. When a noun is the possessor there are two grammatical forms that may occur. One of these forms involves using the third person possessive pronoun (singular or plural) as in the above examples, followed by the possessor noun. The following examples illustrate this type of possessive construction:

i gima'-ña si Rosa
'Rosa's house'

i lepblo-ña i estudiante
'the student's book'

i malago'-ñiha i taotao
'the people's wish'

i lahi-ña si Pedro
'Pedro's son'

The other form that can occur when a noun is the possessor is sometimes called the *construct form*. This form does not use the possessive pronouns, but it does involve the final excrescent *n* that we saw earlier in the modification constructions such as *tendan Filipino.* This excrescent *n* occurs when the possessed noun stem ends with a vowel. The construct form of the possessive is probably used more frequently than the full form which uses the possessive pronoun and the noun. The following examples will illustrate the differences between the full possessive form and the construct form:

Full Possessive Form	*Construct Form*
i gima'-ña si Rosa	i gima' Rosa
i lepblon-ña i estudiante	i lepblon estudiante
i malago'-ñiha i taotao	i malago' taotao
i lahi-ña si Pedro	i lahen Pedro
i haga-ña i rai	i hagan rai

There is probably a degree of difference in meaning between the full possessive form and the construct form, but the difference is difficult to translate. For example, the phrase *i gima'-ña si Rosa* might be translated as 'Rosa's house', while *i gima' Rosa* might be translated as 'the house of Rosa' and might be used when one is talking about the house as a location rather than as something that belongs to Rosa.

Possession with Classifiers. The *classifiers* of Chamorro were discussed earlier in section 3.5.0. They are often used in possessive constructions when the thing possessed is animal, edible, inanimate, or drinkable. The classifiers are listed again here:

na'	'edible things'
ga'	'non-human animals'
iyo	'inanimate objects'
gimen	'drinkable things'

Of these four classifiers the first three are commonly used, the last one much less so.

The use of *na'* and *ga'* is obligatory in possessive constructions. One does not say **i mannok-ku* for 'my chicken'. The statement would have to be made in one of the following ways:

i na'-hu mannok	'my chicken (to eat).
i ga'-hu mannok	'my chicken (pet).

The classifiers will take all of the possessive pronouns, as the following paradigm will show:

Guaha na'-hu guihan.
'I have a fish (to eat).'

Guaha na'-mu guihan.
'You have a fish.'

Guaha na'-ña guihan.
'He has a fish.'

Guaha na'-ta guihan.
'We have a fish.'

Guaha na'-mami guihan.
'We (excl.) have a fish.'

Guaha na'-miyu guihan.
'You (pl.) have a fish.'

Guaha na'-ñiha guihan.
'They have a fish.'

The other classifiers—*ga'*, *iyo* and *gimen*—also follow this paradigm.

The classifier *iyo* is possibly being used less in modern Chamorro than in earlier times. It is still commonly used in many places in the sense of 'belongs to'.

Iyo-ku i lepblo.
'The book belongs to me.'

Iyo-ña ayu na guma'.
'That house belongs to him.'

Iyon-mami na lepblo enao.
'That book belongs to us.'

When *iyo* is followed directly by a noun, the excrescent *n* must be used:

iyon tasi	'belonging to the sea'
iyon lahi	'belonging to the man'
iyon tano'	'belonging to the earth' or 'terrestrial'
iyon langet	'belonging to the sky' or 'heavenly'

Possessive Pronouns as Subject. In certain constructions the possessive pronouns are used as actor of the sentence. It was pointed out in section 3.3.2 that certain verbs always take the possessive pronouns as subject pronoun when used in the non-future tense. They are *ya-*, *alok* and *ga'o*:

Ya-hu chumocho.
'I like to eat.'

Ilek-hu "no".
'I said "no".'

Ga'o-ku guihan.
'I prefer fish.'

The possessive pronouns are also used as subject pronouns in many questions which contain either *hafa* or *hayi* as the question word. Some sample questions will illustrate:

Hafa lini'e'-mu?
'What did you see?'

Hafa malago'-mu?
'What do you want?'

Hafa bidada-ña?
'What is he doing?'

Hafa guinahan-miyu?
'What do you have?'

Hayi lini'e'-mu?
'Who did you see?'

Hayi inatatan-mu?
'Who are you taking care of?'

Some of the above questions could be phrased differently without using the possessive pronouns. The meaning, of course, is somewhat different. Contrast the following sets of sentences:

Hafa un li'e'?
'What did you see?'

Hafa lini'e'-mu?
'What was it that you saw?'

Hafa un hatsa?
'What did you lift?'

Hafa hinatsa-mu?
'What was it that you lifted?'

It will be noticed that the questions that can be phrased two different ways take the infix -*in*- when the possessive pronoun functions as subject. This is the *Goal Focus Infix* which will be taken up later in this chapter. The important thing to notice here is that when the Goal Focus Infix is used, the possessive pronoun form is obligatory.

VERBALIZATION

4.5   Verbalization is the name given to the process of converting a noun (or nounlike word) to a verb. The resulting verb is almost always intransitive. This process was partly described in sections 3.3.2 and 3.3.5. The process of *verbalization* will be reviewed here again.

Verbalizer-um-. Almost any noun can be converted to a verb-like word—a word that can function as a predicate—by adding the verbalizing infix -*um*-. Some examples that show this conversion are given here:

Root Word		Affixed Form
metgot	'strong'	Mumetgot i lahi.
		'The man became strong.'
saga	'place'	Sumaga yo' gi gima'.
		'I stayed at the house.'
pulan	'moon'	Pumulan i palao'an.
		'The woman had her menses.'
tasi	'sea'	Tumasi i bayineru.
		'The sailor went to sea.'
halom	'into'	Humalom i patgon gi eskuela.
		'The child went into the school.' or
		'The child started school.'

Plural Verbalizer man-. When the subject is plural, the plural verbalizer *man*- is used in place of -*um*-. The above sample sentences are given here with plural subjects:

Manmetgot i lalahi.
'The men became strong.'

Mañaga siha gi gima'.
'They stayed at the house.'

Manasi i bayineru siha.
'The sailors went to sea.'

Manhalom i famagu'on gi eskuela.
'The children went to school.'

Verbalizer -ma-. It was shown in section 3.5.3 that certain words take *ma*- as the verbalizer instead of -*um*-. There seems to be no way to determine why certain words take *ma*- instead of -*um*-. The words that take *ma*- will have to be considered as belonging to a special irregular paradigm. Some of the root words that take the verbalizer *ma*- are repeated here:

Root Word		Affixed Form	
ta'chong	'seat'	Mata'chong yo'.	'I sat down.'
fondo	'bottom'	Mafondo gue'.	'He sank.'
cho'cho'	'work'	Macho'cho' gue'.	'He worked.'
udai	'ride'	Ma'udai yo'.	'I rode.'

When the above affixed forms are made plural, the prefix *man-* is added to the affixed form:

> Manmata'chong siha.
> 'They sat down.'
>
> Manmafondo i famalao'an.
> 'The women sank.'
>
> Manmacho'cho' i lalahi.
> 'The men worked.'
>
> Manma'udai i famagu'on.
> 'The children rode.'

The verbalization process is applied when one wishes to form a verblike predicate from a noun or other part of speech. The verbalizer is also found in constructions that might be called *infinitives*. Some examples with the verbalized forms underlined are given here:

> Malago' yo' macho'cho'.
> 'I want to work.'
>
> Ti siña yo' mata'chong.
> 'I can't sit down.'
>
> Ya-ña pumeska.
> 'He loves to go fishing.'
>
> Ti siña yo' humuyong.
> 'I can't get out.'
>
> Manmalago' siha manma'udai.
> 'They want to ride.'

Other Verb Forming Affixes. Some of the other affixes that were discussed in section 3.5.3 might be considered verb forming affixes because they can convert non-verbs to verblike words. However, they cannot be placed in the same class of affixes with *-um-* and *ma-* for the following reason: in certain syntactic environments where the "infinitive" construction discussed above is required, the verbalizing infix *-um-* (or some form of it) must occur in addition to another affix.

For example, the prefix *e-* 'hunt for' is a verb forming affix because it can convert a noun to a verblike word, as in the following example:

> panglao 'crab'   Épanglao na dos.
>   'You two go look for crabs.'

However, in sentences where the infinitive construction is used, the verbalizing infix *-um-* is also required:

Malago' yo' umepanglao.
'I want to go crab-hunting.'

Some other affixes that might be included in the class of verb forming affixes are included here:

na'-	+ gasgas	'clean'	→	na'gasgas	'to clean'
fa'-	+ baba	'bad'	→	fa'baba	'deceive'
fama'-	+ taotao	'man'	→	fama'taotao	'act like a man'

THE VERB PHRASE

4.6   In section 3.3.2, Verbs in Chamorro, we saw the various types of affixes that occur with verbs. We have also seen how other types of words can be converted to verbs by using different affixes. In this section we will examine the *verb phrase* in Chamorro. To try to discuss every conceivable verb pattern in Chamorro would not be feasible. Hence, for the purposes of this discussion we will select basic types of verb phrases that are found in Chamorro.

Like the noun phrase (cf. 4.1), the verb phrase has a headword (or nucleus), which is usually some type of verb. The verb phrase may also contain some additional items, depending on the kind of verb that is used as the headword. There are five basic types of headword that are found in the verb phrase. These will be examined separately.

Transitive Verb Phrase. A transitive verb phrase has a transitive verb as its headword. A transitive verb is defined here as one that takes a *hu*-type subject pronoun and a specific object. Some verbs that fit this description of transitive are *li'e'* 'see', *pacha* 'touch', *hatsa* 'lift', and *tuge'* 'write'. To illustrate an expanded transitive verb phrase we will use the verb *tuge'*.

The minimum transitive verb phrase must include a transitive verb and a noun phrase. This can be expressed by the following rule (which is followed by a sample sentence.):

$VP \rightarrow V_t + NP$

Hu <u>tuge'</u> i katta.
'I wrote the letter.'

This minimum transitive verb phrase can be expanded by including different types of modifiers. For example, we could add a modifier of location:

VP→V$_t$ + NP + Loc.

Hu tuge' i katta gi eskuela.
'I wrote the letter at school.'

The VP could also be expanded by adding an adverb (or modifier) of manner (abbreviated as Mod$_{Man}$). The preferred position for this modifier of manner is before the NP. We can show this in our rule by placing the Mod$_{Man}$ before the NP, or we could show it following the NP, and later change its position by a Transformational Rule. For the present, we will show the modifier of manner occurring in our rule before the object NP:

VP→V$_t$ + Mod$_{Man}$ + NP

Hu tuge' chaddek i katta.
'I wrote the letter quickly.'

And the VP can also be expanded by adding a modifier of time:

VP→V$_t$ + NP + Mod$_{Time}$

Hu tuge' i katta nigap.
'I wrote the letter yesterday.'

It is possible, of course, to include all three types of modifiers in an expanded transitive verb phrase:

VP→V$_t$ + Mod$_{Man}$ + NP + Loc + Mod$_{Time}$

Hu tuge' chaddek i katta gi eskuela nigap.
'I wrote the letter at school quickly yesterday.'

Since the modifiers are all optional in the VP we can show this in our rule by placing the modifiers in parentheses. Whenever anything is put in parentheses in a grammar rule it is considered optional. Our rule for the transitive verb phrase will now look like this:

VP → V$_t$ (Mod$_{Man}$) + NP (Loc) (Mod$_{Time}$)

This rule simply states that a transitive verb phrase in Chamorro contains an obligatory transitive verb and noun phrase. It may also contain optional modifiers of location, manner, and time.

How many other transitive verb phrases do you think can be constructed following this formula?

NOTE: All transitive verbs in Chamorro can be "de-transitivized" by the prefix *man-*. This will be taken up later in the discussion of Definite-Indefinite Object Constructions. It is also important to remember that the modifier of manner can be shifted around to different places within the VP, and can also be shifted to a position where it becomes a sentence modifier.

Defective Verb Phrase. The term *defective verb* is used here to describe a subgroup of transitive verbs that do not follow the same syntactic patterns as the regular transitive verbs. They are all listed among the Irregular Verbs in section 3.3.2. The *defective verbs* which can also be considered transitive verbs are as follows:

gai	'have'
tai	'not have'
guaha	'have'
taya'	'not have'
alok	'say'
ga'o	'prefer'
ya	'like, prefer'
iyo	'belong to'

Each of these defective verbs can take an object NP and the modifiers of location, manner, and time. They differ from the transitive verb phrases in the way that the subject and object are expressed. Contrast the following sentences:

Transitive Verb	Hu pacha i salape'.	'I touched the money.'
Defective Verbs	Guaha salape'-hu.	'I have money.'
	Gai salape' yo'.	'I have money.'
	Ga'o-ku salape'.	'I prefer money.'

Each of the above sentences can take modifiers in the VP. See if each of the defective verbs can take the modifiers of location, manner, and time.

The rule for the Defective Verb Phrase can be expressed like this:

$$VP \rightarrow V_{def} + NP \ (Loc) \ (Mod_{Man})(Mod_{Time})$$

Intransitive Verb Phrase. The major difference between the intransitive verb phrase and the ones already discussed is that the intransitive verb does not take an object NP. The intransitive verb can, however, take the modifiers of location, manner, and time. Some examples of intransitive verb phrases are given below.

NOTE: Even though the subject NP appears following the headword, it should not be considered as part of the VP.

Malagu gue' para i eskuela chaddek nigap.
'He ran to the school quickly yesterday.'

Mamokkat yo' ginen Susupe despasio nigap.
'I walked from Susupe slowly yesterday.'

Humalom yo' gi gima' listo gi painge.
'I went into the house quickly last night.'

The rule for the intransitive verb phrase can be expressed by the following formula:

$$VP \rightarrow V_{int} \ (Loc) \ (Mod_{Man}) \ (Mod_{Time})$$

(It is understood at this point that the subject NP follows the intransitive verb in the non-future tense. The subject NP does not appear in our formula for the intransitive verb phrase).

Existential Verb Phrase. The existential verb phrase is different from the intransitive verb phrase because the *existential verbs* do not take the same affixes as the other intransitive verbs. There are two existential verbs, *gaige* 'be, exist' and *estaba* 'used to be'. (These verbs are also listed under Irregular Verbs in section 3.3.2.)

The existential verb phrases can take the modifiers of location and time, and perhaps some adverbs of manner. The existential verbs differ from the regular intransitive verbs because they will not take the affixes *-um-* or *ma-*. The following sentences illustrate the existential verb phrases:

Gaige gue' gi eskuela pa'go.
'He is at school now.'

Estaba yo' giya Rota gi ma'pos na sakkan.
'I used to be in Rota last year.'

The formula representing the existential verb phrase is:

$$VP \rightarrow V_{ex} \ (Loc) \ (Mod_{Time})$$

Adjective Phrase. The *adjective phrase* is included here in the discussion of verb phrases because the adjective in Chamorro can function as the predicate of a sentence. The adjective phrase is very similar to an intransitive verb phrase except that it will not take the modifier of manner. The adjective phrase can, however, take an intensifier. Following are some examples of adjective phrases as predicates:

Maolek i taotao.
'The man is good.'

Dánkolo i lepblo.
'The book is big.'

Gof yommok i ma'estro.
'The teacher is very fat.'

The rule for the various types of verb phrases in Chamorro can be summarized by the following representation:

$$
VP \rightarrow \left\{ \left\{ \begin{matrix} \begin{Bmatrix} V_T \\ V_{def} \end{Bmatrix} + NP \\ \begin{Bmatrix} V_{int} \\ V_{ex} \\ Adj. \end{Bmatrix} \end{matrix} \ (Mod_{Man}) \right\} \ (Loc) \ (Mod_{Time}) \right\}
$$

This formulaic representation states that a verb phrase can have any one of the five types of headwords: the transitive verb, defective verb, intransitive verb, existential verb, or adjective. If the verb is transitive or defective, it must take a NP object. All of the verb phrases except those containing an adjective may take a modifier of manner. All the verb phrases may take the modifiers of location and time.

We will see later in the section on embedded sentences that some verb phrases include another sentence. For the time being, the above description will account for most of our basic verb phrases. The reader can probably think of many examples of verb phrases that don't follow our rules. Those exceptions will be better understood when we examine the section on the focus system of Chamorro.

PLURALIZATION

4.7   The Chamorro grammar system shows the difference between plural and non-plural among the verbs, nouns, and pronouns, and in some cases the adjectives. Notice that the distinction made here is between plural and non-pural rather than between plural and singular. This is because Chamorro also distinguishes between dual and plural in the verb system.

Plural of Intransitive Verbs and Adjectives. All of the intransitive verbs, existential verbs, and adjectives (when they form a predicate) take the plural marking prefix *man-* when the subject is plural, i.e. three or more. If the subject is singular or dual the plural marker is not used. The following examples will illustrate:

Singular:
    Humanao yo' para Saipan.
    'I went to Saipan.'

Gaige yo' gi banko.
'I am at the bank.'

Mumagof yo' gi gipot.
'I became happy at the party.'

Dual:
Humanao siha para Saipan.
'They (2) went to Saipan.'

Gaige siha gi banko.
'They (2) are at the bank.'

Mumagof siha gi gipot.
'They (2) became happy at the party.'

Plural:
Manhanao siha para Saipan.
'They went to Saipan.'

Manggaige siha gi banko.
'They are at the bank.'

Manmagof siha gi gipot.
'They became happy at the party.'

Transitive verbs do not take any plural marking affixes when the object of the verb is definite. However, when the object is not definite, the plural marking prefix must be used when the subject is plural. Notice the following set of sentences. In the first sentence the object of the verb is definite; in the second sentence the object of the verb is not definite:

Definite Object:
Ma li'e' i gima'.
'They saw the house.'

Indefinite Object:
Manmanli'e' siha guma'.
'They saw a house.'

Notice that the verb in the second sentence has two prefixes which sound and look the same. They must be interpreted as two separate prefixes. One of them is the *Plural Subject Marker* while the other is the *Indefinite Object Marker*. The evidence for this analysis is that when the subject is singular and the object is non-specific, one prefix *man-* is used, as in the following sentence:

Manli'e' yo' guma'.
'I saw a house.'

The prefix *man-* in this sentence is the Indefinite Object Marker.

This will be discussed again later in the section on Definite and Indefinite Objects.

Plural of Nouns. Most nouns are made plural by one of two methods. (There is a small group of irregular nouns that will be discussed in the following subsection.) If the noun functions as a predicate in a stative sentence, it is pluralized by the prefix *man-*. (This prefix was described as a plural verbalizing prefix in section 3.5.3.) This is illustrated in the following examples:

Noun		*Stative Sentence*
estudiante	'student'	Manestudiante siha. 'They are students.'
ma'estro	'teacher'	Manma'estro hamyo. 'You are teachers.'
ma'gas	'boss'	Manma'gas siha. 'They are bosses.'
emfetmera	'nurse'	Manemfetmera hit. 'We are nurses.'

When nouns do not function as predicates of stative sentences, they are usually pluralized by adding the word *siha* following the noun. This word is identical in sound and shape to the third person plural pronoun *siha*. For purposes of grammatical analysis they can be considered the same morpheme. The following sentences will illustrate how *siha* is used as a plural marker for nouns:

Singular Form	*Plural Form*
Metgot i estudiante. 'The student is strong.'	Manmetgot i estudiante siha. 'The students are strong.'
Malate' i mediku. 'The doctor is intelligent.'	Manmalate' i mediku siha. 'The doctors are intelligent.'
Malingu i ga'lagu. 'The dog was lost.'	Manmalingu i ga'lagu siha. 'The dogs were lost.'
Ñalang i babui. 'The pig was hungry.'	Maññalang i babui siha. 'The pigs were hungry.'

The plural marker *siha* is often omitted. It is not really necessary from a logical point of view because the prefix *man-* is enough to tell us that the subject noun is plural. For example, in the sentence *Manbrabu i mediku* we know that *mediku* refers to more than one because of the prefix *man-* on the word *brabu*. Since the additional plural marker *siha* is grammatically redundant, it is often omitted in speech.

Irregular Noun Plurals. There is a small set of nouns in Chamorro that have irregular plural forms. All of these nouns refer to people. The singular and plural forms of the irregular nouns are listed below:

Singular		Plural	
lahi	'man'	lalahi	'men'
palao'an	'woman'	famalao'an	'women'
patgon	'child'	famagu'on	'children'

A slightly larger subgroup of the irregular nouns are pluralized by the prefix *man-*. These nouns also refer to persons. And some have been derived from verbs through the nominalizing process of reduplication. The following list will show the nouns that are pluralized by adding *man-*. (It should be stressed that these nouns are pluralized by the prefix *man-* even when they are not functioning as predicates. The regular morphophonemic changes caused by *man-* will be observed except where another type of affixation, e.g., reduplication has already taken place, as in the case of the derived nouns.)

Singular		Plural	
pale'	'priest'	mamale'	'priests'
saina	'parent'	mañaina	'parents'
che'lu	'sibling'	mañe'lu	'siblings'
ga'chong	'friend'	mangga'chong	'friends'
sakke	'thief'	mañakke	'thieves'

Derived Nouns:

kiko'ko'	'harvester'	mankíko'ko'	'harvesters'
pápaki	'gunner'	manpápaki	'gunners'
títuge'	'writer'	mantítuge'	'writers'
fáfahan	'buyer'	manfáfahan	'buyers'

Ask yourself how many additional nouns are there that can be pluralized by the prefix *man-* when they do not function as the predicate of a stative sentence?

The question word *mangge* is also pluralized by adding the prefix *man-*. This is the only one of the question words that is marked for plural, as in the following examples:

Singular	Plural
Mangge i lepblo?	Manmangge i lepblo (siha)?
'Where is the book?'	'Where are the books?'

Mangge i lahi? Manmangge i lalahi?
'Where is the man?' 'Where are the men?'

The fact that *mangge* is the only question word that is pluralized can be accounted for by the fact that it is a contracted form of *manu nai gaige*. Thus we can assume that the entire phrase, including the existential verb *gaige*, has been pluralized.

BASIC SENTENCE TYPES

4.8   If you were to examine a text of Chamorro, either written or spoken, you would discover that the sentences of the text would, for the most part, be quite different from each other. At least they would appear to be quite different from each other. For example, look at the sentences from the following recorded narrative:

> Un tiempo estaba un patgon na'an-ña si Jose. Si Jose katotse años ha' trabia, lao sumen brabu na patgon. Kada dia humanao ya machocho'cho' gi un riku na taotao. Ha papasto i ga' este i taotao siha chiba yan kinilu. Ha titife' ibas. Guaha lokkue' nai macho'cho' gi kusina ya ha chocho'gue todu i nisisidat este na taotao i riku as Tun Francisco. Anai esta tres años maloffan, humanao si Jose para as Tun Francisco ya ilek-ña, "Tun Francisco, esta tres años nai macho'cho' yo' guini ya malago' yo' na bai deskansa."

When we see such a variety of ways to put sentences together—and the above passage is only a very small sample —we can see that the task of describing their structure can be an enormous one.

What the linguist-grammarian must try to do is determine the *basic sentence types* of a language. (Some grammarians, such as Paul Roberts, call them the "kernel sentences.") Once these basic sentence types for a language have been established, the linguist then tries to find the rules which enable the native speaker of the language to form longer and more complex sentences from the basic sentence types.

Put in another way, linguists assume that every language has a limited number of basic sentence types. From this limited number of basic sentence types, the native speaker of the language can generate an infinite number of longer, more complex sentences by various linguistic devices. For example, he may convert a statement to a question, an active sentence to a passive sentence, or a positive statement to a negative statement. He may also add an unlimited number of modifiers, change the emphasis from object to subject, or change the tense from present to future. In short, a native speaker of any language can produce an incredible variety of sentences when he is speaking. However, according to current linguistic theory, his great variety of sentence structures all come from a small core of basic sentence types.

According to the present analysis, Chamorro has at least four basic sentence types. There may be more than four, but it appears that most Chamorro sentences can be derived from one of these four basic types. These four types are *transitive, intransitive, stative,* and *existential.* They will be discussed separately below.

Transitive Sentence. One of the four basic sentence types is called the *transitive sentence.* As its name would suggest, the sentence must contain a transitive verb, a subject, and a direct object of the verb. Following are some examples of transitive sentences:

Subject	Pron. + Verb	Object
I taotao	ha utot	i tronkon hayu
I patgon	ha baba	i petta.
I taotao	ha tanom	i tronko.
Si Jose	ha pasto	i guaka.

It should be observed that the word order can be changed without significantly changing the meaning as the following sentences show:

Pron + Verb	Subject	Object
Ha fahan	si Juan	i chandia.
Ha gimen	i neni	i leche.
Ha hatsa	si Jose	i kahon.
Ha chonnek	i palao'an	i kalesa.

(Some Chamorro speakers claim that the word order in the second set of sentences above is the preferred order. In any case, both types of word order are permissible.)

It is possible to construct many variations of the above sentences. For example, we could take the sentence *Ha fahan si Juan i chandiha* and transform it to any of the following:

Si Juan fumahan i chandia.
Finahan i chandia as Juan.
Mamahan si Juan chandia.

The main point here is that the three sentences above are *transformations* (to use the linguistic term) of the basic transitive sentence *Si Juan ha fahan i chandia*. Put in another way, the three sentences above are *derived from* the basic transitive sentence *Si Juan ha fahan i chandia*. They are *derived sentences*.

In the sections to follow, and especially in the section on the *focus system*, we will examine more closely the ways in which derived sentences are formed from basic sentence types.

Intransitive Sentence. The second basic sentence type is the *intransitive sentence*. The basic elements of an intransitive sentence are an intransitive verb (see 3.3.2 and 4.6) and a subject. Some examples of basic intransitive sentences are given here:

Verb	Subject
Umo'o'o'	i gayu.
Bumabaila	i palao'an.
Ma'udai	i taotao.
Gumupu	i páharu.
Manmata'chong	i famalao'an.
Humanao	gue'.
Manhanao	hit.

It was pointed out in section 4.6 that the intransitive verb can take various types of modifiers, as can the noun phrase (cf. 4.1). The above sentences are simply examples of basic intransitive sentences which are capable of being expanded in a variety of ways.

Stative Sentence. Stative sentences are sentences that do not have a verb in the predicate. The predicate may consist of a noun or modifier that does not have any verbalizing affix (cf. 4.5). The following are examples of stative sentences:

Predicate	Subject
Mediku	si Juan.
Ma'estro	gue'.
Manmediku	i lalahi.
Manma'estro	siha.
Dánkolo	i patgon.
Dikike'	i ga'ga'.
Malingu	i guaka.
Malangu	i mediku.
Hafkao	bidada-mu.

(Some linguists prefer to call the predicate of a stative sentence a *comment* and the subject a *topic*. Thus, a stative sentence could be described as a sentence consisting of a verbless comment and a topic about which the comment is made.)

When a verbalizing affix (such as *-um-* or *man-*) is added to the predicate of a stative sentence, it then becomes an intransitive sentence. The reason for claiming this change in status is that an intransitive sentence can take a modifier of manner while a stative sentence cannot.

Existential Sentence. The term *existential sentence* is used to cover those sentences which describe the existence or nonexistence of something. The verbs that occur in the existential sentences are included among the irregular verbs in section 3.3.2. The irregular verbs that are generally found in existential sentences are *gaige, estaba, guaha, taigue, taya', gai,* and *tai.* Some sample existential sentences are given here:

> Gaige yo' gi eskuela.
> Estaba yo' gi eskuela.
> Guaha salape'-hu.
> Taigue i estudiante.
> Taya' salape'-hu.
> Gai salape' yo'.
> Tai salape' yo'.
> I desehu taya' bali-ña.
> I desehu gai bali.

This concludes the present discussion of the four basic sentence types in Chamorro. There are undoubtedly other basic sentences that do not fit the four basic patterns given here. Nevertheless, it is felt that most sentences in Chamorro can be derived from one of these four basic sentence types.

Try going back to the short text given at the beginning of this section to see if you can identify the sentence types used in that passage. Remember that most of the sentences used there (and in our daily speech) are *derived sentences.* That is, we use sentences in our regular communication that have been derived through transformations of basic sentence types.

DEFINITE-INDEFINITE OBJECTS

4.9   One of the very important features of Chamorro grammar is the way in which it requires the speaker to distinguish between a *definite object* and an *indefinite object* in sentences that may be considered transitive. This distinction between the two types of objects is formally made by changes in the structure of the verb, the subject pronoun, and the article used with the object (see section 3.3.2 for earlier discussion of this topic).

The following sentences will show the changes that take place in the verb, subject pronoun, and article when we change a definite object to an indefinite object:

Definite Object	*Indefinite Object*
Hu li′e′ i lepblo.	Manli′e′ yo′ lepblo.
'I saw the book.'	'I saw a book.'
Un taitai i lepblo.	Manaitai hao lepblo.
'You read the book.'	'You read a book.'
Ha pacha i tronko.	Mamacha gue′ tronko.
'He touched the tree.'	'He touched a tree.'

The changes that take place when the subject is singular are these:

1. Indefinite Object Marker *man-* prefixed to verb.
   (Note the accompanying morphophonemic changes.)
2. *hu*-type subject pronoun → *yo′*-type subject pronoun.
3. Definite article *i* is dropped from object NP.

When the subject NP includes a noun, the *yo′*-type subject pronoun is not included in the Indefinite Object sentence:

Si Juan ha li′e′ i lepblo.	Manli′e′ lepblo si Juan.
'Juan saw the book.'	'Juan saw a book.'

When the subject NP is plural, the Plural Marking Prefix *man-* is also added to the Indefinite Object sentence. This prefix should not be confused with the Indefinite Object Marker *man-*. The following sentences illustrate how both prefixes can occur together:

Ta li′e′ i lahi.	Manmanli′e′ hit lahi.
'We saw the man.'	'We saw a man.'
En taitai i lepblo.	Manmanaitai hamyo lepblo.
'You (pl.) read the book.'	'You (pl.) read a book.'
Ma pacha i tronko.	Manmamacha siha tronko.
'They touched the tree.'	'They touched a tree.'

In section 3.3.2 it was shown that there are three types of *special transitive verbs* in Chamorro. They are considered special for one of the following three reasons:

1. The form used with the indefinite object is different from the form used with the definite object, but one form is obviously derived from the other. Examples of this type are:

Definite Object	*Indefinite Object*
tuge' 'to write'	mangge'
Hu tuge' i katta.	Mangge' yo' katta.
'I wrote the letter.'	'I wrote a letter.'
tufok 'weave'	mamfok
Ha tuge' i kannastra.	Mamfok gue' kannastra.
'He wove the basket.'	'He wove a basket.'
tife' 'to pick'	mamfe'
Hu tife' i ates.	Mamfe' yo' ates.
'I picked the sugar apple.'	'I picked sugar apples.'
tufong 'count'	mamfong
Un tufong i kinilu siha.	Mamfong hao kinilu siha.
'You counted the sheep.'	'You counted sheep.'

(For a description of how the Indefinite Object form is derived from the Definite Object form see section 3.3.2.)

2. A completely different verb form is used for the definite and indefinite object constructions. There is probably only one pair of verbs that fits this pattern:

Definite Object	*Indefinite Object*
kanno' 'to eat'	chocho
Hu kanno' i ates.	Chumocho yo' ates.
'I ate the sugar apple.'	'I ate sugar apples.'

(It should be noted that the word *boka*—from the Spanish word *boca* 'mouth' —can be used with both definite and indefinite objects. When used with indefinite objects the prefix *man-* is used.)

3. A single form only exists for both Indefinite Object and Definite Object constructions. When an article is used to mark the object, it is *ni*. There are probably only four verbs in this category, as listed below:

	malago'	'want'
Malago' yo' ates.		'I want a sugar apple.'
	maleffa	'forget'
Manmaleffa siha ni lep-blon-ñiha.		'They forgot their books.'
	mañotsot	'repent'
Mañotsot gue' ni bida-ña.		'He repented what he did.'
	munhayan	'finish'
Munhayan hao ni lepblo.		'You finished the book.'

It is not unusual at all to find a Chamorro sentence in which the Transitive Definite Object form of the verb is used but no object is expressed in the sentence. When this happens, we can assume that both the speaker and the listener have the definite object in mind because it has been named in a preceding sentence. The following brief dialogue will illustrate:

> A. Kao ya-mu guihan?
> 'Do you like fish?'

> B. Hunggan, gof ya-hu.
> 'Yes, very much.'
> Hafa na klasen guihan este?
> 'What kind of fish is this?'

> A. Tarakitu. I amigu-hu ha konne' nigap.
> 'Tarakitu. My friend caught (it) yesterday.'

In the last sentence the Definite Object form of the verb *konne'* is used but no object is expressed in the sentence. Obviously both the speaker and listener understand that *tarakitu* is the specific object that was caught.

Indefinite Object and Intransitive Sentences. In some instances the Indefinite Object form of the verb is used when the sentence appears to be intransitive: that is, the sentence appears to have no object at all. The following pair of sentences will illustrate:

> A. Hafa bidada-ña?
> 'What is he doing?'

> B. Manespipia gue'.
> 'He is looking around.'

Even though there is no apparent object of the verb *espia* in the response to A's question, the sentence must still be considered a transitive sentence with an Indefinite Object that is simply not specified. It must be considered a transitive sentence because intransitive verbs must take either *-um-* or *ma-* when they occur with singular subjects. *Espia* is a transitive verb. When the object is not specified, as in the sentence above, the Indefinite Object Marker *man-* can be used. The sentence *Manespipia gue'* might better be translated as 'He is looking around (at things in general).' This translation suggests that an object is included in the speaker's mind. Perhaps this explanation will help in showing that the sentence is a transitive sentence rather than an intransitive one.

THE FOCUS SYSTEM

4.10   The *focus system* of Chamorro is a very important syntactic feature of the language. It is probably the most significant syntactic feature of Chamorro with regard to the identification of Chamorro as a Philippine type language. Even though the focus system of Chamorro is different from those found in the languages of the Philippines, similarities are sufficient to establish the fact that Chamorro is a close relative of Tagalog, Ilocano, and Cebuano, all of which have elaborate focus systems.

The term *focus system* is used here because most modern grammars of Philippine languages use the term to describe the same type of syntactic structure. Since the concept is completely absent from European languages, it is not easy for a speaker of English to comprehend. The earlier grammars of Chamorro make no mention of the system. A somewhat formal statement of the concept of focus is given by Virginia Morey in her article on Ata, a Philippine language.

> Focus is the formally marked relationship of orientation between the verb and a particular substantive phrase. The focus affix of the verb determines whether the focused substantive phrase is the object, direction, subject, or accessory of a particular clause. (1964:83)

To put it another way, the Chamorro speaker must indicate through the syntactic structure of his utterance which of the substantive elements is the "theme" of the utterance, or what, in his own conceptual framework, is at the heart of the utterance.

Rather than try to explain in an abstract way how the focus system works in Chamorro, let us look at some concrete examples of the five different types of focus constructions in Chamorro.

Actor Focus. The *actor focus* construction is used in Chamorro when the focus (or emphasis) is on the actor. (The actor is the one that performs the action, and is usually the subject of the sentence.) The actor focus involves the use of the emphatic pronouns (cf. 3.4.1) and the actor focus affixes *-um-* and *man-*. The following pair of sentences will show the contrast between actor focus construction and a nonfocus construction:

Non-focus	*Actor Focus*
Hu li'e' i palao'an.	Guahu lumi'e' i palao'an.
'I saw the woman.'	'I am the one who saw the woman.'

The essential elements of the actor focus sentence above are the emphatic pronoun *guahu* and the infix *-um-*. If the actor of the sentence is expressed by a proper name, the emphatic pronoun can be omitted, as in the following example:

Non-focus	*Actor Focus*
Si Juan ha li'e' i palao'an.	Si Juan lumi'e' i palao'an.
'Juan saw the woman.'	'Juan is the one who saw the woman.'

The above actor focus sentence could be expressed differently. For example, one could say *Si Juan ayu i ha li'e' i palao'an* or *Si Juan ayu i lumi'e' i palao'an* 'Juan is the one who saw the woman.' But this is the long way of saying something for which Chamorro has a very convenient syntactic device.

The prefix *man-* is used instead of *-um-* when the object is indefinite:

Actor Focus, Definite Obj.	*Actor Focus, Indefinite Obj.*
Guiya lumi'e' i palao'an.	Guiya manli'e' palao'an.
'He is the one who saw the woman.'	'He is the one who saw a woman.'
Si Juan lumi'e' i palao'an.	Guiya Si Juan manli'e' palao'an.
'Juan is the one who saw the woman.'	'Juan is the one who saw a woman.'

NOTE: There are good reasons to consider the verbalizing affix *-um-* (cf. 3.5.2) the same as the actor focus affix *-um-*. In an intransitive sentence such as *Humanao si Pedro* 'Pedro went' we could say that the focus is on *Pedro* since there isn't anything else in the sentence except the verb *hanao*.

Another reason for considering the two *-um-* affixes one and the same is that it is used in all "infinitive" constructions regardless of whether the infinitive is transitive or intransitive. Note the following sentences which contain the "infinitive" constructions:

Intransitive Infinitive	*Transitive Infinitive*
Malago' yo' gumupu.	Malago' yo' lumi'e' i lahi-hu.
'I want to fly.'	'I want to see my son.'

On the other hand, there are good reasons for making a distinction between the verbalizer *-um-* and the actor focus marker *-um-*. For example, in a question where the focus is clearly on the actor, the actor focus infix must occur in the verb, as in the following question:

Hayi lumi'e' i palao'an?
'Who is the one who saw the woman?'

Contrast the above sentence with the following one where the focus is on the goal (and where the verb takes the goal focus infix *-in-*):

Hayi lini'e'-mu?
'Whom did you see?'

It is more convenient, it appears, to distinguish between the actor focus infix *-um-* and the verbalizing infix *-um-* even though there is an obvious relationship between them.

Goal Focus. The *goal focus* construction is used in Chamorro when the focus (or emphasis) is on the goal. (The goal is usually the direct object of a verb.) The goal focus construction involves the use of the goal focus infix *-in-* and the use of the articles *i, si, nu, ni,* and *as* (cf. 3.4.6). The following pair of sentences will show the contrast between a goal focus construction and a non-focus construction:

Non-focus	Goal Focus
I lahi ha li'e' i palao'an. 'The man saw the woman.'	Lini'e' i palao'an ni lahi. 'The man saw <u>the woman</u>.' or 'It was the woman that the man saw.'
Si Pedro ha li'e' si Maria. 'Pedro saw Maria.'	Lini'e' si Maria as Pedro. 'Pedro saw <u>Maria</u>.' or 'It was Maria that Pedro saw.'

Notice the importance of the use of the articles *i, si, ni,* and *as.* It is clear that the articles *i* and *si* are used to mark the NP that is in "focus" while the articles *ni* and *as* mark the non-focused NP's. The importance of these articles can be illustrated by the following sentences:

Lini'e' i lahi ni palao'an.
'The woman saw the man.'

Lini'e' ni lahi i palao'an.
'The man saw the woman.'

Lini'e' si Maria as Pedro.
'Pedro saw Maria.'

Lini'e' as Maria si Pedro.
'Maria saw Pedro.'

It is the article, not the word order, that marks the actor and goal in Chamorro grammar when the goal focus construction is used.

The earlier Chamorro grammars treat this type of construction very differently. Safford (1909: 91) interprets the infix *-in-* as a marker of past definite or preterite verb tense. Von Preissig (1918:20) describes it as a passive voice construction. Costenoble (1940:312) also considers it a passive voice construction. Even though many Chamorro speakers will translate goal focus constructions by using the English passive voice, such a translation does not reveal the true meaning of this Chamorro construction. Moreover, there is a passive voice construction in Chamorro which uses the prefix *ma-*. This will be discussed in some detail later in section 4.12.

Perhaps the concepts of actor and goal focus can be seen more clearly if we contrast the two types of constructions. In the actor focus construction the actor emerges as the focal point or theme of the statement:

> Si Pedro lumi'e' i palao'an.
> 'Pedro saw the woman.'

In the goal focus construction the goal emerges as the theme of the statement:

> Lini'e' i palao'an as Pedro.
> 'Pedro saw the woman.'

Tied in with the goal focus infix *-in-* are the articles *i/si* and *ni/as*. Both *i* and *si* are used to mark the goal. *Si* is used to mark personal names; *i* is used with all other nouns.

Ni and *as* are used to mark the non-goal NP's of the sentence. *As* is used to mark personal names; *ni* is used with all other nouns. *Ni* is in all likelihood a contracted form of *nu i*, and it is pronounced by many speakers as *ni'*. It is always possible to use *nu i* instead of *ni* in this construction.

When the goal includes a demonstrative, the article is not used, as in the following sentence:

> Guinaiya enao siha as Pedro.
> 'Pedro likes those.'

There is probably a syntactic-semantic relationship between the goal focus infix *-in-* and the nominalizing infix *-in-* (cf. 3.5.2). However, we will maintain a distinction between the two.

When the actor is plural, the prefix *ma-* occurs with the verb, as in the following sentence:

Maguaiya si Maria ni famagu'on.
'The children love Maria.'

This prefix raises a theoretical problem of whether the plural goal focus marker *ma-* is the same as the Passive Marker *ma-*, to be discussed in 4.12 below. No doubt there is a relationship between the two, and perhaps they are the same. There is an interesting point that should be noted about the difference between the singular and plural goal focus constructions. In the two sentences below both subject and object are included:

Singular	*Plural*
Lini'e' i ma' estro ni patgon.	Mali'e' i ma'estro ni famagu'on.
'The child saw the teacher.'	'The children saw the teacher.'

In the plural sentence the subject can be omitted to give us:

Mali'e' i ma'estro.
'The teacher was seen.'

However, in the singular form the actor/subject must be included because the sentence **Lini'e' i ma'estro* is considered incomplete.

Causative Focus. The *causative focus* construction is used in Chamorro when the focus is on the thing that is caused to do or become something. This is a very awkward way to describe the causative focus. The "thing" referred to may be animate or inanimate, and it may perform an action or it may become something as a result of an action. Some examples of the causative focus construction, which involves the use of the *causative prefix na'-* and the articles *i, si, nu, ni,* and *as,* will illustrate how it works.

The simplest kind of causative focus construction contains a subject actor, the causative prefix plus a stem, and an object of the causative. The stem may be any type of content word. The following examples illustrate this kind of construction:

Causative + Modifier

Hu na'gasgas i kareta.
'I cleaned the car' or 'I caused the car to be clean.'

I mangga ha na'malangu i patgon.
'The mango made the child sick' or 'caused the child to be sick.'

I palao'an ha na'mahgong i neni.
'The woman calmed the baby' or 'caused the baby to be calm.'

(Notice that the *hu*-type pronouns are used with the simple causative construction.)

Causative + Intransitive. When a verb occurs with the causative prefix, the *base form* of the verb is used (see section 3.3.2):

Hu na'fakmata gue'.
'I caused (made) him wake up.'

Ha na'fatto yo'.
'He made (let) me come.'

Ha na'famokkat i ga'lagu.
'He made the dog walk.'

Si Jose ha na'baila i che'lu-ña.
'Jose made (let) his sister dance.'

Notice that the causative in Chamorro can be translated by the English words 'cause,' 'make,' and 'let'. To the Chamorro speaker the concept of causing something to happen and letting it happen are apparently similar.

When a transitive verb occurs in a causative focus construction, there are two objects: the object of the causative and the object of the main verb. The object of the causative always takes one of the *focus marking articles i* or *si*; the object of the main verb takes one of the articles *ni* or *as*. The following sentences will illustrate how the articles are used in the causative focus construction:

Causative + Transitive

Hu na'sugon i lahi ni kareta.
'I made the man drive the car.'

Hu na'kanno' i ga'lagu ni katne.
'I let the dog eat the meat.'

Hu na'akka' i ga'lagu as Pedro.
'I made the dog bite Pedro.'

Hu na'ayao si Pedro ni salape'.
'I lent (caused to borrow) Pedro the money.'

The causative prefix *na'-* is one of the most productive prefixes in Chamorro in that it is frequently used to make *complex words*. (cf. 3.2) Listed below are a few examples showing how this prefix is used to form verbs from non-verb stems:

Stem		*Verb with Causative Prefix*	
maolek	'good'	na'maolek	'fix, make good'
bubu	'angry'	na'bubu	'anger'
annok	'apparent'	na'annok	'reveal'

la'la'	'living'	na'la'la'	'activate'
fache'	'mud'	na'fache'	'smear, liquefy'
haspok	'full'	na'haspok	'satiate'

Referential Focus. The *referential focus* construction in Chamorro has a fairly wide range of meanings, and there seems to be a certain amount of overlap between the referential focus and the *benefactive focus* (to be discussed in the following section). The range of meanings covered by the referential focus can be illustrated by the following sentences. The first sentence in each pair is a non-focus sentence; the second includes the referential focus suffix *-i*:

Non-focus	*Referential Focus*
Mama'tinas yo' kafe.	Hu fa'tinasi hao kafe.
'I made some coffee.'	'I made some coffee for you.'
Kumuentos yo'.	Hu kuentusi hao.
'I talked.'	'I talked to you.'
Tumo'la' yo'.	Hu to'la'i hao.
'I spit.'	'I spit at/on you.'

The rules for the referential focus construction seem to fit in neatly with the overall pattern for the various focus constructions. They are as follows:

1. Only *Hu*-type subject pronouns are used.
2. The base form of the verb (or that which occurs in the future) is the stem to which the referential focus suffix *-i* is added.
3. The referential object NP is always marked by the focus marking articles *i* or *si*.
4. If there is another object of the verb, it is marked by the articles *ni* or *as*.

The following sentences will illustrate the use of the four articles:

Hu fa'tinasi si Paul ni kafe.
'I made the coffee for Paul.'

Si Paul ha sangani si Rita ni estoria.
'Paul told the story to Rita.'

Ha ututi i guafi ni hayu.
'I cut the wood for the fire.'

Hu pachayi si Pedro as Jose.
'I touched Jose for Pedro.'

Notice that the addition of the suffix *-i* causes *vowel raising* (see 2.7.3) in stems that have a mid vowel in the final syllable. The following examples will show this feature:

Stem		*Suffixed Form*	
kuentos	'talk'	kuentusi	'talk to'
utot	'cut'	ututi	'cut for'
tuge'	'write'	tugi'i	'write to'
fugo'	'squeeze'	fugu'i	'squeeze for'

There are three allomorphs of the referential focus suffix. They are -*i*, -*yi*, and -*gui*. The rules that determine which of the allomorphs will occur are as follows:

1. If the stem ends with a vowel or the diphthong *ai*, the suffix is -*yi*:

kanta	'to sing'	Hu kantayi si Rita. 'I sang for Rita.'
taitai	'to read'	Hu taitayi si Rita. 'I read to Rita.'

(Notice that the glide of the diphthong is lost when the suffix is added; see section 2.1.4.)

2. If the stem ends with a consonant, the suffix is -*i*:

kuentos	'to talk'	Hu kuentusi si Maria. 'I talked to Maria.'
tuge'	'to write'	Hu tugi'i si Maria. 'I wrote to Maria.'

3. Some stems that end with <u>ng</u>, <u>f</u>, or <u>ao</u> take the allomorph -*gui*:

huyong	'to go out'	Hu huyonggui si Pedro. 'I went out for Pedro.'
li'of	'dive'	Hu li'ofgui si Pedro. 'I dived at Pedro's.'
hanao	'to go'	Hu hanagui si Pedro. 'I went to Pedro.'

(Notice again that the glide of the diphthong is lost when the suffix is added.)

However, there are other stems ending with <u>ng</u> that take the suffix -*i*, as in the following examples:

tufong	tufungi
songsong	songsungi
fongfong	fongfungi
hagong	hagungi

Certain verbs in Chamorro do not occur without this suffix. For example, the word *apasi* 'to pay' never occurs as a verb without the suffix *-i*. It is derived from the root *apas* which means 'salary'.

In addition, there are some verbs in Chamorro that have incorporated the suffix so that it no longer appears to be a suffix. One such example is the word *chatge* 'to laugh at'. This word undoubtedly comes from the word *chalek* 'to laugh'. However, we cannot add the referential focus suffix to *chalek* to get a form such as **chaliki*. Probably in older Chamorro this form was permitted, but in modern Chamorro the suffix has become an inseparable part of the verb *chatge*. (See 2.7.4 for a discussion of the process involved in this type of morphophonemic change.)

The verbs *atte* 'pour in' and *na'i* 'give' also include the referential focus suffix. This can be demonstrated by observing the manner in which the articles *i* and *ni* are used in connection with these two verbs, as in the following sentences:

> Ha atte i basu ni limonada.
> 'He poured the lemonade into the cup.'
>
> Ha na'i i patgon ni leche.
> 'He gave the milk to the child.'

The article *-i* marks the NP that is in focus, while the article *ni* marks the NP that is not in focus.

Benefactive Focus. The *benefactive focus* construction is used in Chamorro when there is a benefactor—something or someone for whom something is done. The benefactive focus construction uses the suffix *-iyi* and the articles.

A puzzling factor about the benefactive focus construction is its relationship to the referential focus construction. Some verbs will take the referential focus suffix *-i* and the benefactive focus suffix *-iyi*, while others will not. Perhaps the benefactive form is in a stage of transition and is not used as much as it once was to distinguish between referential and benefactive focus.

There are at least two possible reasons for this somewhat puzzling situation. One is that the meaning of statements using the referential focus is sometimes ambiguous. For example, the sentence *Hu kantayi si Maria* could mean 'I sang for Maria' (for her pleasure) or 'I sang for Maria' (in her place). This same ambiguity exists in the English sentence 'I sang for Maria.'

Another possible reason for the confusion lies in the fact that the two suffixes (*-i* and *-iyi*) are very similar in shape.

As stated before, some verbs will take only the referential

focus suffix. *Tuge'* 'to write' is one of them. Notice the two possible meanings of the following sentence:

Hu tugi'i si Pedro ni katta.   'I wrote the letter to Pedro.'
                                 'I wrote the letter for Pedro.'

Other verbs, however, take the referential suffix *-i* and the benefactive suffix *-iyi* in order to show a clear distinction in meaning, as the following examples will show:

Referential	*Benefactive*
Hu sangani si Pedro ni estoria.	Hu sanganiyi si Pedro ni estoria.
'I told the story to Pedro.'	'I told the story for Pedro.' (in his stead)
Hu kuentusi si Pedro.	Hu kuentusiyi si Pedro.
'I talked to Pedro.'	'I talked for Pedro.' (in his stead)

The opinion of native speakers of Chamorro that I have consulted has been somewhat divided on the use of the benefactive focus suffix with all verbs. The consensus seems to be that the benefactive construction is understandable when used with all verbs, but most Chamorro speakers would probably use the referential focus suffix *-i* unless there is a need to draw a specific contrast between the referential meaning and the benefactive meaning.

The suffix-*iyi* has allomorphs that are similar to the allomorphs of *-i*. If the stem ends with a consonant, the suffix is *-iyi*. For example, *sangan* becomes *sanganiyi*. If the stem ends with the diphthong ao, the suffix is *-guiyi*, as in *hanao→hanaguiyi*. If the stem ends with a vowel, the allomorph *-yiyi* occurs, as in *Bai hu siniyiyi si Juan ni lata-ña ni pigas-ña* 'I will put the rice in the container for Juan.'

In addition, there are some outstanding examples of unpredictable sound changes that occur with the word. When the benefactive focus suffix is added to the stem *fatto* 'to come', we get *fattoiguiyi*, as in *Hu fattoiguiyi si Pedro* 'I came for Pedro.' Another example is *fo'na* 'in front of' which becomes *fo'naigue,* as in *Ha taftaf gue' ya ha fo'naigue* 'He was early and so he went ahead.'

There may be other examples of these irregular morphophonemic changes in the language. Thus far, however, these are the only ones that have been encountered by the author.

It was pointed out in section 3.4.5 that there is an alternative way of expressing the benefactive in Chamorro by using the Spanish preposition *para*. For example, both of the two sentences below are considered perfectly acceptable:

> Ha hatsayi si Pedro ni acho'.
> 'He lifted the stone for Pedro.'

> Ha hatsa i acho' para si Pedro.
> 'He lifted the stone for Pedro.'

Perhaps the presence of the alternative Spanish form has contributed to the ambiguous nature of the benefactive and referential focus suffixes.

The following chart and sample sentences may help to show the function of the articles and their relationship to the verb affixes for the five different focus constructions:

Focus	Verb Affix	ARTICLES				
		Actor	Goal	Causative Actor	Referential NP	Benefactive NP
Actor	-um- man-	i/si	i/si	——	——	——
Goal	ma- -in-	ni/as	i/si	——	——	——
Causative	na'-	i/si	ni/as	i/si	——	——
Referential	-i	i/si	ni/as	——	i/si	——
Benefactive	-iyi	i/si	ni/as	——	——	i/si

Actor:	Si Juan sumangan i estoria.
Goal:	Sinangan i estoria as Juan.
	Sinangan i estoria ni lahi.
Causative:	Si Juan ha na'sangan si Pedro ni estoria.
	I palao'an ha na'sangan i lahi ni estoria.
Referential:	Si Juan ha sangani si Pedro ni estoria.
	I lahi ha sangani i patgon ni estoria.
Benefactive:	Si Juan ha sanganiyi si Pedro ni estoria.
	I lahi ha sanganiyi i patgon ni estoria.

Multiple Focus Constructions. It is not unusual in Chamorro to find more than one focus affix occurring simultaneously with a single verb stem. We will not attempt here to explore all of the possible combinations, but some examples will be given:

Actor/Causative
    Guahu muna'gupu i papaloti.
    'I am the one who made the kite fly.'

(Notice that the infix *-um-* metathesizes to *mu-* when it occurs with the causative prefix *na'-*.)

Actor/Referential
    Guahu gumalutiyi ni babui ni hayu si Pedro.
    'I am the one who hit the pig with the stick for Pedro.'

Goal/Referential
    Si Maria ginalutiyi as Pedro ni babui ni hayu.
    'Pedro hit the pig with the stick for Maria.'

Goal/Causative
    Nina'maleffa hao ni estudiu-mu ni kontrata-ta.
    'Your study caused you to forget about our agreement.'

Actor/Causative/Referential/Goal
    Guahu muna'hinatsayi si Maria as Pedro ni neni.
    'I am the one who caused Pedro to lift the baby for Maria.'

Try to generate more sentences that include two or more of the focus marking verb affixes.

An interesting theoretical question (for which we do not now have an answer) is this: when there is a multiple focus construction, which one seems dominant in the sentence?

TOPICALIZATION

4.11   The primary purpose of the focus system, discussed in the preceding section, is to permit the speaker to place emphasis—or focus—on one of the elements of the sentence. The speaker may use an actor focus construction if the focus is on the actor, a goal focus construction if the focus is on the goal, and so forth.

In addition to the grammatical device of the focus system, the speaker may wish to place additional emphasis on one of the elements of the sentence. This is done through a process that is called *topicalization*. This grammatical process enables the speaker to bring out one of the elements of the sentence as the *topic* of the sentence, i.e. the part of the sentence that he wishes to emphasize.

Topicalization is accomplished primarily through the placement of the topic at the beginning of the sentence. When a particular element of the sentence is placed at the beginning, additional changes in the syntax may be required. Notice the following set of intransitive sentences, all of which might be loosely translated as 'The man went to Garapan.' The first sentence might be considered "neutral." In other words, none of the focus constructions are used and there is no particular topic or emphasized element in the sentence. In the other three sentences the topic is underlined.

1. Humanao i taotao para Garapan.
2. <u>I taotao</u> humanao para Garapan.
3. <u>I taotao</u> yuhi i humanao para Garapan.
4. <u>Para Garapan</u> i hinanao-ña i taotao.

In sentence 2 the topic is *i taotao*. This topicalization is accomplished simply by shifting the subject NP to the beginning of the sentence. No other changes are required. In sentence 3 the topic *I taotao* occurs again. In this sentence there is more emphasis on the subject NP than in sentence 2 because of the additional changes that can be seen in the rest of the sentence. (Basically, the verb *humanao* has been nominalized and now forms part of the subject NP *i taotao yuhi i humanao*; the sentence can now be considered a *stative sentence*; cf. 4.8)

The topic of sentence 4 is the location *para Garapan*. The locative element has been topicalized by placing it at the beginning of the sentence and by using a nominalized goal focus form of the verb *hanao*. Sentence 4 is also a stative sentence since the verb was nominalized and incorporated into the locative NP *para Garapan i hinanao-ña*.

Various elements of transitive sentences can also be topicalized through a combination of the grammatical processes described above used with actor and goal focus constructions. Notice the following set of transitive sentences which share the common meaning of 'The man sold the car.'

5. Ha bende i taotao i kareta.
6. <u>I taotao</u> ha bende i kareta.
7. <u>I taotao</u> bumende i kareta.
8. <u>I taotao</u> i bumende i kareta.
9. Binende i kareta ni taotao.
10. <u>I kareta</u> binende ni taotao.
11. <u>I kareta</u> yuhi i binende ni taotao.

Sentence 5 is nonfocus and has no particular topic marked for emphasis. Sentence 9 shows the goal focus construction, but no topic is marked for emphasis. In sentence 6 the emphasis is on the topic *i taotao* since it occurs at the beginning of the sentence. In sentence 7 there is more emphasis on the NP *i taotao* because the verb now contains the actor focus infix *-um-*. In sentence 8 the subject NP is emphasized even more because the verb *bende* has been nominalized and incorporated into the subject NP.

Sentence 9 shows a simple goal focus construction which has the effect of placing some emphasis on the object NP *i kareta*. However, in sentence 9 there is nothing marked as the topic, that is, nothing in the sentence has been singled out for special emphasis. In sentence 10 the object NP has been topicalized by placing it at the beginning of the sentence. And in sentence 11 the object NP is emphasized even more by the same process that we saw in sentence 3, namely, the nominalization of the verb and the incorporation of the verb into the goal NP.

Topicalization is a fairly complex grammatical process. It is used very frequently when the speaker wishes to place emphasis on one or another of the parts (or constituents) of the sentence. In some cases the only change that is involved is the relocation of the topicalized part of the sentence so that it occurs at the beginning. In some instances additional changes in the verb are required. We will not go into the formal details of the changes that take place in the verb at this time. The following sentences will illustrate topicalization in a transitive sentence that contains modifiers of manner, time, and place. How would you describe the differences in meaning of these sentences?

12. Hu tuge' i katta chaddek gi eskuela nigap.
13. Chaddek hu tuge' i katta gi eskuela nigap.
14. Gi eskuela hu tuge' i katta chaddek nigap.
15. Nigap gi eskuela hu tuge' i katta chaddek.
16. Nigap gi eskuela chaddek hu tuge' i katta.
17. Nigap gi eskuela hu tuge' chaddek i katta.

Can you think of additional ways to achieve topicalization of particular elements of a sentence? It is very probable that the use of stress and juncture (cf. 2.6.2 and 2.6.4) play an important role in topicalization in spoken Chamorro.

PASSIVE VOICE

4.12   The *passive voice* in Chamorro is not as clear cut as we might like it to be for purposes of describing the language. Both Costenoble (1940:314–316) and Safford (1909:61) describe two forms of the passive voice. One of the forms uses the infix -*in*- (which we have defined as goal focus) while the other uses the prefix *ma*-. Safford claims that the passive voice is formed by using -*in*- when the agent is singular or dual, and by *ma*- when the agent is plural. Costenoble sets up a "subjective genitive passive" which uses -*in*- and an "objective genitive passive" which uses *ma*-.

In our analysis we have stated that the infix -*in*- is used in goal focus constructions when there is an agent and when the focus is on the goal of the action. The passive voice is another construction which uses the prefix *ma*- and which contains no agent. The following sentence is an example of a passive voice construction in Chamorro:

> Masangan na maolek iya Guam.
> 'It is said that Guam is good.' or 'They say that Guam is good.'

In this particular sentence it is difficult to ascertain whether the prefix *ma*- is actually a passive marker or the third person plural pronoun *ma* meaning 'they.' And in most cases it doesn't make any difference whether the gloss is 'they', as in the English impersonal 'They say that war is cruel,' or straight passive, as in 'It is said that war is cruel.'

In other cases, however, it is easier to determine that the verb with the prefix *ma*- is clearly a passive construction rather than a verb with the third person plural pronoun. Compare the grammatical structures of the following two sentences:

> (1) Manlinalatde i famagu'on ni ma'estron-ñiha.
> 'The *children* were the ones that were scolded by their teachers.'

> (2) Manmalalatde i famagu'on gi eskuela.
> 'The children were scolded at school.'

Sentence (1) above contains the goal focus infix -*in*- which places the emphasis on the goal 'children'. Sentence (2) contains the passive prefix *ma*- which also has the effect of placing some emphasis on the goal, but only when there is no subject actor.

If, in the second sentence, the *ma*- were the subject pronoun *ma* meaning 'they,' then the preceding plural marking prefix *man*- would not be permitted. Notice the contrast between the following two sentences:

> Ma lalalatde i famagu'on.
> 'They are scolding the children.'
> Manmalalalatde i famagu'on.
> 'The children are being scolded.'

When the goal is plural, the function of the passive marker *ma-* is quite clear. However, when the goal is singular, the sentence can then be ambiguous, as is the following:

Malalalatde i patgon.
'The child is being scolded,' or 'They are scolding the child.'

In order to avoid this ambiguity in the writing system we write the pronoun *ma* as a separate word and the passive marker *ma-* as a prefix. Thus, we get the following:

Ma lalalatde i patgon.
'They are scolding the child.'

Malalalatde i patgon.
'The child is being scolded.'

Verbs containing the passive prefix can be nominalized through the process of reduplication (cf. 3.3.5 and 4.3). The following examples will illustrate this process:

Root		Root + Passive		Reduplicated Form	
kanno'	'eat'	makanno'	'be eaten'	mámakanno'	'edible'
gimen	'drink'	magimen	'be drunk'	mámagimen	'drinkable'
chupa	'smoke'	machupa	'be smoked'	mámachupa	'smokeable'
tuge'	'write'	matuge'	'be written'	mámatuge'	'writeable'
taitai	'read'	mataitai	'be read'	mámataitai	'readable'

The passive marker *ma-* is probably related to the *ma-* found in so many modifiers, such as *malingu, malangu, magof* and *ma'i'ot,* and it may also be related to the verb prefix *ma-* discussed in 3.5.3. Perhaps some day the riddles surrounding *ma-* can be answered.

ASPECT

4.13   The term *aspect* is used to describe a syntactic feature that is somewhat similar to tense in that it shows the completion or noncompletion of an action. We might even say that it is related to, but different from tense (which will be discussed in the following section).

There are two types of aspect in Chamorro: *continuative* and *noncontinuative.* Continuative aspect means that the action is continuous, or at least is not completed. It is somewhat similar to the "progressive" *-ing* verb forms in English, as in "I am walking," or "I am eating." The Chamorro speaker uses the continuative aspect when the action is habitual, continuative, or taking place at the time of speaking. As Safford puts it, "It makes indefinite the time of the completion of the verb's action." (65) It is used in both future and nonfuture tense. (cf. 4.15)

The continuative aspect is marked by reduplication of one of the words in a clause, usually the verb. Noncontinuative aspect is simply unmarked. Following are some examples of words that show continuative and non-continuative aspect:

Noncontinuative		*Continuative*	
sága	'stay'	sásaga	'staying'
hugándo	'play'	hugágando	'playing'
táitai	'read'	tátaitai	'reading'
égga'	'watch'	é'egga'	'watching'

Notice that the stressed vowel and preceding consonant of the stem are always reduplicated, and that the primary stress remains on the reduplicated syllable. Notice also that when the syllable that is reduplicated consists of a single vowel, an excrescent glottal stop is always placed between the two succeeding vowels.

Following are some short sentences that illustrate the difference between noncontinuative and continuative aspect:

Noncontinuative	*Continuative*
Sumaga gue' giya Agaña.	Sumasaga gue' giya Agaña.
'He lived in Agaña.'	'He is living in Agaña.'
Para un saga giya Agaña.	Para un sasaga giya Agaña.
'You will stay in Agaña.'	'You will be staying in Agaña.'
Hafa bidan-ñiha?	Hafa bidan-ñiñiha?
'What did they do?'	'What are/were they doing?'

It should be pointed out that the stem that is reduplicated is not always a root. Nor is it always a verb. In the last example above, the first syllable of the pronoun *ñiha* is reduplicated because that is the syllable of the stem that carries the primary stress. Following are some additional examples of reduplication of stems that are not verbs, yet the syntactic function of the reduplication constitutes continuative aspect:

Falak i *sasa*ddok. (Noun *saddok* is reduplicated.)

Hafa *kumeke*ilek-ña? (Prefix *ke-* is reduplicated.)

*Guagua*ha interes-hu para ta adelanta este na isla. (Irregular verb *guaha* is reduplicated.)

Uniku rimediu i para ta sodda' mo'na i inali*gagao*-ta. (Nominalized form of aligao is reduplicated.)

At this time the precise rules for reduplication for continuative aspect are not completely understood. Usually, if the predicate contains a verb form, the verb is reduplicated. When the predicate does not contain a verb, the headword of the predicate is usually reduplicated. Then, of course, there are the exceptions, such as the peculiar word *falak* which does not occur in the reduplicated form; rather the location word that occurs with *falak* is the word that gets reduplicated.

The rules for using the continuative aspect are not completely clear either. As stated before, it is used when referring to actions that have not been completed. But this is an over-simplified statement of the rule which is undoubtedly more complicated than this. Only a Chamorro speaker can really know when it is appropriate to use the continuative or noncontinuative aspect in his speech.

Following are some sentences from a recorded Chamorro text. When you find the reduplicated-continuative form in the sentence, try to determine why the reduplicated form was used rather than the nonreduplicated form:

Lao cha'-miyu nina'fanpininiti sa' hami ni famagu'on-miyu ti bai in sedi enao.

Un huhungok i famagu'on mane'essalao bota si Castro.

Ti ha distitingge i taotao kao hafa rasa-ña.

Sakkan pot sakkan ni masilelebra ha' este i gipot San Isidro.

Kada sakkan ma gopte manggupot, ma gogopte si San Isidro.

The reduplication in the last example above is especially puzzling for the non-Chamorro speaker to understand. In the first clause the verb *gopte* occurs in the nonreduplicated form, while in the second clause it is reduplicated. Perhaps further research by a native speaker of Chamorro will provide further insight into the question of when the reduplicated, continuative aspect is used.

Another structure in Chamorro that might be considered part of the aspect system of the language is the prefix *ke*-. This was described as a Derivational Affix in section 3.5.3. The meaning of this prefix and the way it is used in Chamorro syntax might suggest that it be considered a part of the aspect system, different from but somewhat related to the reduplicated verb forms. In-

terestingly, when the prefix *ke-* is used, it is often reduplicated, as
in *Hafa kumeke'ilek-ña*?

TENSE

4.14 In Chamorro the verb is marked for *tense*. The word tense is used
here in the traditional sense of a syntactic feature that denotes the
location of an action or event in time. Chamorro has two tenses:
future and *nonfuture*. The verb phrase is marked for future tense
and unmarked for the nonfuture. If the verb phrase has the future
tense markers, it will be considered future tense even though it
may not always translate into the future tense of another language.
If the verb phrase does not have the future tense markers, it will
be considered nonfuture, which includes past and present.

There are several markers for future tense in Chamorro. The
most common one is the function word *para*. (The term "function
word" is used here to refer to a word that has a specific syntactic
function but no real semantic content.) There are, of course, at
least 3 words in Chamorro spelled *para*. The future marker *para*
always precedes a verb phrase, as the following examples will
show:

> Para u saga giya hami
> 'He will stay at our place.'

> Hafa para un bida?
> 'What will you do?'

> Para ta fañocho gi ega'an.
> 'We will eat in the morning.'

The word *siempre* is sometimes used in place of *para* when
the speaker wishes to indicate strong determination. Thus, we
might get either of the following two sentences:

> Para bai hu falagui i kareta-hu.
> Siempre bai hu falagui i kareta-hu.

Both sentences mean something like 'I will go and get my car,'
but the second sentence, because of *siempre,* suggests a stronger
determination.

Another marker for future tense in Chamorro is the function
word *bai* which is used only with the first person singular and
first person plural exclusive pronouns, as follows:

> Para bai hu saga giya Susupe.
> 'I will stay in Susupe.'

Para bai in fañaga giya Susupe.
'We (excl.) will stay in Susupe.'

NOTE: The word *bai* is rather puzzling because, to my knowledge, there is nothing quite like it in any of the other languages of
the Philippines or Micronesia. The origin of the word is not
known for certain. Safford lists the word as *béa*, and says that
it is used in the first person singular(1909:101). Costenoble
lists two forms, *bay* and *boy*, and says that it is "possibly" from
the Spanish *voy*, the first person singular form of the Spanish
verb *ir* 'to go' (1940:307). It was suggested by Professor William
Labov (personal communication) that the Chamorro word *bai*
might come from the widely used Pidgin English form *bye'm bye*,
which is used in Melanesian and Hawaiian Pidgin as a future
marker.

Whatever the origin of *bai* may be —and it is probably from
Spanish *voy*—it must be considered one of the markers of the
future tense in Chamorro. In normal, everyday speech it is often
omitted.

Another marker for future tense in Chamorro is the function
word u̲ which is used with third person. The following examples
will illu̲strate:

Para u̲ tuge' i katta.
'He/she will write the letter.'

Para u̲ ha tuge' i katta.
'They (2) will write the letter.'

(*u* may also occur in first person plural inclusive, as in *Para u ta
tuge' i katta*, but it is not obligatory.)

The remaining markers for the future tense in Chamorro are:

a. The base form of the verb is always used.
b. Hu-type pronouns are always used, even with intransitive
   verbs.
c. Verbs which ordinarily take *man-* in the non-future tense
   must take *fan-* in the future tense.

A paradigm of a transitive and an intransitive verb phrase
is given here to illustrate the rules for the formation of the future
tense in Chamorro:

Transitive Verb *li'e'*

Para bai hu li'e' i lahi.	'I will see the man.'
Para un li'e' i lahi.	'You will see the man.'
Para u li'e' i lahi.	'He/she will see the man.'

Para bai in li'e' i lahi.	'We (excl.) will see the man.'
Para (u) ta li'e' i lahi.	'We (incl.) will see the man.'
Para en li'e' i lahi.	'You (pl.) will see the man.'
Para u ha li'e' i lahi.	'They (2) will see the man.'
Para u ma li'e' i lahi.	'They (pl.) will see the man.'

Notice that in the last two sentences the distinction is made between 'they two' (dual) and 'they plural'. This is the first example we have seen of this dual/plural distinction which is very common in languages of the Pacific. Notice in the following paradigm that the dual/plural distinction is shown in all of the nonsingular forms. Notice also that only the pre-posed *hu*-type pronouns are used with the future form of intransitive verbs:

Intransitive Verb *saga*

Para bai hu saga giya Yigo.	'I will stay in Yigo.'
Para un saga giya Yigo.	'You will stay in Yigo.'
Para u saga giya Yigo.	'He/she will stay in Yigo.'
Para bai in saga giya Yigo.	'We (2, excl.) will stay in Yigo.'
Para bai in fañaga giya Yigo.	'We (pl., excl.) will stay in Yigo.'
Para (u) ta saga giya Yigo.	'We (2, incl.) will stay in Yigo.'
Para u ta fañaga giya Yigo.	'We (pl., incl.) will stay in Yigo.'
Para en saga giya Yigo.	'You (2) will stay in Yigo.'
Para en fañaga giya Yigo.	'You (pl) will stay in Yigo.'
Para u ha saga giya Yigo.	'They (2) will stay in Yigo.'
Para u fañaga giya Yigo.	'They (pl.) will stay in Yigo.'

Notice that the dual/plural distinction is maintained only with the intransitive verb through the use of the plural prefix *fan-*.

Some people might consider the word *debidi* another future marker, since it is always followed by a future verb construction. *Debidi* might also be considered a marker of *mode* (cf. section 4.15).

To summarize: there are two tenses in Chamorro, future and nonfuture. Future tense is marked by the use of certain structure words and verb forms that are described in the preceding paragraphs.

Future tense verb forms are often used in Chamorro where

they would not be used in English. Future tense forms are used in Chamorro when there are two actions, one of which is future relative to the other, even though they both occurred in the past. Notice the tense structure in the two clauses of the following sentences:

> Humanao gue' antes di bai hu fatto.
> 'He left before I came.'

In general, Chamorro speakers tend to use the future verb form following *antes di* whether they are describing a past activity or one that is yet to happen. The fact that one activity took place before another one suggests that the second action is future relative to the first action. Some speakers might prefer to use the nonfuture verb forms in both clauses, as in the sentence:

> Humanao gue' antes di matto yo'.
> 'He left before I came.'

MODE

4.15   *Mode* (sometimes *mood*) is a grammatical term used to describe the manner in which the action or condition expressed by the verb is stated. That is, the action may be expressed as conditional, factual, doubtful, reported, imperative, and so on.

In Chamorro it will be necessary to posit only one mode, the *imperative* (or command mode), which is formed by using the same form of the verb that occurs in the future tense. The following examples show the future verb tense and the imperative forms:

Future	*Imperative*	
Para u gimen i setbesa. 'He will drink the beer.'	Gimen.	'Drink.'
Para bai hu chocho. 'I will eat.'	Chocho.	'Eat.'
Para bai hu falagu. 'I will run.'	Falagu.	'Run.'

Both the Indefinite Object Marker *man-* and the Plural Marker *man-* change to *fan-* in the imperative mode. If both prefixes occur with the same stem, only the first one undergoes the change:

> Taitai i lepblo. 'Read the book.'
> Fanaitai. 'Read.'
> Fanmanaitai. 'Read (all of you).'

Some might think it would be appropriate to consider other modes in Chamorro, such as the indefinite, conditional, obligatory, and quotative. This does not seem to be warranted because each of these concepts is brought out in Chamorro by the use of a single word that is added to the phrase. The following sentences will illustrate:

Indefinite: Buente bai hu saga giya Susupe
'Maybe I will stay in Susupe.'

Conditional: Yanggen bai hu saga giya Susupe...
'If I stay in Susupe...'

Obligatory: Debidi bai hu saga giya Susupe.
'I must stay in Susupe.'

Quotative: Sumaga gue' hun giya Susupe.
'It was reported that he stayed in Susupe.'

Other *mode* type concepts are taken care of in Chamorro by affixes and structure words like the above examples. (Cf. 3.5.3 for additional examples.) Therefore, it seems best to posit only the imperative mode for Chamorro as a mode that is reflected in the verb structure.

NEGATION

4.16   There are a number of ways to show *negation* in Chamorro. Some negative words have the effect of negating an entire clause. Others may negate single words in a clause, while still others may stand as a single-word negative response. These will each be discussed separately.

ti. The negative word *ti* is probably the most commonly used form of negation. It usually converts a positive clause to a negative, as in the following examples:

Positive	*Negative*
Tumanges si Maria nigap.	*Ti* tumanges si Maria nigap.
'Maria cried yesterday.'	'Maria didn't cry yesterday.'
Umo'mak yo' nigap.	*Ti* umo'mak yo' nigap.
'I bathed yesterday.'	'I didn't bathe yesterday.'
Siña hit manhanao pa'go.	*Ti* siña hit manhanao pa'go.
'We can go now.'	'We can't go now.'
Ha faisen i ma'estro-ña.	*Ti* ha faisen i ma'estro-ña.
'He asked his teacher.'	'He didn't ask his teacher.'

The negative word *ti* can also be used to negate single words, such as a modifier:

Ti dankolo i tronko.   'The tree is not big.'
Ti maolek i korason-hu.   'My heart is not good.'
Ti metgot i patgon.   'The child isn't strong.'

taya'. The negative word *taya'* also has the effect of converting a positive clause to a negative one when the positive clause could have the irregular verb *guaha*. *Taya'* has verblike qualities in that it replaces *guaha* in negative clauses. A possible translation for *taya'* is 'there doesn't exist'. The following examples contrasting *guaha* and *taya'* will show the primary use of this word:

Positive	*Negative*
Guaha asagua-hu.	Taya' asagua-hu.
'I have a spouse.'	'I don't have a spouse.'
Guaha salape'-ña.	Taya' salape'-ña.
'He has money.'	'He has no money.'
Kao guaha kareta-mu?	Ahe', taya' kareta-hu.
'Do you have a car?'	'No, I don't have a car.'

The word *taya'* is often used by itself as a response to a question that might begin with *kao guaha*, as in:

Kao guaha salape'-mu?
'Do you have money?'

Taya'.
'None.'

taya' nai. The negative word *taya'* when followed by the complementizer *nai* means 'never', and it can be used to negativize a complete clause. It often occurs in the reduced form *tatnai* in normal everyday speech:

Taya' nai munangu gue'.   'He never went swimming'.
Tatnai munangu gue'.

Taya' nai dumeskansa siha.   'They never rested.'
Tatnai dumeskansa siha.

When *tatnai* (or *taya' nai*) is used in combination with the negative word *ti*, then the result is positive. Possible translations are 'usually' or 'almost always'. Note the following examples, which may be said to contain a "double negative."

Tatnai ti hagu mas burukento.
'You are usually the noisest one.'

Tatnai ti hagu mas tataftaf guatu asta i che′cho′.
'You are almost always the earliest one there at work.'

Tatnai ti also occurs as *tatne ti* and *tatde ti* in the speech of some people. All of the various forms are shortened forms of *taya′ nai ti*.

ahe′. The word *ahe′* means simply 'no' and it is used in reply to such yes-no questions as the following:

Kao ma′estro hao?	'Are you a teacher?'
Ahe′, estudiante yo′.	'No, I'm a student.'
Kao humanao gue′ para Guam?	'Did he go to Guam?'
Ahe′, sumasaga gue′ giya Rota.	'No, he is staying at Rota.'
Kao ya-mu mangga?	'Do you like mangoes?'
Ahe′, ti ya-hu.	'No, I don't like.'

munga. The negative word *munga* is used in three different ways. It is used in response to questions when something is being offered. Note how *munga* (not *ahe′*) is used in the following sentences:

Kao malago′ hao chumocho?	'Do you want to eat?'
Munga yo′.	'No thanks.'
Kao malago′ hao chupa?	'Do you want a cigarette?'
Munga fan.	'No thanks.'

Munga is also used as a negative word in an either-or situation, such as the following:

Kao para un hanao pat munga hao?
'Are you going or not?'

Finally, *munga* is used very often in the imperative sense of 'don't do' something:

Munga humanao gi gima′.
'Don't leave the house.'

Munga gof atrasao.
'Don't be too late.'

Munga bumuruka.
'Don't make noise.'

Notice how the three negative words *ahe′*, *taya′* and *munga* are used in the following sentences:

Yes-no Question: Kao katpenteru hao? Ahe′.
Guaha question: Kao guaha salape′-mu? Taya′.
Content Question: Hafa hinassoso-mu? Taya′.
Desiderative question: Kao malago′ hao setbesa? Munga.

diahlo. The word *diahlo* (also pronounced *dialu* and *dihalu*) is another negative word used, like *munga*, to decline an offer of something, as in the following example:

> Kao malago' hao chumupa?   Diahlo, si Yu'us ma'ase'.
> 'Do you want to smoke?'   'No, thank you.'

tai. The negative word *tai* is very similar in meaning to *taya'*, but it is different in that it requires a different syntactic pattern. Contrast the following sets of sentences that use *taya'* and *tai*:

> Taya' salape'-hu.   Tai salape' yo'.
> Taya' relos-ña si Maria.   Tai relos si Maria.
> Taya' magagon-niha.   Tai magagu siha.

It is convenient to consider *taya'* the negative counterpart of *guaha*, while *tai* is the negative counterpart of *gai*.

cha'-. The negative word *cha'-* was described in the section on irregular verbs (3.3.2.) along with *taya'* and *munga*. Like *munga*, it is used in imperative statements meaning 'don't' but with the connotation which might be translated as 'you had better not'. It is used with one of the possessive pronouns:

> Cha'-mu ume'essitan.
> 'You had better not joke.'

> Cha'-miyu fanhahanao sin guahu.
> 'You had better not go without me.'

Cha'- can also be used with other pronouns:

> Cha'-hu gumagacha' hao.
> 'I had better not come across you.'

> Cha'-ña munanangga.
> 'He had better not wait.'

ni. The negative word *ni* is used with question words, nouns, and numerals (and possibly other types of words) with a general negative meaning, depending on the word it is used with. Following are some examples that will illustrate the differences in negative meanings when used with different words:

> Ni hayi gumuaiya yo'.
> 'Nobody loves me.'

> Ni manu ya-hu na lugat.
> 'I don't like any place.'

> Ni taimanu agang-mu ti un ineppe.
> 'No matter how you call, I won't answer.'

Ni hafa un cho'gue, ti bai hu malago'.
'No matter what you do, I won't like it.'

Ni ngai'an na hu guaiya hao.
'I will never love you.'

Ni si Jose ti ha li'e' yo'.
'Not even Jose saw me.'

Ni unu matto.
'Not even one came.'

When the word used with the negative word *ni* is reduplicated, the result is an intensification of the negative meaning:

Ni hayiyi gumuaiya yo'.
'Nobody at all loves me.'

Ni manunu ya-hu na lugat.
'I don't like any place at all.'

Ni hafafa bali-mu.
'You are not worth anything at all.'

Ni ngai'a'an fatto-ku America.
'I will never at all come to America.'

When *ni* is used only with the question word, the meaning is frequently 'no matter'.

Ni hayiyi	'no matter who'
ni hafafa	'no matter what'
ni manunu	'no matter where'
ni ngai'a'an	'no matter when'
ni taimanunu	'no matter how'

nunka. The negative word *nunka* is used frequently to mean 'never', as in the following examples:

Nunka yo' nai mandagi.
'I have never lied.'

Nunka si Rosa ni fatta gi eskuela.
'Rosa is never absent from school.'

chat- (*chatta'*). The prefix *chat-*, and the longer form *chatta'*, should also be included in the list of forms that express negation in Chamorro. The usual meaning of this prefix is 'hardly' or 'barely'. See the following sentences:

Hu chatkomprende i leksion.
'I hardly understood the lesson.'

Chatta' hu komprende i leksion.
'I hardly understood the lesson.'

When the prefix *chat-* is used with certain words, it appears to take on some special meanings, as in the following words:

chat + pa'go→chatpa'go 'ugly'
chat + li'e'→chatli'e' 'hate'
chat + fañagu→chatfañagu 'miscarriage'
chat + fino'→chatfino' 'cursing'
chat + guahu→chatguahu 'I'm not feeling well.'

One might wish to include the Spanish preposition *sin* 'without' and the negative prefix *des-* (as in *desafte* 'unroof') in the group of Chamorro negative constructions. The words listed above, however, constitute the most important of the negative words and constructions in Chamorro.

REFLEXIVE VERBS

4.17   There are certain features of reflexive verb constructions in Chamorro that might be considered somewhat unusual when they are compared with the reflexive verbs of other languages, especially English.

A *reflexive verb* construction is one in which the subject and the object of the verb are identical. Some examples of reflexive verb constructions in English are:

I saw myself.
She touched herself.
You cut yourself.

In English the marker for the reflexive is the form of the object pronoun which includes the form *-self*. Virtually any transitive verb in English can take the reflexive construction.

Likewise in Chamorro most transitive verbs can occur in the reflexive construction by using both the *hu-* and *yo'-* type pronouns. These might be considered *optional reflexives* because the verbs may also occur in nonreflexive constructions. Translations of the above English reflexive constructions follow a very similar structural pattern. Note the following translations:

Chamorro	*English*
Hu li'e' maisa yo'.	'I saw myself.'
Ha pachan maisa gue'.	'She touched herself.'
Un chachak maisa hao.	'You cut yourself.'

The key word in these Chamorro reflexive constructions is

maisa. There are several interesting features about this word which should be mentioned here.

a. When *maisa* precedes the object pronoun, the construction is reflexive:

Ha li'e' maisa gue'.
'He saw himself.'

When it follows the object pronoun it must be linked by the particle *na* and the meaning changes from the reflexive meaning to 'alone.'

Ha li'e' gue' na maisa.
'He saw himself alone' or 'He saw only himself.'

b. When *maisa* follows a verb that has a final vowel, the excrescent consonant *n* must occur:

Verb Stem	With maisa
pacha	Ha pachan maisa gue'.
	'He touched himself.'
hatsa	Hu hatsan maisa yo'.
	'I lifted myself.'

c. For continuative aspect (cf. 4.1.3) *maisa* is reduplicated rather than the verb when it is preceded immediately by the verb:

Ha hatsan mamaisa gue'.
'He is lifting himself.'

Hu atan mamaisa yo'.
'I am looking at myself.'

With intransitive verbs *maisa* is not a reflexive marker, but the rule for reduplication still holds. Notice the reduplication for aspect in the following set of sentences, both of which mean roughly 'He is going alone.'

Humanao mamaisa gue'.

Humahanao gue' na maisa.

As a matter of interest, the word *maisa* in Ilokano means 'one'. The reduplicated form *mamaisa* means 'one only', and the verb form (using the verb prefix *ag-*) means 'to stay or be alone'.

In addition to the optional reflexive verbs, there are some verb forms in Chamorro that might be considered *inherent reflexives* because they are used only in reflexive constructions. At the present time the number of inherent reflexive verb constructions in Chamorro is not known. Some examples are given here to illustrate:

Verb Stem	Reflexive Construction
deskuida	Hu deskuida yo' ni patgon.
	'I neglected the child.'

The verb *deskuida* comes from the Spanish reflexive verb *descuidar*. Interestingly, Chamorro also uses the verb in a reflexive form, but Chamorro substitutes its own pronouns.

tohne	Hu tohne yo' gi liga.
	'I leaned against the wall.'

The verb *tohne* should be considered an optional reflexive because it can be used as a non-reflexive verb in the sense of 'prop' or 'support', as in the sentence *Hu tohne i bentana* 'I propped the window open.'

fa'dagi	Un fa'dagi-mu yo' gi asagua-mu.
	'You used me as your excuse to your spouse.'

The last example should probably not be considered a true reflexive construction. Notice that the object pronoun is the possessive pronoun, not the *yo'*-type pronoun that is used in the other reflexive constructions.

Whenever the prefix *fa'-* 'pretend' is used, some type of reflexive construction is often required:

Ha fa'bunita gue' i palao'an.
'The woman pretended to be pretty.'

Un fa'macheng hao gi gipot.
'You made a fool of yourself (pretended to be a monkey) at the party.'

As stated earlier, the number of inherent reflexive verbs in Chamorro is not known at the present time. We can assume, however, that most of the transitive verbs may be considered optional reflexive verbs. The restrictions on their being used in reflexive constructions could come only from semantic unacceptability, such as **Hu gimen maisa gue'*.

COMPOUND SENTENCES.

4.18   Thus far in the discussion of syntax we have looked only at what might be called *simple sentences*—those, consisting of a single subject, a single verb, and other single elements in the predicate such as the direct object, referential object, benefactive object, causative object, modifiers, and so forth. Obviously, Chamorro speakers do not limit themselves to simple sentences when they talk. They have ways of combining sentences together to form longer sentences. One type of sentence that results from combining two or more sentences together is the *compound sentence.*

A compound sentence is one that consists of two or more *independent* (or coordinate) *clauses.* This means simply that the clauses that are joined together are independent of each other except for the semantic connection that is implied in the conjunction that is used. Another way to look at it is that each of the clauses in a compound sentence could be spoken as a separate utterance without joining them together, and the meaning would remain essentially the same. Some examples of compound sentences in Chamorro are as follows:

Chagi fumaisen gue' ya ta fanhita.
'Try asking him and we will go.'

In dilalak ya in gacha'.
'We ran after and we caught up.'

Ti ya-hu guihan lao ya-hu mannok.
'I don't like fish but I like chicken.'

Para u hanao pat para u saga giya hami.
'She will go or she will stay at my house.'

The compound sentences of Chamorro are joined together by one of the following conjunctions: *ya, lao, pat.* (See section 3.4.8 for a more complete treatment of the conjunctions.)

Very often the compound sentences are reduced in one form or another so that instead of having two full sentences joined by a conjunction, we have one full sentence and part of another sentence. When this happens we can say that part of one of the sentences has been deleted. For example, take the following compound sentence:

Hu li'e' i lahi yan i palao'an.
'I saw the man and the woman.'

This sentence comes from the following two simple sentences:

Hu li'e' i lahi.
Hu li'e' i palao'an.

They could be joined by the conjunction *ya* to produce the following compound sentence:

Hu li'e' i lahi ya hu li'e' i palao'an.

Since the subject and verb in both sentences are identical, the second occurrence of them can be eliminated through the linguistic process known as deletion. This would result in the sentence:

> *Hu li'e' i lahi ya i palao'an.

The rules for conjunctions now require that we change *ya* to *yan* since it now connects two identical structures that are not full clauses. The resulting compound sentence (which has been reduced) is:

> Hu li'e' i lahi yan i palao'an.
> 'I saw the man and the woman.'

Following are some additional examples of compound sentences that have been reduced through the deletion of one of the structural elements of the original sentence:

> Ma'pos si Juan yan si Maria.
> 'Juan and Maria left.'
>
> Kao siña hao munangu pat ti siña?
> 'Can you swim or not?'
>
> Kumakati yan chumachalek i palao'an.
> 'The woman is crying and laughing.'
>
> Humanao yo' yan i che'lu-hu.
> 'I went with my brother.'

One can reconstruct the above compound sentences so that the elements that were deleted are restored. The following example will illustrate further how this should be done:

> Original Sentences: Ha chagi lumi'of.
>   Ti siña gue' lumi'of.
>
> Reduced Compound Sentence: Ha chagi lumi'of lao ti siña.

Theoretically, there is no limit to the number of simple sentences that can be joined together to form a compound sentence. Take the following sentence for example:

> I pale' yan i ma'estro yan i estudiante yan i ga'lagu
> manmalagu para i saddok.
> 'The priest and the teacher and the student and the dog ran to
> the river.'

In the above sentence the first three occurrences of *yan* could be eliminated. Likewise, the list of people and animals that ran to the river could be extended indefinitely. Stylistic preferences help to put a limit on the number of subjects or predicates that a single compound sentence contains.

COMPLEX SENTENCES

4.19   Up to this point in our analysis of Chamorro syntax we have restricted ourselves primarily to simple sentences. In the preceding section some attention was given to compound sentences (or sentences with compound subjects and/or predicates), and in section 3.4.8 on Connectors we saw some examples of complex sentences where one clause was joined with another clause in a subordinate relationship to produce a complex sentence. In everyday Chamorro speech we are likely to hear and use more complex sentences than any other type, for they are the forms that a mature native speaker of the language normally uses.

Complex sentences come in numerous forms in Chamorro, as they do in other languages. We will not attempt to list or account for all of the possible complex sentences in the language. Rather, we will attempt to examine some of the general rules and processes that are involved in forming complex sentences.

We must start with the basic assumption that all complex sentences are made up of groups of simple or *basic sentences* (cf. 4.8) that are combined by various syntactic processes to form longer complex sentences. The processes by which we combine shorter sentences into longer ones are generally known as *transformations*. The rules which describe these transformations are generally called *transformational rules*.

A formal study of Chamorro syntax would probably include explicit transformational rules which would describe in detail all of the steps that one goes through when converting a series of basic sentences to a single complex sentence. In this reference grammar we will give only the general rules for incorporating basic sentences into complex ones.

Complex sentences in Chamorro all contain a *main clause* (or matrix clause) and at least one other clause of the following types: subordinate clause, relative clause, and complement clause. Each of these three types will now be discussed separately.

Subordinate Clauses. When a complex sentence is formed by joining a *main clause* with a *subordinate clause,* the process often involves only the addition of the subordinator. This addition causes one of the clauses to be subordinate to the other. Below are some examples that show how two clauses can be combined to form a complex sentence simply by adding a subordinator. The subordinate clause is underlined:

Basic Sentences: Humanao yo'.
                           Bai hu espia hao.

Complex Sentence: Yanggen humanao yo' bai hu espia hao.
                           'If I go, I will look for you.'

Basic Sentences: Humanao gue' para Guam.
                           Mumalangu si nana-ña.

Complex Sentence: Anai humanao gue' para Guam muma-
                           langu si nana-ña.
                           'When he went to Guam, his mother
                           became ill.'

Basic Sentences: Hu bira tatalo'-hu.
                           Un dulok yo'.

Complex Sentence: Gigon ha' hu bira tatalo'-hu, un dulok yo'.
                           'As soon as I turn my back, you stab me.'

Basic Sentence: Hanao para i lancho.
                           Malangu hao.

Complex Sentence: Hanao para i lancho achok malangu hao.
                           'Go to the ranch even though you are
                           sick.'

Basic Sentences: Humanao yo' para Saipan.
                           Taya' salape'-hu.

Complex Sentence: Humanao yo' para Saipan sa' taya'
                           salape'-hu.
                           'I went to Saipan because I had no money.

In some instances it is necessary to delete one of the elements of the subordinate clause. This deletion may be of the subject or the predicate, and its function is to avoid repetition of redundant portions of the sentence. The following examples will illustrate:

Basic Sentences: Ti mangganna yo'.
                           Mangganna i amigu-hu.

Complex Sentence: Ti mangganna yo' lao achok i amigu-hu.
                           'I didn't win but at least my friend did.'
                           (Deletion of verb mangganna.)

Basic Sentences: Ti hu konne' gue'.
                           Kamten gue'.

Complex Sentence: Ti hu konne' gue' sa' kamten.
                           'I didn't take him because he was restless.'
                           (Deletion of subject pronoun gue'.)

Multiple Subordination. We saw that in forming compound sentences we could join together more than two sentences to form longer compound sentences. It is also possible to join more than two sentences together to form a *multiple subordinate* sentence. The following examples of multiple subordination and subordination plus compounding will illustrate:

Basic Sentences:	Otro sakkan maila' ta li'e' hafa.*
	Ti u annok pilon-ñiha.
	Esta munhayan i botasion.
Complex Sentence:	Otro sakkan maila' ta li'e' <u>sa' ti u annok pilon-ñiha sa' esta munhayan i botasion.</u>
	'Next year let us see, because they will not show their feathers (hair) because the voting is finished.'
Basic Sentences:	Masangan ta'lo hafa.*
	Malate' este na taotao.
	Ma "throw out" si John Doe.**
	Humalom gue'.
	Mata'chong gue'.
Complex/Compound Sentence:	Masangan ta'lo na malate' este na taotao <u>sa' gigon ha' ma-"throw out" si John Doe, humalom ha' ya mata'chong.</u>
	'It was told again that this man is intelligent, because as soon as John Doe was thrown out he entered and sat down.'

Deletion of hafa. In two of the basic sentences above we have used the word *hafa* in a peculiar sort of way. It is unlikely that any speaker of Chamorro would ever say a sentence like **Maila' ta li'e' hafa.* We have inserted the word *hafa* in this sentence in order to give it a sense of completeness. Without the word *hafa*, the sentence **Maila' ta li'e'* would be incomplete. In order to complete the sentence we have inserted the *dummy object hafa* which is deleted when the subordinate clause is added. In the sentence *Masangan ta'lo hafa* we can say that *hafa* functions as the *dummy subject*.

This is a linguistic device that is used to help account for the syntactic rules of the language. We will see that it can also be used to help explain the syntactic processes that take place when forming verb phrase complements.

Subordinate clauses in Chamorro can be introduced by any of the subordinators listed in 3.4.8.

---

*This peculiar use of *hafa* will be explained below.
**Since this sentence is taken from a recorded text, a fictitious name is used here in place of the original.

Complement Clauses. Complex sentences can also be formed by combining main (or matrix) sentences with *complement clauses.* Complement clauses differ somewhat from subordinate clauses in the following two ways: (1) They may be introduced by the complementizer *na* or one of the question words: (2) They bear a very close relationship to the verb phrase of the matrix sentence.

Some examples of complex sentences with different kinds of complement clauses are given below. The basic sentences (including "dummy" elements) and the complex sentence that includes them are given. The complementizer and the complement clause are underlined. The dummy element in the basic sentence is marked by *:

Basic Sentences:	Hu tungo' hafa*.
	Si Juan chumo'gue hafa.*
Complex Sentence:	Hu tungo' na si Juan chumo'gue.
	'I know that Juan did it.'
Basic Sentences:	Malago' yo' hafa*.
	Hu tungo' hafa*.
	Kao magahet na mannge' i guihan?
Complex Sentence:	Malago' yo' na hu tungo' kao magahet na mannge' i guihan.
	'I want to know whether the fish is truly delicious.'
Basic Sentences:	Sangani yo' ni hafa*.
	Ngai'an nai bai hu fafatto.
Complex Sentence:	Sangani yo' ngai'an nai bai hu fafatto.
	'Tell me when I will come back.'
Basic Sentences:	Sangani yo' ni hafa*.
	Hayi kumonne' i guihan.
Complex Sentence:	Sangani yo' hayi kumonne' i guihan.
	'Tell me who caught the fish.'
Basic Sentences:	Hu tungo' hafa*.
	Manu nai gaige si Juan?
Complex Sentence:	Hu tungo' manu nai gaige si Juan.
	'I know where Juan is.'

Sometimes the verb tense of the complement sentence is changed from non-future to future, as in the following example:

Basic Sentences:	Malago' yo' hafa*.
	Si Juan ha cho'gue hafa*.
Complex Sentence:	Malago' yo' na si Juan u cho'gue.
	'I wanted John to do it.'

Also, in some cases there is no complementizer to introduce the complement clause. The use of the complementizer appears to be determined by the verb of the main clause, but the details of this grammatical feature have not been worked out. The following sentences illustrate complement clauses that are not introduced by complementizers:

Basic Sentences:	Hu tago' si Juan.
	Humanao si Juan.
Complex Sentence:	Hu tago' si Huan <u>para u hanao</u>.
	'I told Juan to go.'
Basic Sentences:	I mediku ha tago' i malangu.
	I malangu ha kanno' i amot.
Complex Sentence:	I mediku ha tago' i malangu <u>para u</u>
	<u>kanno'</u> i amot.
	'The doctor told the patient to take the medicine.'
Basic Sentences:	Malago' gue' hafa*.
	Lumi' of gue'.
Complex Sentence:	Malago' gue' <u>lumi'of</u>.

In some instances, too, the use of the complementizer appears to be optional, as in the following example:

Basic Sentences:	Malago' gue' hafa*.
	Ha kanno' i mangga.
Complex Sentence:	Malago' gue <u>kumanno' i mangga</u>.
	or Malago' <u>gue' na u kanno' i mangga</u>.
	'He wants to eat the mango.'

As stated earlier, detailed syntactic rules explaining how complement clauses are combined with main clauses to form complex sentences have not been worked out. This discussion, however, should give us an idea of the general characteristics of complement clauses in Chamorro.

Relative Clauses. Relative clauses in Chamorro differ from the complement clauses discussed above in two ways: (1) They are usually introduced by the relativizer *ni* or *nai* (cf. section 3.4.8); (2) They have a special relationship to the NP or the VP of the main clause. The relativizer replaces either the subject or object of the relative clauses. The following examples will illustrate how complex sentences with relative clauses are formed from basic sentences. Notice that in the basic sentences from which a relative clause is formed it is not necessary to set up a "dummy" element. The relative clause is underlined.

Basic Sentences: Humanao si Pedro para Guam.
Hu li'e' si Pedro.

Complex Sentence: Si Pedro <u>ni hu li'e'</u> humanao para Guam.
'Pedro, whom I saw, went to Guam.'

Basic Sentences: Sangani yo' ni na'an i taotao.
Un espipia i taotao.

Complex Sentence: Sangani yo' ni na'an i taotao <u>ni un</u>
<u>espipia</u>.
'Tell me the name of the man you are looking for.'

Basic Sentences: Na'li'e' yo' ni palao'an.
Un guaiya i palao'an.

Complex Sentence: Na'li'e' yo' ni palao'an <u>ni un guaiya</u>.
'Show me the woman who you love.'

Basic Sentences: Kao un tungo' i taotao?
Para un na'i i taotao ni katta.

Complex Sentence: Kao un tungo' i taotao <u>ni un na'i ni</u>
<u>katta</u>?
'Do you know the man to whom you gave the letter?'

NOTE: In the last three complex sentences above there is more than one occurrence of the word spelled *ni*. According to the analysis in this grammar, these are different morphemes. The relativizer *ni* always follows the noun to which the relative clause is directly related. The other *ni* is the article *ni*. The article *ni* could be replaced by the sequence of particles *nu i*; the relativizer *ni* cannot.

The relative clause may be expressed by different constructions within the clause, depending on whether the speaker wishes to use the goal focus or some other. The following example will illustrate:

Basic Sentences: Hu li'e' i taotao.
Si nana-mu ha tungo' i taotao.

Complex Sentences:
Goal Focus—Hu li'e' i taotao <u>ni tiningo' as nana-mu</u>.
Nonfocus—Hu li'e' i taotao <u>ni ha tungo' si nana-mu</u>.

The relativizer *nai* is used when the relative clause relates to location, as in the following examples:

Basic Sentences: Humanao gue' para i lancho.
                  Machocho'cho' i amigu-ña gi lancho.

Complex Sentence: Humanao gue' para i lancho <u>nai macho-</u>
                  <u>cho'cho' i amigu-ña.</u>
                  'He went to the ranch where his friend was
                  working.'

Basic Sentences: Malak iya Guam yo'.
                  Mafañagu yo' giya Guam.

Complex Sentence: Malak iya Guam yo' <u>nai mafañagu yo'.</u>
                  'I went to Guam where I was born.'

Basic Sentences: Manmalagu ham para i eskuela.
                  Manestudia ham gi eskuela.

Complex Sentence: Manmalagu ham para i eskuela <u>nai mane-</u>
                  <u>studia ham.</u>
                  'We ran to the school where we studied.'

This concludes the present discussion of the complex sentences of Chamorro. We have omitted many details here that would be included in a formal statement of Chamorro syntax. Chamorro sentences can be made very complicated by compounding, subordination, complementizing, and relativizing clauses. When the various focus constructions and methods of topicalization are brought in, the sentences can become very intricate indeed. Hopefully these problems will be explored more fully in another, more formal grammar of Chamorro.

Glossary of Linguistic Terms

active voice   A term used to describe a verb form in which the subject performs the action. For example, the sentence *Sumasaga si Juan giya Guam* is active because the subject *si Juan* is also the actor.

affix   A term used to describe any type of bound morpheme that must be attached to a stem. The four types of affixes in Chamorro are: prefix, suffix, infix, and reduplication.

affricate   A type of consonant in between a stop and a fricative. The air flow is stopped completely, then released with audible friction. Examples are *ch* and *y*.

allomorph   A variant of a morpheme that occurs in a specific environment. For example, *-ku* is an allomorph of *-hu*. *-ku* occurs when the stem includes a medial consonant cluster.

allophone   A sound which may be phonetically different from another sound in the language, but it is not significantly different. In other words, it is not a contrastive sound. It is a variant sound of one of the phonemes.

alveolar   A consonant produced by placing the tip or blade of the tongue against the gum ridge (alveolar ridge) just behind the upper teeth.

alveo-palatal   A consonant produced by placing the front part of the tongue on, or in the region of, the gum ridge and the hard palate behind the gum ridge. Alveopalatal consonants in Chamorro are *ch* and *y*.

aspect   A grammatical category which indicates whether an action is completed or continuative. In Chamorro the continuative aspect is marked by reduplication of the verb or one of the other elements in the sentence.

assimilation A phonetic process in which two sounds that are adjacent to or very near each other acquire certain phonetic features of each other.

Austronesian The language family of which Chamorro is a member.

auxiliary verb A verblike word which usually requires a second verb that carries the primary meaning. For example, *siña* in the following sentence is an auxiliary while *gumupu* is the main verb: *Kao siña yo' gumupu?* 'Can I fly?'

base form The form of a word from which other forms are derived. For example, from the base form *falagu* we can derive *malagu*, *malalagu, manmalagu,* and so on.

basic sentence Simple sentences from which compound and complex sentences can be derived.

bilabial A sound produced by using both lips. Examples of such sounds in Chamorro are *p*, *b*, and *m*.

bound morpheme A morpheme that must be attached to another morpheme.

clause A construction containing at least a subject and a verb. It is usually the same as a simple sentence.

closed syllable A syllable that ends with a consonant or a semi-consonant.

complex sentence Any sentence that contains two or more clauses, one of which is subordinate.

complex word A word that consists of two or more morphemes, one (or more) of which is a bound morpheme. For example, *sangani* which consists of *sangan* plus *i*.

compound sentence A sentence that contains two or more independent clauses.

compound word A word that is made up of two or more free morphemes. For example *halomtano'* from *halom* plus *tano'*.

consonant cluster Two or more consonants that occur together without an intervening vowel.

content word Words such as *lahi, hanao, a'paka'* which have meaning as their primary purpose. Contrast with function word.

continuant   A type of sound in which there is no stoppage of the air flow. Vowels, fricatives, and nasals are all continuants.

contrastive sounds   Sounds that contrast in a given language. The substitution of one sound for another will change the meaning of a word. In Chamorro the sounds *l* and *m* are contrastive because the word *lata* means 'can' or 'container' while the word *mata* (where *m* has replaced *l*) means 'eye' or 'face'. We can say that *l* and *m* are phonemes.

defective verbs   Verbs that do not conform to the general rules of other verbs in the language.

derivational affix   An affix whose primary function is to change the meaning of a word to which it is attached. Also called *semantic affix*.

dialect   The variety of a language spoken in a particular area or by a particular group of people.

digraph   A two-letter symbol used to represent a single speech sound. For example, *ch* in Chamorro represents a single consonant sound. Likewise, *ng* represents a single sound in Chamorro.

diphthong   A vowellike sound consisting of a vowel plus a semi-consonant. Also called *glide* because the tongue glides from one position to another during the production of the sound. Examples of words of one syllable that contain diphthongs are *bai, lao,* and *boi.*

distribution   The set of environments in which a particular linguistic form occurs.

etymology   The history and derivation of a word.

exclusive pronoun   A form of the first person plural that excludes the person being spoken to.

excrescent consonant   A consonant that is added to a stem before affixation in order to make the resultant phrase easier to pronounce. For example, the *n* in *lepblon-mami* has no meaning; it is added to the stem *lepblo* to make it sound better.

existential sentence   A sentence that describes the existence or non-existence of something and includes one of the seven existential verbs.

expletive   An exclamatory word or interjection.

focus   A term used to describe a grammatical feature found in many Philippine type languages where verb affixes and the use of articles that mark the NP determine the type of focus.

fossilized prefix   A prefix that has become an inseparable part of a word.

free morpheme   A morpheme that can occur by itself.

fricative   A type of consonant that is made by forming a partial closure with the articulators and allowing the air to pass through the opening with audible friction.

function word   Words which have very little meaning in and of themselves, but have grammatical significance. Words such as *i, si, pat,* and *na* are all function words which have very little meaning but are essential to the grammar.

geminate consonants   Two identical consonants which come together across a syllable boundary. The first consonant is held, then released so that the effect is that of a very long consonant or a double consonant. The following words contain geminate consonants in the Guam dialect: *tommo, fatto, tatte.*

glide   *See* **diphthong**

glottal   A sound produced by closing the vocal cords and releasing them suddenly.

headword   The word that is at the center of a phrase and is usually modified by other words in the phrase.

homonym   A word that sounds like (and is usually written like) another word but has an entirely different meaning.

inclusive pronoun   A form of the first person plural which includes the person being spoken to.

infix   Any affix that is attached internally within a stem.

inflectional affix   An affix whose primary function is grammatical rather than semantic. It has no independent meaning by itself. Also called *grammatical affix.*

initial position   At the beginning of a linguistic unit such as a syllable, word, or utterance.

intonation   The rise and fall in pitch plus the differing degrees of loudness in a speaker's voice while he is talking.

intransitive verb   A verb that does not require, and often cannot take, a direct object.

irregular   Not conforming to the general rule for the language.

juncture   The periods of pause in between words, phrases, or clauses, usually accompanied by characteristic changes in the pitch and stress patterns.

labial   Refers to the use of the lips in the process of articulating a sound.

labio-dental   A sound articulated with the bottom lip and upper teeth, such as the first sound in *fatto*.

liquid   A type of sound that is made with partial closure of the articulators but without friction. Examples are *l* and *r*.

loanblend   A word borrowed from a foreign language but made to conform to the pronunciation or grammatical rules of the borrowing language. Example: from English *type* comes Chamorro *mantataip*.

loanword   A word that has been borrowed from one language into another. If a loanword becomes totally assimilated into the borrowing language, then it becomes a loanblend.

main clause   A clause which can stand alone, or if it occurs in a complex sentence the main clause, it is the one to which the subordinate clause is attached.

medial position   In the middle of a linguistic unit, usually a word.

metathesis   The transposition of sounds and sometimes syllables within a word. For example, the infix *-um-* occurs as *mu-* in such forms as *muna'* and *munangu*.

minimal pair   Two words or phrases that are distinguished by a single contrast. For example, *mata* 'eye' and *lata* 'container'.

mode   A grammatical category which indicates that the mode expressed by the verb phrase may be conditional, factual, reported, doubtful, imperative, and so on.

modifier   A word, phrase, or clause that qualifies another word, phrase, or clause.

morpheme   The smallest unit of speech that has meaning. *Free morphemes* are morphemes that may occur alone. *Bound morphemes* must be attached to another morpheme.

morphology   The study of morphemes and their combination in word formation.

morphophonemics   A term used to refer to the changes that occur in the phonemic structure of morphemes when they are combined with other morphemes. For example, *man* plus *saga* becomes *mañaga* as a result of a morphophonemic change.

NP   A noun phrase consisting of a noun and its modifiers.

nasal   A sound produced with the uvula lowered, thereby allowing the air to escape through the nose. Nasal consonants in Chamorro include *m, n, ñ,* and *ng.*

nominalization   The process by which a word or a phrase is converted to a nounlike unit.

open syllable   A syllable that ends with a vowel.

orthography   A system of spelling a given language.

passive voice   A term used to describe a verb form in which the subject receives or undergoes the action. Usually the actor is not specified. For example, *Mali'e' i palao'an* 'The woman was seen.'

penultimate   The next to the last. The term is most frequently used with reference to syllables. The primary stress in most Chamorro words falls on the penultimate syllable.

phoneme   A significant (or contrastive) sound in a given language. *See* **contrastive sounds.**

phonology   A general term that covers both phonetics and phonemics.

pitch   The highness or lowness of the tone in an individual's speech. In Chamorro, high pitch usually goes with weak stress.

point of articulation   The point where the speech articulators (such as the tongue and lips) meet the immovable speech organs (such as the palate).

prefix   Any affix that is attached to the beginning of a stem.

reduplication   The repetition of all or part of a syllable.

root   A word which cannot be reduced any further in terms of its morpheme structure. It may take affixes to form words.

semantic feature   A distinguishable element of meaning in a word, such as animate, human, inanimate, and so forth.

semantics   The study of the meanings of words.

semiconsonant   A sound that is between a vowel and a consonant and has qualities of both. Semiconsonants occur in Chamorro as the second member of a diphthong.

simple sentence   A sentence containing a single subject and verb phrase. *See* **clause.**

simple word   Any word that consists of one free morpheme.

stative sentence   A sentence that contains a topic and a comment, but no verb.

stem   Any word or morpheme to which another morpheme can be attached.

stop   A type of consonant. When making a stop the flow of air from the lungs is momentarily stopped by closing one of the articulators against one of the points of articulation. The stops in Chamorro are *p t k b d g '*.

stress   The degree of loudness of a syllable. Sometimes the term "accent" is used to describe stress. Chamorro has primary stress (loudest), weak stress (least loud), and secondary stress (between primary and weak).

subordinate clause   A clause that cannot stand alone but must be joined with a main clause in a complex sentence.

subordinator   A word used to introduce a subordinate clause.

suffix   Any affix that is attached to the end of a stem.

syllable   A unit in the sound system of the language which has a vowel as its peak.

syntax   The study of the way words and phrases stand in relationship to one another in larger grammatical constructions.

tense   A grammatical category which indicates the location of an event or action in time. Chamorro verbs show future tense and nonfuture tense.

transitive verb   A verb that takes a direct object.

velar   A consonant produced by placing the back part of the tongue against the velum, or the very back part of the roof of the mouth.

velum   The back of the roof of the mouth; the rear of the soft palate used in making the velar sounds *k*, *g*, and *ng*.

verb phrase A phrase consisting of a verb and its modifiers. The modifiers may include such things as the direct object, location, instrument, and so forth.

verbalizer An affix that has the effect of changing a nonverb to a word that functions like a verb. For example, when the verbalizer *ma-* is affixed to the stem *ta'chong* 'seat', the result is *mata'chong* 'sat down'.

voiced Sounds produced while the vocal cords are vibrating.

voiceless Sounds produced without vibration of the vocal cords.

vowel fronting The process whereby a back vowel is changed to a front vowel as a result of the vowel harmony rules.

vowel harmony The process whereby vowels change in their phonetic quality to become more like a preceding vowel. For example, the vowel *u* in *guma'* changes to *i* when the word *guma'* is preceded by the article *i*, as in *i gima'*.

vowel lowering The process whereby a high vowel becomes a mid vowel as a result of changing an open syllable to a closed syllable, usually through suffixation.

vowel raising The process whereby a mid vowel becomes a high vowel as a result of changing a closed syllable to an open syllable, usually through suffixation.

Bibliography

Aguon, Katherine B. 1971. *Let's Chat in Chamorro.* Agaña, Guam.

Burrus, E. J. 1954. "Sanvitores' Grammar and Catechism in the Mariana Language," *Anthropos* 49:934–960.

Callistus, P. (O. Capuchin). n.d. *Chamorro-Grammar.* Translated from the German original by James R. Grey. Edited and arranged by Junior Pangelinan. Saipan, M. I.

———— 1910. *Chamorro-Wörterbuch; nebst einer Chamorro-Grammatik.* Hong Kong: Typis Societatis Missionum ad Exteros.

Carano, Paul, and Pedro C. Sanchez. 1964. *A Complete History of Guam.* Tokyo: Tuttle.

"Chamorro in Micronesia." 1965. *Anthropological Linguistics* 7(2).

Conant, Carlos E. 1911. "Consonant Changes and Vowel Harmony in Chamorro." *Anthropos* 6:136–146.

Costenoble, H. 1940. *Die Chamoro Sprache.* 'S-Gravenhage: M. Nijhoff.

Dyen, Isidore. 1962. "The Lexicostatistical Classification of the Malayo-Polynesian Languages." *Language* 38:38–46.

F. "Val" C. 1967a. *Chamorro-English Dictionary.* Hong Kong: The Green Pagoda Press.

———— 1967b. *Chamorro-English Guidebook; Words and Phrases of the Marianas Islands.* Hong Kong: The Green Pagoda Press.

Fischer, J. L. 1961. "The Retention Rate of Chamorro Basic Vocabulary," *Lingua* X (1961):255–266.

Fritz, G. 1908a. *Chamorro Gramatik*. Herausgegeben von dem Seminar für Orientalische Sprachen. Berlin: G. Reimer.

—— 1908b. *Chamorro Wörterbuch*. Berlin: G. Reimer.

Hockett, Charles F. 1958. *A Course in Modern Linguistics*. New York: Macmillan.

Kats, J. 1919. *Het Tjamoro van Guam en Saipan Vergeleken met eenige verwante talen*. 'S-Gravenhage; M. Nijhoff.

Mata y Araujo, Luis de. 1865. *Grammatica Chamorro*. Manila. Giraudier.

Mathiot, Madeleine. 1955. *Chamorro Phonemics*. Unpublished Master's thesis, Georgetown University.

Morey, Virginia. 1964. "Distributional Restrictions on Co-occurrence of Aspect and Focus Morphemes in Ata Verbs." *Oceanic Linguistics* 3:69–86.

Preissig, Edward R. von. 1918. *Dictionary and Grammar of the Chamorro Language of the Island of Guam*. Washington, D. C.: Government Printing Office.

Safford, William E. 1909. *The Chamorro Language of Guam*. Washington, D. C.: W. H. Lowdermilk and Co.

Sanvitores, Diego Luis de. 1954. *Lingua Mariana*. Micro-Bibliotheca Anthropos, vol. 14. Anthropos-Institut, Freiburg, Suisse.

Seidin, William. 1960. "Chamorro Phonemes." *Anthropological Linguistics* 2:6–35.

Solenberger, Robert R. 1953. "Recent Changes in Chamorro Direction Terminology." *Oceania* XXIV:132–141.

Spoehr, Alexander. 1954. *Saipan: The Ethnology of a War-Devastated Island*. Chicago; Natural History Museum.

—— 1957. *Marianas Prehistory: Archaeological Survey and Excavations on Saipan, Tinian, and Rota*. Chicago: Natural History Museum.

Thompson, Laura M. 1932. *Archaeology of the Marianas Islands*. Bernice P. Bishop Museum Bulletin 100.

—— 1945. *The Native Culture of the Marianas Islands*. Bernice P. Bishop Museum Bulletin 185.

—— 1947. *Guam and Its People*. Princeton, N. J.: Princeton University Press.

Topping, Donald M. 1963a. *Chamorro Structure and the Teaching of English.* Unpublished Ph.D. dissertation, Michigan State University.

———— 1963b. "Loanblends: a Tool for Linguists." *Language Learning* 13:281–287.

———— 1968. "Chamorro Vowel Harmony." *Oceanic Linguistics* VIII:67–79.

———— 1969a. "A Restatement of Chamorro Phonology." *Anthropological Linguistics* 11:62–77.

———— 1969b. *Spoken Chamorro.* Honolulu: University of Hawaii Press.

Vera, Roman Maria de. 1932. *Diccionario Chamorro-Castellano.* Manila: Cacho Hermanos.

Index

Printed in the USA
CPSIA information can be obtained
at www.ICGtesting.com
JSHW011001070124
54909JS00010B/88